THE CULTURE
OF DIGITAL
SCHOLARSHIP
IN ACADEMIC
LIBRARIES

ALA Editions purchases fund advocacy,
awareness, and accreditation programs
for library professionals worldwide.

THE CULTURE OF DIGITAL SCHOLARSHIP IN ACADEMIC LIBRARIES

Edited by

ROBIN CHIN ROEMER
and **VERLETTA KERN**

UNIVERSITY OF WASHINGTON LIBRARIES

ALA Editions

CHICAGO | 2019

© 2019 by the American Library Association

Extensive effort has gone into ensuring the reliability of the information in this book; however, the publisher makes no warranty, express or implied, with respect to the material contained herein.

ISBNs
978-0-8389-1897-5 (paper)
978-0-8389-1914-9 (PDF)

Library of Congress Control Number: 2019943587

Cover design by Kimberly Thornton. Cover image © Peshkova/Adobe Stock.

Text design in the Chaparral, Gotham, and Bell Gothic typefaces.

♾ This paper meets the requirements of ANSI/NISO Z39.48-1992 (Permanence of Paper).

Printed in the United States of America

23 22 21 20 19   5 4 3 2 1

Contents

PART III ■ ENVIRONMENTS

ROBIN CHIN ROEMER

Introduction

The Culture of Digital Scholarship

What is the culture of digital scholarship, and what distinguishes it from scholarly culture in general? Where do academic libraries come into the equation, and what are the opportunities and challenges inherent to library staff interested in furthering the development of digital scholarship culture at their institutions?

Let's tackle these questions one by one, starting with some background in digital scholarship.

DIGITAL SCHOLARSHIP AND THE CULTURE OF DIGITAL SCHOLARSHIP

Digital scholarship (DS) a highly interdisciplinary term that encompasses any activity that makes extensive use of digital tools and methods for purposes of teaching or research. This focus on digital tools and methods is what distinguishes it from the more general world of scholarship, particularly in the last few years, as the work of digital scholarship has confronted new sets of questions, problems, and values that have yet to be adopted extensively by more traditional academic circles.

Digital scholarship is also strongly shaped by the sheer diversity of its outputs. As a field, it is composed of an unusually wide variety of works and practices, the specifics of which tend to reflect the values, priorities, opportunities, and challenges of the surrounding intellectual and technical environment (to say nothing of the ambitions of its individual practitioners). Consequently, at some institutions, it is the topic of a growing conversation among a handful of supporters—perhaps in one department, perhaps across a few. At others it is a full-blown interdisciplinary movement, with robust centers and centralized services already in place to support its advancement and further diversification. Digital scholarship is, to a large extent, at the mercy of its local contexts and stakeholders—even more so than general academic scholarship, which is indeed saying something.

This assertion brings us back to the idea of a culture of digital scholarship, which extends our original definition by recognizing the tensions that exist between the overarching values of digital scholarship and its inevitable localisms. By adding the lens of culture to the mix, we essentially assert that one must consider digital scholarship alongside its everyday realities, from institutional policies and resources to funding conditions and community dynamics. As the theorist Raymond Williams once wrote, "Culture is ordinary: that is where we must start."[1] To embrace the ordinariness of digital scholarship is thus to flesh out its field of discussion, and in the process make attainable what otherwise could seem too perfect, too specialized to be of use to most of us.

A few quick clarifications are in order here.

First, this book's conscious emphasis on culture does not mean that we are here to reject the many excellent treatments of digital scholarship that cross geographies or that specifically target greater trends in the DS field. As mentioned earlier, there are several important questions and issues being productively discussed by experts at the broadest level of digital scholarship. The difference between our work and theirs is simply that they implicitly ask their audiences to do the labor of putting their conclusions through the filter of local DS culture, whereas we are here explicitly to model that practice on behalf of our readership. We'll discuss more about this in a moment.

Second, it's worth pointing out that a single institution may easily include more than one extant culture of digital scholarship, particularly at large universities where deep research silos may be firmly in place. Academic institutions are not monoliths, despite all the implications of their sometimes-Gothic exteriors. Still, there is something to be said for evaluating digital scholarship at the level of the institution, if only for the efficiency it affords stakeholders who seek to encourage a more robust, collaborative, interdisciplinary culture of digital scholarship "at home." Institutions are also a convenient scoping point for academic libraries, which are typically set up to benefit whole campuses, or at least entire research disciplines, and are accustomed to operating in collaboration with other institution-focused units, in addition to specific departments, centers, and so forth.

Which brings us, conveniently, back to libraries and the role they play in digital scholarship.

LIBRARIES AND THE CULTURE
OF DIGITAL SCHOLARSHIP

Already we have strongly suggested that academic libraries are one of the stakeholders in the project of digital scholarship. The fundamental reason for this is obvious: all libraries, regardless of type, exist in part to encourage the intellectual growth of their communities. That being said, academic libraries have a special relationship to digital scholarship, which is propelled by three main factors.

1. *Digital scholarship is, by a definition, a subset of scholarship.* This is the least exciting of the three factors, but it also the hardest to argue with. All academic libraries pride themselves on supporting some combination of research, teaching, and learning—activities that are significantly impacted by the modern addition of digital tools, methods, and pedagogies. Libraries must constantly adapt to keep pace with new trends in academia, which makes us stakeholders in institutional digital scholarship culture, wittingly or not.

2. *Academic libraries are a consistent hub of digital scholarship.* Ask yourself: where does digital scholarship live at a college or university? The answers across institutions are remarkably inconsistent, in part because there are few predictable structures across institutions where digital scholarship seems to fit and thrive. Libraries and librarians, however, provide an exception to this inconsistency. Not only do they exist across different academic environments, but their contemporary work with collections, instruction, outreach, preservation, archives, and so on, effectively guarantees that any given academic library helps produce, house, and circulate some quantity of digital scholarship on behalf of users.

3. *Digital scholarship and academic libraries share overlapping values.* Several of our contributors will explore this point in depth—but suffice to say, there is a significant degree of overlap between the emerging topics of concern to the digital scholarship field and those of long-standing importance to segments of the academic library world. Access, for instance, is a driving force behind the actions of both communities— as are values of collaboration, interactivity, interdisciplinarity, sustainability, and more. Practically speaking, the result is that academic library staff have much to offer (and learn from) people interested in engaging further in digital scholarship. Libraries' expertise flows in the same direction as digital scholarship—which gives us the potential to be influencers in local digital scholarship culture, in addition to our role as stakeholders.

We may thus agree that academic libraries and proponents of digital scholarship have a kind of default connection, which varies in degree and shape from instance to instance but exists nevertheless within the culture of digital scholarship. The tricky part comes when an academic library—or even an individual staff member—decides to develop this connection or otherwise further the DS culture of the surrounding environment.

It is here that we arrive at the purpose of this book, which is to reveal and unpack the opportunities, challenges, questions, and individual personalities that sit at the nexus of academic libraries and digital scholarship culture. To accomplish this task, however, we will not begin from a universal perspective, but instead from what will appear at first to be a highly local one: a single research university, the University of Washington, located in and around the city of Seattle.

THE UNIVERSITY OF WASHINGTON

Founded in 1861, the University of Washington (UW) is one of the oldest and largest public universities on the Pacific coast of the United States. Originally based in what is now downtown Seattle, the University relocated in the late nineteenth century to its main campus home, on almost 650 acres of scenic bay-front property in northeast Seattle. In 1990, in response to regional

University of Washington Quad

Courtesy of Joe Mabel.

needs, the University added two more campuses: UW Bothell, to the north of Seattle, and UW Tacoma, to the south. Today, across its three campuses, UW (often locally pronounced "U-Dub") offers over 600 degree options across 300 programs and enrolls the equivalent of nearly 58,000 full-time students—a statistic independent of the nearly 55,000 non-degree students who take classes each year via the University's active professional and continuing education wing. However, even with these impressive teaching impacts, UW is still arguably best known as a public research university. Since 1972, for instance, it has continued to receive more federal funding for research than any other US public university and is one of the few institutions in the United States to receive research funding totaling over $1 billon.[2] That's a lot of dollars, and a lot of research—which helps explain the University's consistent investment in academic libraries, of which it has a whopping sixteen. These libraries—which are collectively known by the organizational name of "UW Libraries"—expend over $50 million annually, and employ nearly 450 librarians, professionals, support staff, and student workers (including virtually all of the contributors to this book).

Such numbers, combined with the well-known commercial success of the greater Seattle region (hello, Microsoft, Amazon, and Boeing), help make UW stand out as something of a powerhouse for teaching, research, and

Courtesy of Joe Mabel.

Exterior of Suzzallo Library

innovation—exactly the sort of place in which one might expect to find strong evidence of digital scholarship and its many academic variants. At the same time, numbers cannot always adequately tell the story of a university's digital scholarship culture—and such is the case with UW. Indeed, even as it houses dozens of the world's top programs in the sciences and social sciences, UW has only recently begun to invest explicitly in its digital scholarship profile, placing its progress arguably behind that of similar R1 universities. It does not, for example, have an interdisciplinary center dedicated exclusively to digital scholarship. And while it does have several librarians and library staff with job titles related to digital scholarship, many of these titles are relatively new, with responsibilities still subject to impending change and interpretation.

All this is to say that although UW is a massive, world-class institution with an abundant set of resources in place to support the cultivation of forward-thinking teaching and research, its specific culture with regard to digital scholarship is still in a state of growth—of rapid and well-established growth, but growth nonetheless. As such, for the ten UW-based contributors to this book, nine of whom hail from the UW Libraries, the opportunity to contribute to a more vibrant culture of digital scholarship is neither a distant memory nor a far-off dream. Instead, each of us comes to this topic with an immediate and unique set of goals and opinions regarding how to develop UW's understanding of digital scholarship, digital humanities, digital pedagogy, and more. We are thus in a position that many academic libraries will find relatable regardless of their size: we are the cheerleaders and counselors of a locally burgeoning academic movement in which we possess significant interest, impressive expertise, and uncertain long-term control. By encouraging a greater culture of digital scholarship at UW, we are paving the way for the UW Libraries' success as much as that of our community of active and would-be-active digital scholars. There is lots of excellent work behind us, but also serious work ahead, the details of which we are eager to share through the chapters in this book.

WHY AND HOW TO USE THIS BOOK

Although this book approaches digital scholarship from the foundation of a single academic institution, it is important to make clear that our aim is not to limit readers to a certain mindset or to tout the merits of UW's way of doing things above all others. Rather, our goal with this book is to do something we see as both unique and valuable: to expose the complexities of the culture of digital scholarship by bringing readers into a shared institutional workspace, and by encouraging them (and you) to move around in it in whatever way makes the most sense for their interests, needs, strengths, and concerns. Think of it as a professional "choose your own adventure," set at the University of Washington but designed to reflect the reader as much as its cast of contributing authors. As you'll find, it doesn't hurt that many of our authors come from very different positions and units across the UW Libraries, not all of which agree about the best way to move the relationship between digital scholarship and library services forward at the University or in general.

To further encourage exploration, we have organized this book's chapters into three themed sections: Values, Practices, and Environments. The first section, Values, presents chapters by Robin Chin Roemer, Reed Garber-Pearson, and Maryam Fakouri, who are focused on investigating some of the theories and concepts that underlie the field of digital scholarship, and on how these ideas might ground or uproot a greater institutional culture of DS. Values are, without question, an essential part of how DS is able to create collaborations, reach new audiences, and to bring diverse impacts to research and teaching. And yet, as these chapters make clear, the values behind DS aren't just boxes to be checked and forgotten; rather, they can serve as blueprints for building a better, more stable academic future.

The next section, Practices, presents chapters by Verletta Kern, Perry Yee and Elliott Stevens, and Elizabeth Bedford, who are interested in current actualizations of digital scholarship at the University of Washington and elsewhere. From the assessment of DS to its interaction with complexities of library stewardship, these chapters highlight the academic library's role in contributing to an institution's digital scholarship practices, and the challenges staff may face along the way.

Finally, the third section, Environments, presents chapters by Beth Lytle; Jennifer Muilenburg; John Vallier and Andrew Weaver; and Justin Wadland and Marissa Petrich, whose approach to digital scholarship is predominantly based on the perspective of a particular service, department, or campus. By highlighting the unique concerns of each environment *vis à vis* digital scholarship, this section makes an implicit case for the diversity of DS, and underscores DS's sometimes precarious potential to unite different groups in the interest of greater academic progress. Verletta Kern's conclusion further digests and meditates on the synthesis of these three themes and what they mean together for the culture of digital scholarship at the University of Washington, as well as for any academic library interested in catalyzing DS at home or in general.

And so, we embark on a bit of an experiment: a collection of chapters with a single starting place, but many possible endings. You will find it full of success and failure, ambition and frustration, but always invested in the culture of digital scholarship and in the different ways that academic libraries can contribute to its development and strive to affect change over time.

NOTES

1. Raymond Williams, *Resources of Hope: Culture, Democracy, Socialism* (London: Verso, 1989), 3.
2. Numbers are based on the University of Washington Office of Research's Annual Report for Financial Year 2018.

PART I

Values

1

Public Scholarship

As implied by the title of this book's first section, digital scholarship is a term that implicates not only a set of practices but also a set of values—values that must be exposed and exercised in order for digital scholarship to grow and thrive. In this chapter, I plan to interrogate one of these values in particular: public scholarship, or what it means for a library to support its faculty and students in the cultivation of (more) public impacts and identities with regard to research and digital scholarship work.

BACKGROUND

As the head of Instructional Design and Outreach Services at the University of Washington Libraries, I find myself often thinking about the relationship between digital scholarship and the larger academic values of scalability, accessibility, and diversity. On a fundamental level, this is because my unit's purpose within the Libraries is to help improve the relevance, delivery, and effectiveness of information literacy instruction to students enrolled in online and professional programs, which often involves taking advantage of tools, projects, services, and pedagogies that fall under the broad umbrella of digital scholarship. That said, my current work with instructional design is not the only reason that I became involved in the culture of digital scholarship. Rather, like many mid-career librarians, I am deeply influenced by my previous professional roles—in my case, serving as the librarian liaison to a School of Communication, and, before that, working as a graduate student in a digital humanities-focused research center.

Instructional design, communication studies, and the digital humanities all have strong overlapping interests with digital scholarship, not only because they all embrace technology, but because they each advocate in their own ways for a broader understanding of the audience of research. Is the purpose of conducting research simply to reach other researchers, or is it something greater and more inclusive? Each of these fields argues strongly for the latter viewpoint, and for an intentionality around the benchmarks of research that is not only well beyond the training of most faculty but also outside of their comfort zones.

But let us pause here a moment and return to this idea of public scholarship, and what that concept means in relation to the larger topic of research impact.

RESEARCH IMPACT AND PUBLIC SCHOLARSHIP

Just as digital scholarship is a field that has come to embrace a surprisingly wide range of digital tools and practices, research impact is an area whose default mode has grown to include, rather than exclude, the practices of scholars and behaviors of their outputs. This is because at its core, research impact is essentially driven by a set of questions: What does it mean for a scholar to produce "meaningful" research? What is the real or intended impact of a piece of research, and how can we tell if this impact has occurred? Last, but not least, can different types of impact be compared, or cultivated, or controlled— and if so, what responsibility do researchers have for managing the impacts of their work?

Defining, tracing, and understanding the impact of research is, as one might guess, a tricky business. No two specialties do this quite the same way, which makes having productive conversations about impact across departments, let alone disciplines, a little like discussing politics with extended family at Thanksgiving dinner. It's a mess. At the same time, the subject of research impact does have its own distinct and fascinating history, one which is heavily based on the twentieth century's record of scientific research and publication.

In the nineteenth century, an explosion in the volume of scientific research created a new and desperate need on the part of scholars, students,

and librarians for better ways to filter, organize, and prioritize scholarly information. Of particular importance was a way to cope with the sudden promi-
nence of professional scientific periodicals, which rose in number from
roughly 100 at the beginning of the century to an estimated 10,000 by its
end.[1] Scientific journals and journal articles therefore became the focal point
for early twentieth-century questions of scholarly communication, including
"which print journals are the most essential to read, or subscribe to, or to keep
on the shelf?" For decades, personal, anecdotal, and highly subjective answers
abounded—much as they continue to do today. However, in the early twentieth century, a new type of answer to this question also began to appear, one
based on the application of statistical methods to sets of written publications,
especially journals and journal articles. The result was a new field of study:
statistical bibliography, which later filtered and evolved into relatively catch-
ier names, including *bibliometrics, scientometrics, librametrics,* and a bit later,
informetrics. Of these, *bibliometrics* is the best known by far, and the one we'll
use for the rest of this abbreviated history.

For those of us invested for whatever reasons in the topic of research
impact, it is hard to overstate the influence of bibliometrics on how today's
academic institutions view and evaluate "meaningful" research. Because of
their overwhelming focus in practice on academic journals, the oldest and
best-known bibliometrics are all inevitably based on the analysis of article
citations—citations derived mostly, and for many years exclusively, from
large sets of science-focused journals. Take, for example, the mega-metric of
Journal Impact Factor. Journal Impact Factor (often just called Impact Factor,
or J/IF) was invented around 1955 by Eugene Garfield, an entrepreneurial
scholar with credentials in chemistry, library science, and (in later years) structural linguistics, who also founded the Institute for Scientific Information
(ISI).[2] Its original purpose, according to Garfield, was to help select journals
to be included in the first Science Citation Index—a revolutionary research
discovery and retrieval tool published by ISI in 1963, which later became the
basis for the internationally recognized Web of Science database. To determine which journals were influential enough to be included in the first Science
Citation Index, Garfield suggested a metric that would start with the number
of citations a journal received in a specific year for articles it published in the
previous two years, and then divide that number by the total number of articles published by the journal during the same two previous years.[3] Thus, if a
journal generated 1,000 citations in 1960 for articles published in 1958 and
1959, and published 100 total articles in 1958 and 1959, then it would have a
1960 Journal Impact Factor of 10 ($n = 1{,}000/100$). In 1976, following the success not only of the Science Citation Index but also its follow-up project, the
Social Sciences Citation Index, ISI published the first edition of *Journal Citation Reports,* a stand-alone resource that ranked scientific journals according
to their latest Journal Impact Factors. Today, *Journal Citation Reports* is the

preeminent tool for ranking and comparing academic journals in the sciences and social sciences, although it has since grown to include other bibliometric indicators, and now offers the option to filter its journals into approximately 235 disciplinary sub-categories.

Not shockingly, the new availability of these completely quantitative, seemingly objective means of comparing the influence of different journals was something of a revolution within the halls of mid-to-late twentieth century academia. Researchers, for their part, had at last an alternate means of understanding patterns in scholarly communication to simple word of mouth. Librarians, mindful of their users' needs, had a new set of tools for managing their collections and connecting scholars with relevant research. But it was academic institutions, ever hopeful of increasing the influence of their departments, that took the next significant step, which was to apply statistical methods like those behind Impact Factor to the records of individual faculty, either literally by using Impact Factor as a proxy for faculty publication quality, or by assessing faculty potential through an analysis of their article citation counts over time. The result was, for many research stakeholders, a frustrating oversimplification of what it meant for scholarship to be impactful. Scholars in fields that primarily produced monographs, policy documents, creative works, and other non-article outputs were left looking weak in relation to those in fields that thrived in a world of journal citations. Researchers with continuing ties to professional practice were frequently counseled to pivot their portfolios toward outputs with a higher likelihood of generating academic citations and accolades. To this day, many students and faculty, especially in the sciences, feel pressured to design their careers around citation-based notions of research impact, rejecting opportunities that better match their interests and those of their communities.

Although it would be convenient to blame this turn of events on the existence of bibliometrics, or at least on the popularity of Impact Factor, the reality is, of course, more complicated. "Impact factor is a mixed blessing," Garfield himself was known to say in the decades following his metric's success. "Like nuclear energy . . . I expected it to be used constructively while recognizing that in the wrong hands it might be abused."[4] The question of what it means to use research impact metrics constructively is still a matter of debate institutionally as well as across the disciplines. That said, many major professional organizations have issued explicit statements over the last ten years cautioning institutions and researchers against the use of bibliometric indicators as the primary means of evaluating research; among them the American Society for Cell Biology, IEEE, and the American Mathematical Society.[5] One factor in this pushback is certainly the "abuses" alluded to by Garfield—which tend to occur most egregiously in situations where quantitative indicators of impact are encouraged without mitigating evidence of research or impact quality. However, the other major factor—arguably the more influential of the two, given the timing—is the advent of the internet and subsequent social networking platforms, which have expanded and energized conversations about impact in ways that were unthinkable even at the beginning of the twenty-first century. As society's daily practices of information-seeking and sharing have changed to include digital platforms, peer networks, and nontraditional voices, so too have we seen the infusion of openness, access, interdisciplinarity, individuality, and informality into our mental models of research and impact. It is no accident that the same innovations that gave birth to the field of digital scholarship were also instrumental in reinventing the topic of research impact, giving scholars permission to propose new answers—or re-propose those that had previously been dismissed—to the original question of what makes research meaningful.

One special beneficiary of what I will call this "digital era" of research impact is the concept of public scholarship, which is also sometimes called publicly engaged scholarship, community-engaged scholarship, or community-based scholarship. Its definition, like its name, varies noticeably across the academy—but it is commonly understood to suggest a type of scholarship that has both a serious and intentional connection to public groups, public practice, public outcomes, or all three of these combined. For example, an often-cited 2008 report by the Imagining America consortium of arts and humanities-focused colleges and universities describes public scholarship as follows: "Publicly engaged academic work is scholarly or creative activity integral to a faculty member's academic area. It encompasses different forms of making knowledge 'about, for, and with' diverse publics and communities. Through a coherent, purposeful sequence of activities, it contributes to the public good and yields artifacts of public and intellectual value."[6]

One important feature of this definition, which is expanded upon in the full report, is the idea that public scholarship cannot to be assigned by default to a specific field or department. "Not all scholarship is public scholarship, and not all creative work in the arts is public art or public design," the report explains.[7] And although it's fair to say that the arts, humanities, and social sciences do tend to get the lion's share of attention when it comes to the locus of public scholarship projects, there are enough examples of public scholars in the sciences, particularly the health sciences, to make the term genuinely interdisciplinary in scope.[8]

So why is public scholarship so intertwined with the digital era of research impact—and why is it a core value of the field of digital scholarship? Looking at our working definition, there is nothing especially new or tech-savvy about the idea of public scholarship—and yet instinct tells us that something about its recent manifestation qualifies it as a growing movement.

The first answer, as you are probably already thinking, is that we are living in a critical moment in which both information and technology are viewed by most people as having vast public dimensions, and in some cases, public responsibilities. In the library world, where terms like "open access" and "net neutrality" are both familiar and common, we know this argument well, and have embraced it as our own via our professional organizations, marketing campaigns, and institutional mission statements. At the University of Washington Libraries, for instance, we strive to "advance intellectual discovery and enrich the quality of life by connecting people with knowledge."[9] Thirty years ago, that might have meant helping face-to-face patrons learn to use an OPAC terminal to more quickly locate journal issues in the stacks. Today, however, the bar for "connecting people with knowledge" is considerably higher, and patrons understandably seek information—including research—that conforms to their expectations for instant, cheap, ubiquitous access. For librarians at public institutions and visitor-friendly private entities, these expectations have real repercussions for our purchases and policies, as we strive to make research not only available but convenient for members of our communities, including the nonaffiliated, nonexpert public.

This first answer to the "why now?" question of public scholarship is certainly important—but taken by itself, I would say it slightly misses the point when it comes to the reason public scholarship matters to digital scholarship and to the latest developments in research impact. The real deal—the juicy stuff—comes when we reflect what it means if today's researchers are no longer exclusively confined to producing outputs that one must go to or through, a library to access. Indeed, as Imagining America's definition points out, public scholarship can denote *any* scholarly or creative activity, so long as it is both integral to its academic area and purposeful in its connection to diverse publics. Such a statement is, I think, a direct reflection of the variety of outputs and options that characterizes research—and research impact—in the digital information age. Faculty and students are now able, if not encouraged, to share insights and information not only by publishing in subscription journals but by adding preprint manuscripts to online academic networks, creating project websites, writing for scholarly blogs, sharing recordings on YouTube, posting to Twitter, uploading data to repositories, sitting down for interviews with online publications—basically extending their scholarly footprints in ways that not only make digital discovery of their work more likely, but also public digital discovery. What's more, self-identified digital scholars are better situated to take advantage of this landscape, as their voluntary engagement with digital tools and methods suggests a higher probability of producing "artifacts of public and intellectual value," that is, research outputs that will translate well to at least one publicly accessible online space, and hopefully more than one.

Thanks to these opportunities, and the benefits they imply, it is a much smaller leap for modern-day researchers to imagine the public as an audience for their research, and thus to see their research as potentially part of the project of public scholarship. What differentiates those who do from those who don't is sometimes as basic as the presence of a catalyst—an encouraging policy, a positive role model, an appropriately themed research venue, or simply access to information about the tools, technologies, and methods of planning one's scholarship with community in mind. As academic librarians, we have the power to create some of these catalysts, particularly when it comes to teaching faculty and students about the diverse impacts of digital public scholarship, and how such impacts can be identified, traced, and communicated to stakeholders for maximum understanding.

CASE IN POINT: TWO APPROACHES TO METRICS-BASED IMPACT

To illustrate better what I mean by the diverse impacts of public scholarship in the digital age, I will briefly walk through an example that I have used occasionally to educate faculty and students about the significance of different outputs from a single research project. I'm fond of this example for many reasons, but primarily because (1) it traces the work of a prominent UW researcher, (2) it focuses on research that doesn't appear at first glance to be unconventional for its field, and (3) it closely mirrors my own real-life approach when consulting with researchers about their impact. For librarians looking to create a similar test case for audiences at their own institutions, I recommend searching a database like Scopus or Web of Science for research affiliated with your university or a specific sub-department, and then selecting an article from the results that has a relatively high citation count. This is the exact sequence of actions I performed in 2017 when preparing an example for a talk about impact for the UW Biomedical Research Integrity Program. The result that caught my eye was a 2009 article titled "Effect of Early versus Deferred Antiretroviral Therapy for HIV on Survival"—a scholarly output on a topic with clear potential for public health and public good.[10] Its primary author, Mari Kitahata, is listed as affiliated with UW's Harborview Medical Center—but I was unfamiliar with her record of research and scholarship.

When tracing the impact of an unfamiliar piece of scholarship, it is usually wise to begin with a traditional metrics approach—which is to say, a quick check for citation-based evidence of impact via amenable online indexes like Web of Science, Scopus, and Google Scholar. Thanks to my initial method of discovery, I had already surfaced a record for Kitahata's article in Scopus, which indicated that the work had been cited 747 times, placing it in the ninety-ninth percentile (i.e., compared to Medicine articles of the same age and document type within the Scopus database).[11] By contrast, when I searched for the same article in Web of Science, the article was listed as having 640 citations—still an impressive number, but noticeably lower than Scopus's due to key differences in indexing between the two sources. Bearing this reason in mind, it was not surprising to find that Google Scholar gave an even higher citation count for the article than Scopus: 1,202 citations according to my search at the time, or nearly double what was listed in Web of Science.

Although numbers do not themselves tell the full story of an article's impact, knowing that such high citation counts existed for Kitahata's article was a promising start for its impact profile. Were this article part of an actual researcher consultation, I would have counseled Kitahata to further parse and analyze her citations, using the indexes in question to learn more about the authors who have built on top of her work, including their disciplines, fields, and specific interest in her original research. For most faculty, this blend of qualitative and quantitative information would be more than enough to satisfy their academic curiosity—certainly a more satisfying stopping place than simply regurgitating a journal's Impact Factor on a grant proposal or tenure file.[12] However, let us pretend that having completed this first approach for collecting evidence of impact, we were motivated to try another: in this instance, a check for less traditional "altmetric" impacts of Kitahata's research.

Altmetrics is a term that was coined in 2013 by Jason Priem, who was then a doctoral student in North Carolina but has since become an entrepreneur and vocal advocate of digital public scholarship. Initially a simple portmanteau for "alternative metrics," altmetrics has come to refer to a wide range of digital indicators, all related to scholarly work, but uniquely "derived from activity and engagement among diverse stakeholders and scholarly outputs in the research ecosystem, including the public sphere."[13] In the twenty-first century, virtually every piece of scholarship leaves some sort of a digital trace, whether or not this is the researcher's intention. As a field, altmetrics embraces this shift in scholarly communication and looks to shed light on how different communities of users come across, filter, and use digitally discoverable research to meet their needs, regardless of whether those needs feed back into academic discourse.

To test the likelihood of major altmetric impacts of Kitahata's research, I began by performing a series of experimental Google searches on her name, affiliations, and keywords from her article. These online searches quickly uncovered an impressive number of popular news stories related to the 2009 study, several of which dated back to late October 2008, a full six months before the official article first appeared on the *New England Journal of Medicine* website.[14] As it turns out, Kitahata presented data from her team's study at a major international medical conference in Washington, DC around that time—a presentation which she followed up with a press conference, at which she answered questions for a group of reporters about the study's implications for HIV patients and medical specialists.[15] The date of this press conference corresponded exactly to the earliest of my online news stories, making clear that Kitahata's efforts to share her pre-published research were successful not only by basic scholarly standards, but from the standpoint of public scholarship as well. Indeed, by the time *NEJM* released the full study online in April 2009, stories about Kitahata's research had already appeared in multiple major news venues, including the *New York Times* and *Time.com*. It is worth noting that the 2008 circulation of the *New York Times* alone was approximately 928,000, making the print *and* online publication of these non-scholarly articles arguably the most significant outputs of Kitahata's research from a pure numbers perspective, and an important indicator of her study's probable public impact.[16]

Following this tentative exploration of the broader outputs of Kitahata's 2009 research, I performed some formal searches on the altmetrics generated specifically by the publication of the *NEJM* article. In the altmetrics world, nearly any online community space has the potential to collect data about users' engagement with a digitized research output, from institutional repositories to Twitter and Facebook. That said, there are only a few major tools available for aggregating these metrics into convenient categories of engagement, which gives librarians interested in altmetrics a fairly stable place to start a consultation if asked. Of these tools, the two most popular are the Altmetric Bookmarklet, a free browser plug-in available from Altmetric, and PlumX Metrics, an Elsevier-owned product that is employed most frequently inside of Scopus. Together, these tools gather, organize, and vaguely attempt to interpret third-party digital usage and engagement metrics from select scholarly blogs, social media, video sites, repositories, popular media, online reference managers, Wikipedia, and more. However, in the same way that it's important to search multiple indexes when gathering citation counts for a given scholarly article, it's essential to check multiple tools and sources when tracing the altmetrics of a given scholarly output.

For instance, when I compared the Altmetric bookmarklet data about Kitahata's article to data gleaned from its PlumX profile in Scopus, I found numerous discrepancies, such as the number of times the article had been saved by Mendeley users (thirty-five "readers" according to Altmetric; six according to PlumX). To resolve this, I went directly to the Mendeley online network, which led to me to discover that, due to variations in how the article's citation had been entered by different Mendeley users, the actual metric should have been closer to 121 readers, dwarfing the estimates of both Altmetric and PlumX. As this anecdote illustrates, the current value of altmetric aggregators is not so much the specific numbers they show as the breadcrumbs that open up further qualitative and quantitative investigation across larger online spaces. Not only did these tools inspire the idea of searching community-driven reference managers like Mendeley, they pointed me toward mentions of the article in nineteen international health policy documents, nine clinical database citations, and the Wikipedia page for the "Management of HIV/AIDS." Each of these source types points toward a different key audience for Kitahata's findings and underscores the value of making one's research widely available on digital platforms outside of proprietary databases, either through open access publishing or alternative research outputs.

Based on these extensive altmetric traces, it seemed safe to conclude that Kitahata's article had a huge impact all across the public web, as great as (or arguably greater than) what we saw in our citation-based approach to determining its impact. It is thus an excellent example of how far public scholarship can go, particularly when researchers put in additional effort toward marketing their work to a variety of audiences. That I as a librarian had the ability to surface these impacts is an equally important takeaway. Expertise in navigating impact-focused tools is not the sole provenance of LIS professionals, but it is a skill we consistently bring to the table, and an ability much appreciated by researchers who may be uncertain about metrics and how to use them.

ACADEMIC LIBRARIANS, RESEARCH IMPACT, AND DIGITAL PUBLIC SCHOLARSHIP

Just as each academic library has its own approach to how it supports faculty and students' research goals and pursuits, no two libraries are exactly the same in how they understand and promote research impact services to patrons, and especially to digital and public scholars. At the Washington University in St. Louis (WUSTL) School of Medicine, for example, a team of librarians in the Bernard Becker Medical Library not only offer patrons tailored "publishing and evaluation services" via a robust "research impact" subject guide, but they also coauthored an original online tool for the assessment of biomedical research impact.[17] This tool, widely known as the Becker Model, is a free and downloadable framework for tracking research diffusion and locating indicators of biomedical impact, including benefits to community health, the economy, clinical practice, legislation, and interdisciplinary research areas.[18] By contrast, Virginia Tech (VT) University Libraries offers patrons assistance via its creatively titled "Tell Your Story: Impact and Engagement" online guide, which focuses on basic information about professional identity, how to make one's work available, and a variety of both traditional and alternative research metrics.[19]

As an aside, it is interesting to note that VT is one of a small but growing number of academic libraries—including the University of Washington—that has hired or is in the process of hiring a dedicated "research impact librarian" or equivalent.[20] As VT's job advertisement explains, "The [Research Impact Librarian] position supports the VT community in discovering, tracking, and communicating the impact of research, scholarly, educational, and creative works in increasingly open environments."[21] One can easily see a nod to digital and public scholarship in its reference to "increasingly open environments," although no explicit mention is made of these fields within the posting.

Although resources at WUSTL and VT help illustrate some of the nuances in how whole libraries are choosing to develop and promote diverse research impact services, it is fair to say that many academic libraries are not at the stage where they are ready to invest institutionally in research impact as a service, nor digital public scholarship as a topic. Reasons for this hesitance often involve what a library lacks: a lack of time on the part of staff, a lack of funding to purchase certain research impact tools, or a lack of support from library leaders who do not see one or both of these areas as a priority for public services. Whatever the reasons, the practical result is that that the work of kick-starting impact services and digital public scholarship conversations may fall heavily on a small and eclectic group of motivated library staff—or even just one staff member, who may, unfortunately, turn out to be you. The good news is that individuals can and do make a huge difference when it comes to advocating for expanded impact services and digital public scholarship. The bad news is that such work is usually time-consuming, is not included in one's job description, and can be lonely work without the solid bolster of collegial or supervisory support.

For example, when I first started getting interested in broader forms of academic scholarship and impact, I was working as a communication librarian in a mid-sized academic library with a colleague who was equally (or more!) passionate about these areas from the disciplinary perspective of the sciences. However, when I left my job in 2013 to become the instructional design librarian for the UW Libraries, I suddenly found myself part of a much larger department, without a designated partner to aid in promoting research impact services to faculty and students. Indeed, it took me over a year of working at UW before I began to see inklings of how I might practically contribute to research impact in the context of my new university. By then, I had gained a better understanding of the formal and informal structures at work within UW Libraries—but more importantly, I had made stronger connections with my colleagues, which let me imagine new, more appropriate ways of approaching the topics of impact and scholarship that matched their needs and interests as much as my own.

BRINGING IT ALL TOGETHER: RESEARCH IMPACT AND DIGITAL PUBLIC SCHOLARSHIP AT UW LIBRARIES

The UW Libraries' activities in the realm of research impact and digital public scholarship are obviously personal to me—but they also form a useful snapshot of what a library looks like when it is in the process of transitioning to a more visible investment in impact services and public scholarship. That said, as other chapters in this book make clear, UW Libraries is a highly complex organization, with multiple different campuses, branches, subcultures, priorities, and challenges that add twists and turns to our particular path toward a culture of digital public scholarship. Consequently, I will focus the next portion of this chapter on three types of efforts that have successfully been piloted or adopted within the Libraries' largest branches on the UW Seattle campus—and less on those efforts that may exist in our smaller branches, or on our more community-specific campuses of UW Bothell and UW Tacoma.

1. Student-Focused Events and Workshops

The most significant way that UW Libraries has incorporated impact and digital public scholarship into its services is via its portfolio of cosponsored campus events, which are frequently targeted at students who self-identify as active researchers. Cosponsored events are especially attractive venues for promoting emerging topics in research to students, not only because of the marketing advantages they offer over purely Libraries-based events, but for the focus they tend to lend such topics by positing them in the context of a discipline, program type, or other specialized identity realm. Student-focused events also have another distinct advantage: they seed interest in digital public scholarship among researchers who are open to developing their practices and priorities (a quality that is far less common in faculty researchers, even those who are still considered "early career"). Functional (e.g., non-liaison) librarians in our two largest library branches—the Suzzallo and Allen Libraries and Odegaard Undergraduate Library—have been instrumental to creating and furthering both these one-off and recurring opportunities, because their activities tend to work across disciplinary lines, and thus connect the Libraries to other campus units with equally broad interests in student learning, research, or success. In addition to my participation as head of Instructional Design and Outreach Services, other contributing librarians have included the head of the Research Commons, the head of Teaching and Learning, and the digital scholarship librarian, who are themselves experienced collaborators with one another.

Example @ UW: Research Smarter, Not Harder

"Research Smarter, Not Harder" was a graduate-student-focused library workshop developed by a team within the Suzzallo and Allen and Odegaard Libraries as part of the UW Center for Teaching and Learning's (CTL) annual pre-fall TA/RA Conference.[22] Clocking in at seventy-five minutes, this well-reviewed and popular workshop—it regularly drew more than 100 conference attendees, with others waitlisted—promised to introduce students to "research and information management tips and tools," including "how to use key databases, evaluate citation managers, and set up email and RSS alerts for new research publications."

In 2013, when I first joined the Libraries' planning team for the conference, we proposed adding a short section on the basics of research impact and online research visibility to the conference outline. The proposal was accepted, and in 2014 I taught a new twelve-minute segment on how to Discover Top Sources, including Web of Science's *Journal Citation Reports,* the Scimago research group's free Journal and Country Rank tool, Google Scholar Profiles, and the scholarly online network Academia.edu.[23] The next year, in 2015, I was invited to repeat this segment, at which point I expanded its content to include more nuanced information about the difference between traditional citation-based impact indicators and more publicly amenable digital indicators of research engagement (i.e., bibliometrics versus altmetrics). I also got consent from my fellow presenters to upload a copy of the revised 2015 workshop slides to the LinkedIn-owned hosting service SlideShare, where they have since been viewed over 620 times.[24]

In the end, content about the ways that different stakeholders discover and prioritize research continued to be included in the Research Smarter, Not Harder workshop until 2017, when the CTL staff decided to sunset the TA/RA Conference's focus on research (and instead offer conference programming exclusively related to TAs' teaching needs). By then, however, the precedent of promoting information to students about research impact and digital public engagement had been effectively set, opening the door to other library events and opportunities.

2. Online Guides and Support Portals

Online guides and portals represent another key way that UW Libraries has begun to more seriously invest in research impact and digital public scholarship. Although most portals are not particularly interactive or dynamic, they do have certain advantages over student-focused events: they are inherently scalable, require much less work and maintenance, and allow users opportunities to engage with research resources, skills, and issues at an individual pace and point of need. Reusability is another notable benefit of using online portals as a means of promoting impact and digital public scholarship issues, as many portals are published via platforms that specifically allow for the instant duplication of select content across guides, or even the sharing of whole guides across otherwise unaffiliated institutions. Indeed, thanks to strong affinities with the open access movement, it is relatively simple for librarians interested in impact, public scholarship, and digital scholarship to find examples of online guides and portals that are already licensed for use with attribution by their authors.[25] The University of Pittsburgh's University Library System, for example, has created a highly detailed online guide on altmetrics under a Creative Commons Attribution 4.0 International License, while at the same time acknowledging its debt to the creators of four other impact-focused guides, including staff at Iowa State University, Duke University Medical Center, and the University of Waterloo.[26]

Example @ UW: Impact-Related LibGuides

At UW Libraries, we use Springshare's popular LibGuides platform to publish our online guides, which we further subdivide into five community groups: "UW Libraries," representing the main Seattle campus' subjects and departments; "Tacoma" and "Bothell," representing programs and needs on UW's two non-Seattle campuses; and "Law" and "HSL," representing the more specialized research needs of users of the UW Law Library and UW Health Sciences Library.

Searching these groupings for page hits related to keywords like "metrics," "research impact," and "digital scholarship" reveals a surprisingly accurate portrait of how these topics have permeated each of the different segments of the UW Libraries organization. For instance, the relatively high number of impact-related hits in the HSL grouping are the result of an Impact Factors research guide that was created by biomedical and translational sciences librarian Diana Louden to support health sciences faculty, students, and researchers.[27] The guide is by far the UW Libraries' most comprehensive source of online information about research impact, with pages on Journal Impact Factor, Author Impact Factor, Article Impact, and Documenting Your Research Impact—the last of which specifically discusses the Becker Model, altmetrics, and the advantages of making one's work more visible online, á la digital scholarship if not digital public scholarship. Likewise, the high number of digital scholarship-related hits in the UW Libraries grouping is indicative of a handful of specific online portals, including a robust digital scholarship research guide managed by our digital scholarship librarian, a scholarly publishing and open access guide managed by our director of scholarly communication and publishing, and a digital humanities guide managed by our digital collections curator. Together, these resources illustrate how the librarians on UW's main campus have sought strategically to position digital scholarship not only as a subject in its own right, but as a sister issue to scholarly publishing, the humanities, and other academic areas in which faculty may already have established interests.

3. Assessments and Related Pilots

The third major way that UW Libraries has started to upgrade its position relative to both research impact and digital public scholarship is via our assessment activities, an area for which we are well-known within the academic libraries world.[28] Assessments can be powerful tools for both individual librarians and whole departments that are hoping either to test the waters or enhance buy-in for digital scholarship and its implied values. Targeted surveys and needs assessments, for example, are often deployed by libraries with budding digital research programs in order to determine the size and scope of a community and that community's need for certain categories of support. Certainly on the UW Libraries' main campus, we have employed a variety of assessment methods over the last three years to better understand the direction of our digital scholarship activities, led mostly by the efforts of our digital scholarship librarian as well as the Libraries' director of assessment and planning.[29] There are two key reasons for the timing of this uptick, one of which was the identification of digital scholarship as a focus area within the UW Libraries' 2014–2017 Strategic Plan; the other was a series of major decisions to hire, reallocate, or otherwise retitle certain Libraries staff to make explicit their responsibilities regarding digital scholarship and digital initiatives.[30] This same pattern has held true on UW's two non-Seattle campuses, where increases in the number of Libraries staff dedicated to digital scholarship have translated directly to increased collection of local data about digital scholarship practices and needs.[31]

Assessment, staffing, and strategic planning have thus become something of a power triad for the UW Libraries' maturation as an active proponent of digital scholarship across the UW community. However, as in the case of online guides and portals, it remains to be seen exactly how the Libraries should translate this dynamic to the official creation of more specific digital scholarship services, including those that focus on impact and public scholarship.

Example @ UW: Research Impact Pilot Assessment Project

In 2017, I participated in a small-scale impact-focused assessment project based on the results of the UW Libraries' 2016 Triennial Survey of the relevant needs and interests of UW students, staff, and faculty.[32] In the survey, 53 percent of faculty respondents indicated that they would be interested in library services to help assess the impact of their research and scholarly activities, including 61 percent of the health sciences faculty and 75 percent of the business faculty.

The resulting effort—dubbed the Research Impact Pilot Assessment Project—was a two-quarter collaboration led by our director of planning and assessment. The project team included me, a second member of the Libraries' Assessment Team, and two librarian liaisons from the Foster Business Library Health Sciences Library, respectively. Together, we successfully interviewed four UW faculty members (three in health sciences and one in business) about their impact-related research needs and provided them with sample Research Impact and Attention reports, which I compiled for participants by running one or more of their major research outputs through a series of citation-based tools, altmetric-indicating tools, and other digital sources of public research impact. From these interviews, we learned that tenure requirements for both health sciences and business faculty are still largely focused on journal-based impact metrics, which limited faculty's interest in collecting evidence of impact in the form of altmetrics or other digital indicators. At the same time, somewhat confusingly, interviewees did express a strong desire for help "translating" research impact for grant applications, which when pressed, they described in terms of demonstrating their research's potential to impact the public through government policy, patient care outcomes, and global practices, all of which are better captured through altmetrics than through traditional journal-based metrics.

This tension between what researchers say they need in terms of impact metrics and what they say they want in terms of larger, actual research impacts is challenging for librarians to navigate. As such, institutions that wish to pursue research impact support for faculty—including the UW Libraries—must be extremely careful in how they collect information about the specific needs of researchers and be sensitive to the inherent contradictions that may exist across different departments, or even within individual departments, based on where faculty stand in their understanding of impact and digital public scholarship.

MOVING FORWARD: IMPACT, DIGITAL PUBLIC SCHOLARSHIP, AND YOU

In this chapter, I have striven to show that the cultivation of digital scholarship is thoroughly inseparable from the cultivation of digital scholarship's values—which include, but are by no means limited to, public scholarship and impactful research practices. At the same time, where such cultivation begins (or ends) is almost never easy to determine, which means some degree of frustration is likely to arise, even if support is present and interest in growth already evident among stakeholders. Consequently, it is essential for libraries and librarians who are passionate about the field to not only think intentionally about the opportunities and roadblocks that exist within their institutional landscapes for the values associated with the digital scholarship, but also to be flexible about their plans for addressing these values over time. Some aspects of digital scholarship can be addressed today, whereas others may require significant periods of waiting, experimentation, and mundane forms of advocacy that can feel suspiciously like failure.

Happily, there is a bright side, and it goes back to the underrated power of individuals to shape their own expertise when it comes to digital public scholarship, research impact, and more. Each of us has the ability to expand our skills when it comes to public scholarship, even if it's as basic an action as signing up for a one-time webinar. In the case of public scholarship, there are countless resources at your disposal, from journals to whole conferences. For impact, there are numerous free tools ready for you to download and experiment with, and online portals ready to be read or reused with a click of a mouse.

Regardless of the specifics, the point I would leave you with is this: advocacy for impact and public scholarship is a skill that can be learned and that does make a difference to the future growth and success of digital scholarship culture. And although few of us start our careers in positions where such skills are required, it is truly surprising where one's career may someday lead, and what opportunities may open up along the way when one is willing to make one's interests visible and public.

Takeaways

- Digital scholarship is deeply entwined with public scholarship values.
- Digital public scholarship is the result of researchers who think about their impactful practices in advance, not just after the fact.
- Librarians invested in public scholarship have a role to play at multiple stages in the DS process, including the planning and assessment of DS output impact.
- Although it can be hard for an individual library employee to be the first to support research impact and digital public scholarship, individuals can and do contribute meaningfully to the cultivation of new digital scholarship practices, values, and projects.

FURTHER RESOURCES

Meaningful Metrics: A 21st Century Librarian's Guide to Bibliometrics, Altmetrics, and Research Impact, www.ala.org/acrl/sites/ala.org.acrl/files/content/publications/booksanddigitalresources/digital/9780838987568_metrics_OA.pdf.

Scimago Journal and Country Rank, https://www.scimagojr.com/.

Altmetrics Conference, www.altmetricsconference.com/.

Metrics Toolkit, www.metrics-toolkit.org/.

NOTES

1. William H. Brock, "Science," in *Victorian Periodicals and Victorian Society*, ed. J. Don Vann and Rosemary VanArsdel (University of Toronto Press, 1994), 86.

2. Eugene Garfield, "The History and Meaning of the Journal Impact Factor," *JAMA* 295, no. 1 (2006): 90, doi:10.1001/jama.295.1.90.

3. The first edition of the Science Citation Index included 613 journals, which accounted for a whopping 1.4 million references. The whole index took up five printed volumes, with much of the information appearing in type as small as 3.5 point. See Ronald Rousseau, Leo Egghe, and Raf Guns, *Becoming Metric-Wise: A Bibliometric Guide for Researchers* (Cambridge: Elsevier Ltd., 2018), 103.

4. Eugene Garfield, "Journal Impact Factor: A Brief Review," *Canadian Medical Association Journal* 161, no. 8 (October 19, 1999), www.garfield.library .upenn.edu/papers/journalimpactCMAJ1999.pdf.

5. See, respectively, the San Francisco Declaration on Research Assessment, https://sfdora.org/read/; "IEEE Statement on the Appropriate Use of Bibliometric Indicators," https://www.ieee.org/content/dam/ieee-org/ ieee/web/org/pubs/ieee_bibliometric_statement_sept_2013.pdf; and "The Culture of Research and Scholarship in Mathematics: Citation and Impact in Mathematical Publications," https://www.ams.org/profession/leaders/ culture/CultureStatement09.pdf.

6. Julie Ellison and Timothy K. Eatman, "Scholarship in Public: Knowledge Creation and Tenure Policy in the Engaged University A Resource on Promotion and Tenure in the Arts, Humanities, and Design," in *Imagining America* (2008), 6, http://imaginingamerica.org/wp-content/ uploads/2015/07/ScholarshipinPublicKnowledge.pdf.

7. Ibid., 5.

8. At the same time, it is fair to say that public scholarship in the sciences can look a bit different than in the arts or humanities. For example, it is frequently categorized under the auspices of the highly disciplinary "science communication" movement, which advocates for better, clearer, more purposeful communication of scientific research to public practitioners and nonexperts in general. Another reason public scholarship looks different in the sciences is the recent implementation of federal public access policies for NIH and NSF grant recipients, which revealed challenges some scientists face (or perceive themselves to face), in making their research accessible to members of the public. As well, did I mention that faculty scientists still face significant pressure to focus on citation counts and Journal Impact Factor? Pressure to demonstrate achievement in the context of bibliometrics can make the path toward public scholarship for many academic scientists a little more complicated, depending on their access to institutional support structures. Health sciences faculty tend to receive

more support for public scholarship because of departmental missions that explicitly value public outcomes and public partnerships.

9. "Libraries Mission, Vision, and Values." University of Washington Libraries. www.lib.washington.edu/about/intro/mvv.

10. Mari Kitahata et al., "Effect of Early versus Deferred Antiretroviral Therapy for HIV on Survival." *New England Journal of Medicine* 360, no. 18 (2009): 1815–26, https://doi.org/10.1056/NEJMoa0807252.

11. Scopus provides citation benchmarking in the metrics portal of their articles whenever possible.

12. For what it's worth, the publishing journal for Kitahata's article is the *New England Journal of Medicine,* which in 2011 had an IF of 53.298. Whether or not Kitahata's article achieved more than fifty-three citations in 2011 (i.e., two years following its publication, per the IF formula), I didn't deign to check—because *it really doesn't matter* compared to the article-specific citation counts available in 2017, eight years after publication.

13. From outputs of NISO's 2015 Alternative Assessment Metrics Project. See *Outputs of the NISO Alternative Assessment Metric,* National Information Standards Organization, https://www.niso.org/publications/rp-25-2016-altmetrics.

14. Examples of popular and trade-focused news sites that reported on the study in October 2008 include NBCNews.com, FOXNews.com, MedPageToday.com, and WebMD.com. By comparison, Kitahata's scholarly article first appeared on the *New England Journal of Medicine* website on April 30, 2009.

15. An edited transcript of this press conference can be found online at "Starting HAART: Should 500 Become the New 350?," *The Body,* October 26, 2008, www.thebody.com/content/art49164.html.

16. Numbers are from an Audit Bureau of Circulations report on newspaper circulation for the six-month period ending September 30, 2008.

17. Bernard Becker Medical Library, "Research Impact: Home," Washington University St. Louis, https://beckerguides.wustl.edu/impact.

18. Bernard Becker Medical Library, "Accessing the Impact of Your Research," Washington University St. Louis, https://becker.wustl.edu/impact -assessment/how-to-use.

19. Ginny Pannabecker, "Tell Your Story: Impact and Engagement," Virginia Tech University Libraries, https://guides.lib.vt.edu/TellYourStory/Home.

20. At UW, this position is the Research Impact and Social Work Librarian, situated within our Health Sciences Library.

21. The original VT job ad was posted to http://listings.jobs.vt.edu/postings/82228, although it has since been closed to viewing. This text is taken from a Mid-Atlantic Medical Library Association version of the job listing, available at https://macmla.org/research-impact-librarian-at-virginia -tech-blacksburg-virginia/.

22. In 2017, this event was revised and rebranded by the Center for Teaching and Learning as a more teaching-focused TA Conference; see https://www.washington.edu/teaching/programs/ta-conference/. For a sample schedule from a previous workshop iteration, see www.washington.edu/teaching/files/2015/09/Whats-Where-When-TA-RA-Conf-20151.pdf.

23. Although similar to *Journal Citation Reports* in structure, *Scimago Journal and Country Rank* (SJR) calculates its journal rankings using a slightly different formula and using citation data collected from Scopus instead of Web of Science. https://www.scimagojr.com/aboutus.php.

24. University of Washington Libraries, " Research Smarter, Not Harder" (presentation at the UW TA/RA Conference September 2015), https://www.slideshare.net/uwlibeo/uw-libraries-research-smarter-not-harder.

25. The most common way that authors do this is by including a visible Creative Commons license icon on their guides. It can be freely downloaded from the Creative Commons website. That said, there are different types of Creative Commons licenses—some of which do not restrict reuse to noncommercial purposes, and some of which do restrict adaptations of a work, even for noncommercial purposes. Because of this variability, it's important to double-check the conditions of a guide's license before, for example, deciding to make it the foundation of your institution's online portal for digital public scholarship. For more information, see https://creativecommons.org/share-your-work/licensing-types-examples/.

26. University of Pittsburgh Library, "What Are Altmetrics?" https://pitt.libguides.com/altmetrics.

27. University of Washington Health Sciences Library, "Impact Factors Research Guide," http://guides.lib.uw.edu/hsl/impactfactors.

28. For a snapshot of the major assessment activities of the UW Libraries, see www.lib.washington.edu/assessment/.

29. See chapter 4 of this book for more details about how the UW Libraries has deployed such assessments in service of digital scholarship.

30. Interestingly, one of the first UW Libraries positions to be retitled in this way was our Dean of Libraries, Betsy Wilson, who was appointed Vice Provost for Digital Initiatives by the Provost in summer 2013. See www.lib.washington.edu/about/strategicplan/2014 and www.libwashington.edu/about/news/announcements/dean-lizabeth-betsy-wilson-is-appointed-vice-provost-for-digital-initiatives.

31. See chapter 10 for more details on activities outside of the main UW campus.

32. University of Washington Libraries, "Triennial Survey," www.lib.washington.edu/assessment/surveys/triennial.

2

Digital Citizenship

Teaching Research Identity and
Accountability to Undergraduates

When initially approached about contributing to this book, I was skeptical of my ability to address the culture of digital scholarship at the University of Washington (UW). My roles at the UW Libraries do not specifically address scholarship nor publishing. But as the online learning librarian, I do directly respond to and develop strategies for teaching research using available digital tools and platforms. And as the liaison to UW's online bachelor's degree completion program in Integrated Social Sciences (ISS), I collaborate on curriculum development, co-teach core courses and create online outreach projects with academic advisers. The work is highly collaborative and very much embedded in the workflow of the ISS program. My work does not center on the Libraries' collections nor the production of scholarship by faculty, but rather is about enhancing student learning and experiences. In this chapter, I hope to make a case for why every library worker who teaches or works with students has a role in changing scholarship practices through the possibilities of digital scholarship, the practices of digital citizenship, and the cultivation of conversations around researcher voice and identity. To do this, I'll begin with a meditation on some of the theories and literature related to scholarship and identity, discuss how my own background as an undergraduate affects how I see the possibilities for digital scholarship, and end with a look at how these pieces intersect with my work at the University of Washington.

DIGITAL TOOLS AND THE MEANING OF DIGITAL SCHOLARSHIP

The influx of digital tools and the Free Web over the past twenty years have expanded the bounds and meanings of scholarship enormously. Today's researchers and students have ready access to an abundance of information and perspectives, from peer-reviewed secondary literature to Tweets directly from the president of the United States. Digital self-publishing and social media have especially altered the landscape of whose voices *get* to be heard, breaking down traditional print-based publishing barriers. Virtually anybody with a device and the ability can now publish for free via a wide selection of online blogging platforms and services, which provide authors with the opportunity to give life to perspectives, partnerships, and voices that are not fully represented or promoted in academia.

When recognized for these qualities, we can see how the digital landscape has enormous possibilities for reframing scholarship as directly accountable to, and collaborative with, communities beyond the academy. The digital realm provides an opportunity to question what scholarship is and whom it is for, by making intentional changes not only in our theoretical understandings of scholarship and production, but also in our practices as educators and librarians. As stakeholders in information literacy, we are called to intentionally teach students to connect with and participate in a larger world of digital citizenship and scholarship. Students no longer only consume scholarship, but can actively develop it. If we can continue to frame digital scholarship as not just a product of technology, but as the practice of equity, accountability, and social justice, then we move toward more ethically driven practices of scholarship, and those that benefit a larger diversity of people and communities.

A NEW ORDER OF DIGITAL CITIZENSHIP

In 1997, Jon Katz introduced a new social class: the digital citizen. These technological activists, as Katz described them, were going to change the landscape of community and political engagement by "harnessing the power of new media and playing to a sold-out world venue."[1] That individuals would actively participate in and revolve their entire social and political lives around the internet now seems entirely unexceptional for the majority of us. But pre-2000, those who were using the internet for both speculation and dissemination were limited to the more technical, educated, and afflu-ent.[2] Much has evolved around the Free Web since Katz's initial writings, but there is still much we can learn from his observations, because they repre-sent visions of engagement that many of us now take for granted. Although the vast majority of us have become indoctrinated digital citizens, many of the ways that the internet has changed community engagement have not yet reached the landscape of scholarship and publishing.

What was initially exciting about the Free Web for Katz was the way that ideas evolve. "Ideas almost never remain static," he wrote. "They are launched like children into the world, where they are altered by the many different envi-ronments they pass through, almost never coming home in the same form in which they left."[3] Today we can see the evolution of ideas through comment-ing features, social media shares, and even news opinion pieces. To shift public discourse can be a simple matter of having a large number of followers or find-ing the appropriate channel in which to share an idea. The turnaround time for this kind of openly published information can be swift, and the period for feedback nearly instant, particularly if we consider commenting features to be a form of community review. However, the speed at which information travels openly on the web is not the value that I am trying to articulate, but rather the ability it affords individuals to build on and transform ideas. Schol-arship and thinking never happen in a vacuum; they are always informed by life experiences and community. The Free Web makes this overt in ways that traditional scholarship and publishing do not, particularly for students who do not actively or regularly publish their research and writing.

My own experiences with writing and research as a student reinforce these observations about the transformative power of the web. Much of the research I took part in as an undergraduate student during the early 2000s consisted of visiting the library and conducting ethnographic interviews with people in my physical proximity. The sources for my course research came almost entirely from the university library, as if all the knowledge and theories applicable to academic research was contained and housed by the library itself. The library's collections appeared to represent knowledge depth on any given topic. If I wanted information or perspectives outside of what I could find in the library, I had to talk to someone with the necessary expertise, either by traveling to them in person or by contacting them over the phone. But, of course, that assumes that I could identify the existence of those gaps in the first place.

Although this story may at first appear to extoll the value of libraries in my own learning development, it is actually quite the reverse. The fact that I believed an academic library, even that of a large R1 university, could ade-quately represent knowledge in all its fullness is a testament to the limited kinds of research that were promoted and valued during my time as an under-graduate student. And my faith in the library system to contain and represent that totality of perspectives and information was a barrier to seeking out information from and connecting to people with experiences that could inform my ideas and practices. At one point, for example, I was doing research on the judicial processes that undocumented migrants go through in Southern Arizona when detained crossing the border. I uncovered government documents and court reports, newspaper articles, and even some research studies. But there was no database of oral histories to draw from, nor were there sources made by and for migrant voices that could adequately represent those experiences. I did not find this odd, because my experience with academic research led me to believe that those kinds of experiential voices were not expert enough to be included in scholarly research conversations. I eventually found a researcher on campus who incorporated me into a study that involved going directly to communities most impacted by migration policies. This researcher made explicit the requirement that I stand witness to the activism happening around migrant rights, and explained that to be an effective volunteer, I would need to spend time gaining trust and building relationships. I spent my weekends with No Más Muertes placing water in strategic areas along the Arizona-Mexico border.[4] I sat in on countless trials at the detention center and offered my labor and time to organizers in the community. I followed the people already invested in the work and collected their stories. The resulting testimonies were a stark contrast to those of the government documents and data that had earlier informed my research understandings. This discrepancy is a flaw of scholarship and higher education that can only be addressed through a research platform that includes and is driven by more public voices. We must strive both to find gaps in what information is available and to fill those gaps. Digital scholarship practices offer opportunities for more voices to aid and facilitate this expansion through community participation.

My own experiences as an undergraduate student are a helpful lens to examine the role of digital tools in the general work of student researchers. The development of digital tools allows students to be in conversation with writing and community projects outside of the scholarly world, something that many students understandingly find challenging during short quarter and semester terms. Incorporating community partners online does not preclude the importance of making direct and meaningful connections with people and conducting one's own methods for research, but it expands the possibilities drastically. I find it encouraging when the students I work with already gather information outside of formal research channels by expounding on their own experiences and knowledge, speaking with family and peers, and using free search engines to surface social media discussions. These skills are often informally acquired, but digital scholarship practices require that information literacy instruction intentionally emphasizes them in an academic context, all while calling critical attention to the lack of openness in proprietary library sources. This kind of openness in the emergence of ideas and gathering of information is the new digital citizenship that will enable students to participate actively in shaping their communities.

PUBLIC VOICES: SUPPORTING RESEARCHER IDENTITY AND ACCOUNTABILITY

One of the challenges for students who are considering adding their voices to the scholarly record is the lack of real and perceived support for the inclusion of personal identity in the same space as research output. Traditional scholarship has left the researcher's identity largely out of the writing and publishing process, creating a misconception that scholarship can be neutral and anonymous, or that research questions can be asked outside of our own identities and cultural contexts. Because scholarship is a form of power, those who wield it must ask questions that are itself grounded in self-reflection and interrogate how their work may be affecting other communities' lived experiences. Brittney Cooper, professor of Women's and Gender Studies and Africana Studies at Rutgers University, and cofounder of the Crunk Feminist Collective, expands on this dilemma when writing about the highly contested scholarship produced to justify transracial identity claims. Cooper exemplifies this using the example of Rachel Dolezal, a white woman and former Washington State NAACP president, who was called out by the media for identifying as Black. In 2017, scholar Rebecca Tuvel, a white cisgender woman, theorized on the justification of Dolezal's identity claim in the prominent journal *Hypatia* by pursuing the connections among the socially formed designations of transgender and transracial. Tuvel argued that "since we should accept transgender individuals' decisions to change sexes, we should also accept transracial individuals' decisions to change races."[5]

Although Cooper acknowledges that scholars must ask difficult questions that challenge current thinking, and may even be unpopular or harmful, she pays close attention to how and when identities are used to privilege and leverage research questions. For example, Tuvel's scholarship ignores the deep history of harm in racial appropriation, while also associating trans people with gender appropriation. The history of the two are distinct and cannot be conflated, and Tuvel's scholarship threatens harm to people who experience continued discrimination due to racism and/or cisnormativity. It also lends permission to white people by ignoring the complex systems of whiteness and white privilege that are inevitable to living as a white person in the United States. Trans women of color are four times more likely to be victims of violence than the general public.[6] Tuvel's research cannot be separated from these systems of violence and may even contribute to it. Tuvel asks these questions as a white cisgender woman, a position from which she can speak without facing the repercussions of her theories. As a Black woman, Cooper does not have the privilege of being uninvested in the politics of a transracial identity. "If I woke up one day, told people I identified as a white woman, and insisted that I be able to move about the world as one," Cooper writes, "well, I hope you see the absurdity of such a position."[7] This scholarship around transracial and transgender identity teaches us that standard research practices do not necessarily take into account the causal or implied impacts on lived experiences. Academic research and publishing have the power to inflict harm on individuals and communities; changing the tide of traditional scholarship and publishing requires that we actively train researchers to value community relationships and be accountable beyond the borders of a classroom, peer-review circle, or institution. If we leave accountability and subject responsibility up to the peer-review process and Institutional Review Boards, as in the example above, we risk providing safety only to the institution and to the largely white body of researchers who produce academic scholarship.

The importance of accountability also comes up in the work of Indigenous scholars such as Shawn Wilson, who have been practicing, writing about, and teaching decolonizing methodologies and participatory action research before digital scholarship became a way to bridge community and scholarly interests. Wilson articulates an Indigenous research paradigm as one that values relational accountability. The researcher must establish respectful and genuine relationships with the ideas being studied, including understanding the development of the self in a cultural context. This Indigenous praxis of relational accountability is meant to ensure that the research conducted by Indigenous scholars "will be honoured and respected by their own people."[8] Wilson's entire text builds a relationship with readers. Through various experiences and relationships, such as letters to his sons, stories from his own life, and interview segments from those that influenced him, we learn to understand how Wilson developed his research questions. Although these principles were written specifically to guide working with Indigenous communities, I believe they have the capacity to guide accountable research practices more broadly. If all research that works with people and communities can be framed as needing to be held directly accountable to and building relationships with those people, then we have a more ethical praxis for producing scholarship that echoes community-driven interests and creates pathways for building trust between research practices and communities.

Digital scholarship in itself offers the possibilities to connect researchers with communities more smoothly. Depending on the community, communication and trust can be established across various platforms with information being shared and exchanged more frequently. The publication of that scholarship acquires more possibilities for being accessible outside of the academic context. Most importantly, students can more easily hold themselves accountable to making their work more widely available and accountable to those they wish to impact. An example I continually return to is the work of Moya Bailey, professor of Culture, Societies and Global Studies at Northeastern University and sustainer of the Allied Media Conference. Bailey sought consent from Black and transgender women, including Janet Mock, to look at the hashtag #girlslikeus and how it shapes health and visibility for Black trans women.[9] Bailey's line of questioning guides my own teaching practices, and is one that all library workers who are involved in research can evaluate and incorporate into their practice, as they look to not only identify community collaborators in research, but also to create new resources for communities and to transform the self through new research understandings (see appendix A for sample questions used with students to reflect on community accountability). Each reflective question at the end of Bailey's essay leads to building collaborative consent and making sure that the research itself is answering questions that are not only valuable to a scholarly context, but also to the community being examined.

UNDERSTANDING MY OWN EXPERIENCES WITH RESEARCH IDENTITY

After graduating from college, I made an intentional decision to work outside of higher education, putting my time into community-driven projects in order to better understand my own place within the larger communities I inhabited socially, politically, and geographically. However, prior to that time, I loved being an undergraduate student. As a white, middle-class person with two educated parents, it was an expectation that I would attend college, and I did not encounter any financial barriers to attending an in-state university. Space and resources allowed my family to prioritize education and so I was able to make learning an almost full-time job. That comfort allowed me to expand and question the world around me in ways that I do not see as available to a majority of the current students I work with, due to their financial limitations and family or work responsibilities. In my junior year, I was offered opportunities to take graduate seminars where I proudly cited Judith Butler, Michel Foucault, and Gayatri Spivak. I spent countless nights at the university library unpacking and trying to echo the language of the scholars I was reading for class. At home alone, I would sometimes read my own papers aloud with wonder, thinking "this sounds so smart—I wrote this!" But persistent questions of doubt found me nevertheless: "What does this even mean? Where does all this information go now?" My experiences had allowed me to explore many theoretical understandings of inequities, yet overall I found school an inadequate means for translating these theories into actionable projects, particularly in terms of research practices (I had not yet gotten involved in the migrant research project).

My final project for a Chicana Feminisms course was a zine I created in partnership with *Las Sinfronters,* a queer women's organization I had been working with. Because I had been struggling to apply my theoretical learning to the work I was doing outside of school, I proposed the idea of a zine to my professor as an alternative final project. The zine included an extensive bibliography of community resources as well as a literature review of the scholarly sources that had shaped my construction of the project. The bulk of the zine was populated with interviews with local activists working in queer and immigrant women's health. Upon completion, the zine was distributed to a local zine library and community organizations and was read not only by my classmates and professor, but also by the community of people I had interviewed and was writing about. This was a rare moment in my undergraduate career, and one that still shapes my relationship to academic research. Although the level of consent I created with my collaborators was minor compared to projects like Bailey's, I expanded my audience and therefore knew that I had to be accountable to reflecting not only the voice representation, but the needs of the community. My project had to provide a pathway for improving conditions and structural barriers and had to be dispersed to the right people to have an effect. Community-engaged research was not a standard component of my learning, but something I asked special permission to try. Today this zine project could still be a zine, or be a web page, a series of social media posts, blog entries, or even a BuzzFeed list, and through all these platforms could be distributed widely and among many communities.

MY GUIDING WORK: THE INTEGRATED SOCIAL SCIENCES PROGRAM

As an online librarian who works in an instructional design unit at the University of Washington, I often hear from my library colleagues about their concerns for effective teaching. Some of the more common issues that I have heard include not being integrated into the academic process, and not understanding fully the needs of the students we work with. It can be challenging to provide useful feedback and guidance on a research project without understanding a student's process and context. I am fortunate to work within a program that has integrated me so thoroughly into the context and core operations of the degree, which has allowed me to collaborate and experiment with faculty, students, and academic advisors in ways that might be difficult for many liaisons. I know that not all library workers have the privilege of close networking within their departments and programs, so my own experiences may help to provide ideation and inspiration for building digital scholarship ethics into your own programming and teaching.

Integrated Social Sciences is a fully online bachelor's degree–completion program, providing a curriculum that teaches skills transferable outside of the University. The mission of the program is to provide equitable access to education, use technology to enable community connection, and inspire holistic learning. Through seven thematic areas in the social sciences, the curriculum uses self-reflection and integrated activities to encourage an examination of how an individual's experiences shape the world. Students in the program are often older than "traditional" college students, and the majority work full-time and have significant family obligations. Although some students intend to apply to graduate school, many want to complete their degree for personal reasons or to move forward in their career trajectories. The program's high-touch academic advising model ensures that students experiencing academic or personal barriers get personalized help in navigating their courses early on. Because of this the completion rate is astoundingly high for a program of its kind.

When I started working with the program in 2016, my involvement as co-instructor, curriculum co-developer, and librarian were all implicitly expected. This expectation has enabled me to understand better the needs and interests of students, get to know them more deeply than I would otherwise, and take part in shaping the curriculum from an information literacy perspective. "Embedded" doesn't quite describe the inherently strong collaboration we have between faculty and staff.

Because of the nature of collaboration and freedom I have within the curriculum, and the program's emphasis on highlighting research skills beyond the classroom, I get to continually practice incorporating research skills that speak to transforming scholarship practices. Two cornerstones of the curriculum are a set of social science "keywords" that students create throughout their time in the program and an electronic portfolio that serves as a capstone project for degree completion. Students are expected to research each keyword in historical and semiotic contexts and to have implications beyond theory. Writing and researching social science keywords within the context of the program require that students know *why* they are interested in their keywords and what impacts they would hope to see from their research inquiries. All of these keywords live in an electronic portfolio created through Google Sites, which also houses a biography, bibliographies, various media created by students, and personal statements on learning. Our most recent collaborative project is building an assignment based on digital storytelling that will have students create digital narratives that will be central to presenting their electronic portfolios.

The level of meta-reflection that is already built into the curriculum lends enjoyment to talking with students about voice, positionality, and accountability. Unlike peers in other programs, ISS students are publishing their writing on the web, and are often sharing these portfolios with employers, prospective graduate schools, and their peers. They are already producing digital scholarship and through the many assignments that require personal statements are positioning themselves within the larger landscape of research and inquiry practices.

Negotiating the tensions between students creating digital works and ensuring student privacy is a concern that is still being addressed through lessons on citation, copyright, and intellectual property, and through the use of an institutional Google account. Entire lessons in the curriculum are devoted to understanding the specific communication contexts and tools of a website, and students are encouraged to think of their work as personal and scholarly websites. Lessons on citation practices in research stress that students own whatever they create in the program and is their intellectual property. Portfolios are created in UW Google Sites and are, by default, only accessible to those with a UW affiliation. Students are not required to publicize their portfolios but are given directions on how to make their work openly available and searchable and to consider the purposes of doing so in relation to their identified audience and purpose. What is still missing from these lessons is the presence of intentional and overt conversations on privacy risks associated with creating web content outside of an institutional account.

STRATEGIES FOR TEACHING RESEARCH SKILLS

In an effort to make this chapter not only theoretically compelling but practical, I will now review four tangible applications of digital scholarship for library workers that teach, based on my own experiences with online, hybrid, and face-to-face instruction.

1. Blogs

When I started my position as the UW Libraries' ISS librarian, my first order of business was updating the ISS research guide to include community organizations, blogs, and other non-scholarly sources as centerpieces of the program.[10] My revised research guide intentionally highlights very few proprietary resources, due in part to the potentially short amount of time that ISS students may stay in the program, but also due to the nature of the program itself. My guide's focus is on teaching students to find many different source types through open and free platforms, with the goal of having students fluent in an array of research strategies, including those based in the Free Web.

Blogs are one of the most powerful resources on the Free Web for examining the ways that inquiries emerge. When I work with students, they are often seeking general arguments to establish their own claims; however, these general arguments are rarely found in peer-reviewed journal articles. Students do not see the "conversation" that emerges in the shaping of inquiry, and blog articles offer a lens into the construction of these ideas and arguments. As a librarian instructor, I have been influenced by the teaching practices of Anne-Marie Deitering and Kate Gronemyer, who use blogging networks to teach students how scholars produce knowledge in conversation with one another.[11] My own interpretation of this examination of knowledge formation is a "jigsaw" activity, which I have used frequently in teaching lower-level composition students (see appendix B). In a jigsaw, students divide into several groups, each of which reviews a preselected piece of information around a chosen topic. After the initial examination, they divide into groups that have one representative from each original group. Working in these formations, students compare and contrast the preselected pieces of information using a worksheet or other method of source evaluation. Through the activity, their line of discussion is directed toward observing how each piece of information may inform others and be "in conversation." This activity works well as a twenty-five minute in-class exercise and can be done online through asynchronous discussion groups. An individual activity or assignment alternative to the jigsaw is to have students search blogging networks like ResearchBlogging to find recent developments in assigned research topics.[12] A series of prompted questions or worksheet can lead students through "seeing" the conversations develop between writers and researchers. Jigsawing blog articles and other popular forms of digital writing is a mechanism for students to delve into how inquiries are developed with more general language. By using blogs and other forms of digital writing to teach inquiry, my hope is that students can see how their own work and voices can be represented and integral as part of larger research conversations.

2. Assignment Types

Undergraduate students get a lot of practice writing papers, and the majority of those papers rarely leave the confines of the classroom or are set in larger conversation with current inquiry. As an instructor I am continually interested in consulting with faculty about alternative assignments that may prompt their students to contribute differently to (digital) scholarship. By providing students with a multitude of assignment types to express their learning and knowledge, instructors create better opportunities to examine writing for a general or specific public audience, creating works that can be consumed outside of academia. Exploring assignments that are digitally produced more easily places student voices and experiences in conversation with current scholarship. With this consciousness, I have listed some assignment alternatives that I currently use or am in process of incorporating into my teaching.

> **Digital Storytelling.** As mentioned earlier, the culminating project of the ISS program is an electronic portfolio in which students display their scholarship and interests. Much of this portfolio work has been heavily text-based, so I am working with an ISS faculty member to translate their course paper assignment into a digital storytelling project. In the assignment, students use psychoanalytic theories to examine how collective memory creates trauma around an international phenomenon. They use narrative to create a multimodal,

multimedia object that they are encouraged to make a part of their portfolios. Digital storytelling provides a project for knowledge translation, whereby students produce research findings to be disseminated and understood by a more generalized audience, rather than being relegated solely to the realms of academic readership. Digital storytelling inherently creates more space for creativity to emerge, bringing identity and experiential knowledge into the formal learning space.[13]

BuzzFeed List. This one is somewhat more difficult to get faculty on board with, as BuzzFeed is so far outside the regular norms of academic scholarship practices. BuzzFeed Community is a platform that allows users to create their own lists. [14] It's a fantastic way to create space for students to generate objects that feel both playful and approachable in digital places. The idea behind this assignment is that students use skills and knowledge developed through course topics to create a publicly searchable list that uses evidence to explain a topic or argue a point.

Wikipedia Editing. Although I have not yet done this in any of my teaching, I have been in conversation with faculty colleagues about the value of requiring students to edit an existing Wikipedia page (or create new pages based on their topics of interest). Wikipedia editing provides students a direct application toward digital and public scholarship, and also demonstrates a collaborative process toward creating knowledge via a widely accessed digital platform.

3. Research Examples

One of my favorite examples to show students when talking through research accountability is the many projects associated with the slogan "nothing about us without us." This slogan has been used by disability-rights organizations since the 1990s to ask that members of the group(s) affected by policy decisions be invited to participate in those decisions. It has been used by organizations affiliated with HIV rights, LGBTQIA rights, and sex workers' rights to call for more community participation in research projects and policy making. For teaching purposes, the slogan is often enough to denote to students the significance not only of including voices of those impacted by the research questions being asked, but of collaborating with the people who are most impacted by the topic of study. For example, when teaching ISS students how to research HIV and sex workers rights, I sometimes use the report *Nothing About Us Without Us* as a resource in a jigsaw activity.[15]

Other examples that I use of community-accountable research are those produced locally on campus by the UW Center for Human Rights. The Center's hands-on research practices take students to communities impacted and seek directly to involve a community's concerns and needs in the research process. Of particular relevance to my teaching are the reports generated by the Center around law enforcement, immigration rights, and border detainment in Washington State. For library instructors at other universities, it can be especially useful to find nearby research centers and identify professors who may work in these communities and therefore be familiar to the students you teach, thus illustrating that research practices can be very local and can have very tangible effects. I dedicate workshop time during class for students to identify their own questions of accountability. These same questions can be used for an online quiz or assignment (see appendix C for a sample worksheet.)

4. Consultation Prompts

Working one-on-one with students in a face-to-face class is one of my favorite teaching scenarios, as it's where I'm most likely to learn enough about students' interests and background to better support them in their research. If a face-to-face instruction session is long enough, I may spend a majority of the time walking around and talking briefly with each person. When online, this technique often takes the form of a discussion board or open office hours. In my ISS librarian role, I recently created an optional assignment (see appendix D) where students can receive extra credit by meeting with me one-on-one online. In preparation, students are asked to devise a series of questions about their research or the research process, and then meet with me synchronously (via phone, video conferencing, or in-person). Questions may be simple and broad; for example, "can you help me to understand what is expected of me?" They may also be very specific, for example, "which article database and search terms can you suggest I use for my topic?" After the meeting, students write a summary of what they have learned and reflect on their next steps. In the rush to complete their assignments, many ISS students, leave out key components of their research, such as personal interests and possible social impacts. It's quite easy to fall into the habit of following the path of least resistance when there is only a short amount of time to complete an assignment. However, I have found that once I get students talking about their personal investment in a particular topic (rather than what has already been written about a topic), their excitement for completing the research project intensifies. Here is a list of questions I use to help students reflect on their own research accountability.

- What do you already know about this topic?
- What questions do you still have that, when answered, will help you to understand this topic in more depth?
- What is your personal relationship with this topic? What events or contexts in your life have led you to study this topic? (Note that I don't ask students to share this with me, but only encourage them to think about it. They often do share it, however.)

- Who might be impacted by this topic? How might you include their voices in your bibliography? Is there a way that you can collaborate with those individuals or communities?
- What are your unique contributions to this topic? What impact do you intend your research questions to make?
- What are your social and/or ethical responsibilities in representing this topic?

A NEW ETHICS OF SCHOLARSHIP

In this chapter, I have attempted to demonstrate how digital scholarship practices are tied to a set of ethical shifts that have the ability to aid in transforming traditional scholarship into community-driven projects that intentionally advance equity and could break down structural barriers to access. There is space in this project for each of us in all our capacities. You need not be a dedicated scholarly communication librarian or publishing librarian. I have focused on teaching practices that initiate a shift from scholarly expertise to experiential knowledge, but there are many ways that library workers can be involved in promoting equitable information through digital scholarship—from examining licensing agreements and vendors to shifting the resources that are highlighted in a research guide.

As library workers and educators, it is our responsibility to champion this shift in scholarship to be more open and inclusive, so that students not only see themselves represented in research but are also actively producing it. Shifting this landscape of publishing requires library workers to examine how we talk about scholarship, how we teach scholarship, and how we use technologies and digital spaces to communicate. It should compel each of us to promote and practice scholarship that is equitable and accountable. I find that the more I question the traditional roles of a librarian in maintaining hierarchies in scholarship and publishing, the more spaces I find relevant to my own work in the field. The relevance of our jobs can only become more important as we imagine and create new publishing landscapes.

Finally, I want to advocate for the use of imagination in the process of teaching scholarship differently. It can be difficult to imagine what an entirely new landscape could look like without a hierarchy of expertise, proprietary platforms, or physical library collections. But it's worth the effort to reconstruct an imagined reality and to work for a new set of ideals that put students and learners at the center. Our individual and collective imaginations will be critical in expanding and shaping emerging practices in publishing, and without an inventive fantasy of equitable scholarship we risk continued hierarchy, increasing prices, and limited voice representation.

Takeaways

- Digital scholarship practices are inextricably tied to a set of ethical shifts that have the ability to help transform traditional scholarship into community-driven projects that intentionally promote and further equity and social justice.

- Being a student researcher in the digital era involves connecting to and participating in a larger social world of digital citizenship, which opens up many new possibilities for expanding the definition of scholarship.

- It's part of our responsibilities as teaching librarians to instill basic ethics of research accountability and impact in library and research instruction at all levels.

NOTES

1. Jonathan Katz, "The Digital Citizen—A New Type of Grassroots Activism," *Webroot,* https://www.webroot.com/us/en/resources/tips-articles/digital -citizenship.
2. In a survey conducted by *Wired* and the Merrill Lynch Forum, some of the initial demographic assumptions about the connected digital citizen were proven incorrect; however, it was found that over half were male, nine out of ten were white, and all were more likely to be economically well-off. J. Katz, "The Digital Citizen," December 1, 1997, https://www.wired .com/1997/12/netizen-29/.
3. Ibid.
4. "No More Deaths," http://forms.nomoredeaths.org/en/.
5. Rebecca Tuvel, "In Defense of Transracialism," *Hypatia* 32, no. 2 (2017): 263–78.
6. Human Rights Campaign Foundation, and Trans People of Color Coalition, *A Time to Act: Fatal Violence against Transgender People in America in 2017* (Washington, DC: Human Rights Campaign, 2017), https://www.hrc .org/blog/hrc-trans-people-of-color-coalition-release-report -on-violence -against-the.
7. Brittney Cooper, "How Free Speech Works for White Academics," *The Chronicle of Higher Education,* November 16, 2017, https://www.chronicle .com/article/How-Free-Speech-Works-for/241781.
8. Shawn Wilson, *Research Is Ceremony* (Halifax and Winnipeg: Fernwood Publishing, 2008): 59.
9. Moya Bailey, "#transform(ing)DH Writing and Research: An Autoethnography of Digital Humanities and Feminist Ethics," *Digital Humanities Quarterly* 9, no. 2 (2015), www.digitalhumanities.org/dhq/vol/9/2/000209/ 000209.html.

10. See University of Washington Libraries, "Integrated Social Sciences Research Guide," http://guides.lib.uw.edu/research/iss.

11. Anne-Marie Deitering and Kate Gronemyer, "Beyond Peer-Reviewed Articles: Using Blogs to Enrich Students' Understanding of Scholarly Work," *Portal: Libraries and the Academy* 11, no. 1 (2011): 489–503.

12. "Research Blogging," http://researchblogging.org/.

13. For more about digital storytelling at UW, see chapter 5.

14. Information on BuzzFeed Community is available at https://www.buzzfeed .com/community. For a great example of this assignment, see Christina Katopodis, "Using BuzzFeed to Teach Melville," January 31, 2016, https:// christinakatopodis.net/2016/01/31/using-buzzfeed-to-teach-melville/.

15. Sharmus Outlaw et al., *Nothing About Us Without Us: Sex Work, HIV, Policy, Organizing* (Best Practices Policy Project and Desiree Alliance: 2015), www .bestpracticespolicy.org/nothing-about-us-without-us/.

3

Scholarly Communications Outreach and Education

DIFFICULT QUESTIONS ARE OUR FRIENDS

Big, difficult questions can be like unwanted party guests. Sometimes we'd rather talk to anyone else in the room. Their conversations are not neatly bounded. They show up everywhere, and they never leave early. At the same time, difficult questions make conversations more compelling, more urgent. They are A-list influencers who everyone talks about. They are guests from the future, and they are the ones who will who lead us forward. Because of difficult questions we've encountered about technology, rights, and access, we have made great progress toward open access literature and digital scholarship. Yet we still have a lot of work to do.

- How can we leverage technology to foster education and scholarly collaboration globally?
- How can we best support digital scholarship and open publishing, practically and financially?
- How can teaching librarians integrate scholarly communication into one-shot classes?
- How can we expand professional identities so that all librarians realize that they are scholarly communications librarians?

These big questions drive my work now. As a scholarly publishing outreach librarian at the University of Washington (UW), I help to enable digital scholarship initiatives and foster awareness of scholarly communication issues. Because I'm a lawyer as well as a librarian, I encounter specific questions about intellectual property, many of which involve fair use. Other questions touch on contracts, international law, and copyright ownership.

Difficult questions can be uncomfortable because they expose gaps in our knowledge. Thus, they are a form of self-assessment. They show us that we must instruct ourselves before we can offer help to others. Writing about teaching, education experts Grant Wiggins and Jay McTighe explain how essential questions help learners form connections with prior knowledge, which leads to understanding.

> The point of school is . . . to become better at and more assertive about inquiry. . . . Essential questions are ongoing and guiding queries by which we make clear to students that true learning is about digging deeper; it is active, not passive. If we truly engage with a topic, we pursue questions that naturally arise: Why? How? What does this mean? What of it? What is its significance? What follows? These and other vital questions kindle our own meaning-making . . . . Learning to ask and pursue important questions on one's own is the desired result, and arguably key to all genuine lifelong learning.[1]

Difficult questions increase our capacity. They prepare us for the next time we face that issue—and chances are we will see that issue again. And more crucially, they teach us how to learn.

Less than a year ago I was a librarian at a mid-sized private college specializing in creative and media-rich fields. I assisted students at the reference desk and in the classroom. I also conducted outreach about copyright and open resources for students and faculty. My new institution is very different in size (nearly 58,000 students on three campuses), range of departments (aeronautics to urology), and status (public). I am also in a much more specialized role. Yet the questions I received at my former job prepared me for the queries and issues I encounter in the course of my work at the University of Washington. Authors want to use orphan works in scholarly articles. Students remix copyright-protected media for class projects. Faculty weigh publishing opportunities for their own career advancement. Librarians try to reach target audiences at opportune moments. At both institutions, I've sought to bring information policy and scholarly communication alive for stakeholders.

My attitudes toward outreach are shaped by my experiences as a reference and teaching librarian. First, the fundamentals are consistent and simple everywhere. Outreach requires subject expertise and a receptive audience. Start by leveraging interest. I have noticed that all types of people relate to copyright because everyone is both a creator and a consumer of copyright-protected work. Similarly, everyone has been frustrated by an access barrier at some point. People also understand high prices. And people are curious about innovation.

Second, librarians—especially reference librarians—welcome questions and questioners. There's an art to framing questions and a mindset for investigating them. They help us to develop habits of inquiry. Investigations require evaluating multiple perspectives, maintaining a receptive yet critical stance, flexibility, and persisting through ambiguity.[2] Although the process can seem unwieldy, we recognize that big, difficult questions and conversations advance knowledge.

Third, I see digital scholarship and open access scholarly publishing as large, overlapping initiatives to share knowledge for the greater good. They are both grounded in the philosophy that information benefits society, and therefore should be accessible to all. Both evolve from the limitations—technical, economic, and legal—of traditional publishing models. Digital scholarship especially is an augmentation of traditional publishing as well as an alternative to it. Technology now allows various forms of media to be combined in one project. Anyone can be a publisher. At the same time, consumers need information literacy skills to effectively evaluate and use scholarship in any form, old or new.

So, like any librarian, I view scholarly communication and digital scholarship through many overlapping lenses. In the rest of this chapter, I will briefly discuss the lenses that are most important to me, given my interests and experiences to date.

WELCOME TO THE JUNGLE

The term "scholarly communication" ("scholcom" to insiders) encompasses the entire trajectory of scholarship, from creation to dissemination to impact to preservation. It seems everyone has opinions about how works of scholarship should be managed, and the scholcom community is enthusiastically open to debate. Whether or not your job title includes "scholarly," "communication," "publishing," "copyright," "data," "open," "digital scholarship," or "repository," developments in academic publishing influence your work.

To set the stage, legal structures set parameters for our management of copyright-protected works. The threshold for copyright protection is low; any original work of authorship with more than a "modicum of creativity" that is fixed in a tangible medium is automatically protected.[3] The rights it confers are exclusive, and they last a very long time. Together, these legal defaults place a vast number of works in private control for many decades. Contracts determine agreements between individual parties. Meanwhile, economic pressures force libraries to make difficult decisions about how to allocate their budgets. Not all libraries can provide essential services and have funds left to support and preserve new forms of scholarship.

Librarians across functional areas respond to the publishing industry. We have long-standing relationships with publishers, who have proven themselves to be a highly adaptive species. Over time, their business models and products have changed. My peers and I study their new developments and compare publishers' services and their value to the needs of our institutions and stakeholders.

The 1990s marked the transition from bound journals on shelves to digital files available through annually renewable database subscriptions. One of the results of this shift is that libraries today often no longer own copies of many scholarly articles. They license them instead. The advent of digitization coincided with a wave of consolidation in the publishing industry. Since the 1990s, a few major publishers have come to control a large proportion of published scholarly output. According to a study of frequently cited journals published in 2015, five publishers accounted for 30 percent of the papers published in the natural and medical sciences during 1996.[4] This percentage rose to 50 percent in 2006, and then to 53 percent in 2013. Three publishers (RELX Group, Springer, and Wiley-Blackwell) accounted for 47 percent of papers.[5] The social sciences and humanities show similar trends.[6] Also, publishers have developed increasingly complex corporate family structures through strategic acquisitions. For example, Informa, PLC has fifty-six companies in its corporate family tree, including Taylor and Francis, which itself includes Routledge Group.

Along with changing technology and corporate growth, journal subscription prices have steadily increased over time. Publishers began offering subscription packages, often called "big deals." (Not everyone scrutinizes journal packages, but most casual acquaintances have faced the dilemma of preselected cable television subscription packages.) Although it is still possible to subscribe to individual titles—in print, online, or both—those costs have grown as well. *Library Journal* has measured these trends over time. (It explains its methodology and data sources in its annual Periodicals Price Survey.)[7] Results show that the overall cost of journal subscriptions increases every year. Another safe assumption is that science, technology, and medical literature will cost more than other disciplines. Scholarly publishing, like digital scholarship, has the potential make scholarship open to all at a lower cost by eliminating the publisher as the middleman.

In addition, publishers are expanding their portfolios to include tools to preserve and share scholarship. Wiley is "a global provider of content-enabled solutions to improve outcomes in research, education and professional practice with online tools, journals, books, databases, reference works and laboratory protocols."[8] RELX Group, "a global provider of information and analytics for professional and business customers across industries," formerly known as Elsevier, has 156 companies in its corporate family tree.[9] Two of them are well-known examples of horizontal integration. In 2015, RELX Group acquired bepress, a common platform for digital repositories and publishing software.[10] RELX Group had previously acquired Mendeley, a social media site for researchers, in 2013.

Two of Mendeley's main competitors are ResearchGate and Academia .edu.[11] Each platform allows researchers to share articles, network with peers, and track usage statistics of articles shared within the network. Mendeley and ResearchGate include job listings. Mendeley also includes funding opportunities. That's a lot of capability in one site, and all anyone has to do to access it is sign up. Yet this convenience has implications. All three platforms are ultimately for-profit, and use data collected about their users to deliver tailored advertisements.[12] If users permit, Mendeley and Academia.edu gather information from third-party social media profiles such as LinkedIn and Facebook.[13] Mendeley and Academia.edu also retain royalty-free, non-exclusive licenses to use content posted to their sites.[14] These licenses may not be compatible with publisher's terms.

Librarians want researchers to consider how information by and about them might be used in commercial or even potentially threatening ways. This is particularly important as more researchers share their work openly. Researchers working in controversial areas could be at risk if information about them is not treated with care. The Association of College and Research Libraries advises researchers to

- decide where and how their information is published;
- understand how the commodification of their personal information and online interactions affects the information they receive and the information they produce or disseminate online; and
- make informed choices regarding their online actions in full awareness of issues related to privacy and the commodification of personal information.[15]

Further, librarians hope researchers will compare commercial platforms with the benefits of not-for-profit institutional and disciplinary repositories.[16] Above all, librarians want researchers and students to understand that *information has value.*[17]

Many librarians' personal values align with the American Library Association core values of access to information, intellectual freedom, and diversity. We believe these are crucial to democracy and the public good.[18] We encourage lifelong learning and strive for a world in which everyone can research issues of importance and participate fully in civic life. However, academic values and norms, such as peer review, promotion, and tenure, may pressure early-career researchers to publish their work in venues that are inaccessible to much of the public. To advance their careers, scholars may seek to publish their work in the most prestigious journals in their fields. Such high-profile journals may be available only through costly subscriptions. Because librarians value public access, we believe open scholarship, and not only prestigious journal titles, should weigh heavily when a scholar's impact is measured.

BE COMFORTABLE WITH CHANGE AND AMBIGUITY

Fair use jurisprudence, alternative metrics, new publishing models, corporate mergers, emerging technology platforms—all of these aspects of scholarly communication are a lot for a person to monitor. Meanwhile, the development of digital scholarship has been described as "a remarkable undertaking at a time of significant transformation" and "a revolution of the organization of knowledge, a cultural phenomenon of unprecedented sweep and consequence."[19] Heraclitus's time-tested phrase bears repeating: the only constant is change.

Because change is so frequent in the realm of information sharing, the North American Serials Interest Group (NASIG) recommends that all scholarly communication librarians "be prepared to deal with a fast-paced environment and community" and have a core personal strength of "comfort with change and ambiguity": "The ambiguous nature of scholarly communication and academia demands a librarian that is adaptable and comfortable with change. The climate of scholarly communication is in a constant state of flux, and the [scholarly communication librarian] must be able to adapt to changing conditions and expectations at his or her institution and within organizations and associations."[20]

I take a broad view of this counsel and would extend it beyond scholarly communication librarians to include digital scholarship specialists as well. All of us leverage technology to disseminate scholarship, and all operate within the myriad structures of higher education, technology, and law.

Although many changes in scholarly information sharing are fast-paced, others are not. After the Authors Guild sued Google in 2005, it took ten years of litigation for Google's book scanning project to be determined to be a fair use of copyright-protected works. (In contrast, Apple, Inc. released fifteen versions of its iPhone in the ten years since its introduction in 2007.[21] Fair use jurisprudence and cell phones are still developing.)

When changes happen slowly, we live in a suspended state of unknowing. We wait, often impatiently, to see what our new reality will be. But until the future arrives, we need to carry on and get things done. So we set policies, answer questions about intellectual property, and plan for the futures of our organizations using the information we have *at this moment,* knowing that the structures around us are shifting.

To lead ourselves through change, we focus on long-term goals and values. What does a library want to do? What kind of future does it want to create? How might its culture impact its campus and community? Tools change. Staff change. Administrative structures change. Our institutional values, strategic plans, and professional values are beacons through uncertainties. And as we advance toward our visions of scholarly communication and digital scholarship, we will have to research and weigh several concerns.

IT REALLY DOES DEPEND

If your responsibilities include scholarly communications outreach or digital scholarship, you might find yourself speaking with a colleague who wants to digitize historic newspapers and put them online. You might find yourself talking to a graphic designer who is angry because her work was used without permission or payment. You might be invited to speak to students who are parodying a powerful and litigious news channel. You might counsel a professor on options for posting articles she wrote onto her personal website. You might find yourself saying, "It depends . . ." without irony. You might say this because you know that several factors influence how copyright-protected works are treated in academia. Here are a few of your considerations.

Let's start with law. When much of our copyright law was passed by Congress, it was known as the Copyright Act of 1976.[22] In that era it was considered adequate for a household to have one television and access to three channels. Phones connected to wall outlets. Photographic film required processing time. Music was distributed on vinyl discs. Bulky equipment reproduced and distributed copyright-protected works. Although the technology of the 1970s might now seem rudimentary, the copyright laws of the day were complicated enough. Over subsequent decades, copyright laws and practices have developed amid litigation, additional legislation, and extensive innovation.

In the present world of digital scholarship, rights issues multiply and accelerate. Everyone, truly *everyone,* is both a user and a creator of copyright-protected work on a daily basis. A click or two is all it takes to copy or distribute a protected work. With more clicks, users can create derivative works. Each of these actions is an exclusive right of copyright owners.

Although copyright owners have many exclusive rights to their works, their monopoly is not absolute. Federal copyright law, now Title 17 of the U.S. Code, includes limits on copyright protection. These legislative exceptions to copyright are powerful because they provide directions and certainty. If users satisfy all criteria required for an exception, they do not need to seek permission to use a work, and they will not be liable for infringement. Title 17 limitations that benefit libraries and teachers include:[23]

- Section 108 is a highly technical exception that allows librarians to copy works for patrons' personal use or for preservation.

- Section 109 allows libraries to lend and weed physical books and phonorecords.
- Section 110(1) allows instructors to show films in face-to-face teaching situations.
- Section 110(2), known as the TEACH Act, allows "a nondramatic literary or musical work or reasonable and limited portions of any other work" to be digitally transmitted to students provided a number of criteria are met.
- Section 107, the fair use statute, is the most flexible limitation to a copyright holder's rights, and likely the most talked about and relied upon. Whether they stem from initiatives branded as "scholarly communication" or "digital scholarship," many of the queries I receive are questions of fair use. Unlike other limits, section 107 does not have detailed conditions that users must satisfy. Instead, the law describes four factors to evaluate when considering fair use. These familiar factors are

  1. the nature of the work,
  2. the purpose of the use,
  3. the amount and substantiality of the portion used in relation to the whole, and
  4. the effect of the use on the market for the original work.

Each fair use question requires careful deliberation of these factors in relation to its own particulars. It is understandable that many librarians feel insecure evaluating fair use given that experienced lawyers and judges disagree about what is and is not fair. Nevertheless, federal courts have interpreted the four factors many times. We can compare their precedents to our uses to make informed decisions.

Best practices are another form of fair use guidance. As the Association of Research Libraries (ARL) correctly states, "Ultimately, determining whether any use is likely to be considered 'fair' requires a thoughtful evaluation of the facts, the law, and the norms of the relevant community."[24] Over time, communities face recurring dilemmas about using copyright-protected work. So they develop shared practices that they consider to be reasonable in light of their missions—although rights holders may disagree. ARL and other stakeholder groups have worked together to create codes of best practices for a variety of contexts.[25] The codes describe how community members use protected works, and why they consider their uses to be fair. For example, the ARL Code of Best Practices in Fair Use for Academic and Research Libraries describes how librarians might digitize at-risk items for preservation or reproduce materials for disabled patrons.

Contracts determine the obligations of parties in a contractual relationship and can be more restrictive than federal copyright law. Therefore, it is crucial to read them carefully and to negotiate acceptable terms. Some types of contracts are particularly relevant to scholarly communication and digital scholarship.

Hosting platforms such as Omeka, Scalar, and Wix.com each have their own terms of use and privacy policies. Common terms stipulate acceptable behavior, uses of third-party content, and uses of users' personal information. Wix, a for-profit company, may share personal information with third parties or allow them to track users to deliver targeted advertisements. Wix also gives itself a perpetual license to use subscribers' websites for promotional purposes and modify websites as necessary for such purposes.[26]

Database licenses determine who may access licensed content, how the content may be used, and how long an institution has access to licensed content.

Publishing agreements often transfer copyright ownership of articles from authors to publishers. Increasingly, however, authors negotiate to retain rights to their work.[27] Possible contract terms may allow authors to use their own work in classes, post their work on their personal websites, deposit their work into an institutional repository, or use published articles within larger works. Pay attention to which version of the article authors may use: the submitted version, the post-peer review preprint version, or the publisher version.

Institutional open access policies also rely on licenses. Typically, authors grant their institutions a non-exclusive license to exercise all rights under copyright to their scholarly works prior to transferring their copyright to publishers. This policy usually applies to the final peer-reviewed but not-yet-published version of the work. Under policies similar to Harvard's Model Open Access Policy, the institution's license includes the right to allow others—including the author herself—to use the works it covers.[28] Thus authors can continue to use their works in compliance with their employers' open access policy. For example, authors might use the preprint versions of their articles in their own courses or post them on their websites.

The terms of a grant may affect eventual publication and management of resulting research. Many grant-funding organizations and federal agencies require public access to research articles or data resulting from their grants.[29] The following institutions are just a few funders with such a requirement:

NEH Office of Digital Humanities	Wellcome Trust
Ford Foundation	Gates Foundation
Howard Hughes Medical Institute	Smithsonian Institution
World Bank	World Health Organization
William and Flora Hewitt Foundation	Alfred P. Sloan Foundation
American Heart Association	National Institutes of Health

A library's internal policies also affect how digital scholarship is managed. It may have deposit agreements for its institutional repository. Donor agreements may transfer rights to materials donated or, conversely, place usage restrictions on gifts. Some of the intellectual output on campus could be held back from distribution due to its commercial potential. A library might also have policies about digitizing and sharing culturally sensitive materials in its collection.

Finally, risk tolerance and institutional culture influence the treatment of intellectual property. Individual risk tolerance manifests itself in words and actions. Some librarians approach projects with trepidation. Others push forward with confidence. Still others are confused.

At an organizational level, risk tolerance must often be deduced over time, and you may not arrive at a predictive formula for it. Within any organization there are likely to be differing approaches to uncertainty, and any conversations about risk might happen behind closed doors. Do not be disheartened if nobody wants to go on record. It could be that people in your organization disagree about how to proceed with a project or leaders in your organization may not be aware of all of the ways your campus stakeholders use copyright-protected work. Regardless, each situation is different and should be evaluated on its own terms. To get a broad sense of your institutional stance consider its policies, digital presence, structure, and leadership. Are your administrators at the forefront of the open access movement? What is your strategic plan? How does your institution allocate resources to support scholarly communication?

At any type of institution, it helps to have a strong relationship between the general counsel and the library. Explain to your institution's lawyers what the library would like to do. If fair use best practices apply to your situation, share them with your general counsel. They are not librarians, so they may not know about library community norms. Remember they work to protect your institution, so they understandably want to limit any risk to it. At the same time, they want to help your institution fulfill its educational mission. They can bring a fresh, trained eye to your work. So bring them into your circle.

With so many variables to consider—again, this is only a partial list—the path forward is not always straightforward or clear. Your colleagues, faculty, and students have many questions about the materials they use and create—especially in digital scholarship—and they need your expertise. You might find yourself saying, "It depends *because* . . ." in a manner that helps them to evaluate an issue.

TEACHING COMPLEX IDEAS TO BUSY PEOPLE, OR "WILL YOU SPEAK TO MY CLASS FOR TWENTY MINUTES ABOUT COPYRIGHT AND FAIR USE?"

I consider teaching to be a cornerstone of my work. Further, I agree with the ACRL that "every librarian in an academic environment is a teacher."[30] Never mind job titles. As librarians help stakeholders through project planning,

Recommended Resources About Law and Policy

U.S. Copyright Office
   https://www.copyright.gov/

ACRL, "Scholarly Communication Toolkit"
   http://acrl.libguides.com/scholcomm/toolkit/home

ALA, "District Dispatch"
   https://www.districtdispatch.org/

Cornell University Library, "Copyright Term and the Public Domain
   in the United States"
   https://copyright.cornell.edu/publicdomain

Columbia University Libraries, "Fair Use Checklist"
   https://copyright.columbia.edu/basics/fair-use/fair-use-checklist.html

Michael Brewer and ALA Office for Technology Policy, "Fair Use Evaluator"
   http://librarycopyright.net/resources/fairuse/index.php

Center for Media and Social Impact, "Codes of Best Practices in Fair Use"
   http://cmsimpact.org/codes-of-best-practices/
   This site includes codes for journalists, documentary filmmakers, use
   of images in study and teaching, poetry, communication, dance-related
   materials, media literacy education, visual arts, research libraries, and
   more.

Scholarly Publishing and Academic Resources Coalition (SPARC) website,
   especially

   "Authors Rights and Addendum"
      https://sparcopen.org/our-work/author-rights/

   "Article Sharing Requirements by Federal Agency"
      http://researchsharing.sparcopen.org/compare?ids
      =4,9,26&compare=articles

publication, and preservation, information literacy concepts arise at every phase. We teach when we help researchers assign metadata to their files. We teach when we introduce music students to fair use. We teach when we review a publishing contract with a professor. We teach when we explain to a reference patron that the paper he seeks is in a disciplinary repository. As ACRL makes clear, "there are many new 'teachable moments' when the whole scholarly ecosystem is considered."[31]

We usually begin new research projects by gathering information and absorbing it. We're like newcomers to a party that's already in progress, and we seek to understand the conversation before forming our own views and participating in it.[32] To make sense of the scholarly conversation, researchers of all levels must critically evaluate a growing variety of sources, encompassing data, video, audio, text, and more. Moreover, a scholarly object might be dynamic and interactive, like a video game. ACRL acknowledges the need for information literacy skills in this context: "Information literacy programs have to address finding, evaluating, using, citing, and creating a much wider range of material types, and include more emphasis on the technological and rights issues of working with different kinds of media. Digital literacies are fundamental to the goal of developing lifelong learners in that they prepare students to be effective and critical users of information."[33]

Eventually, we use our findings to produce new scholarship, which takes on increasingly creative forms. Regardless of the medium used, information creation is a process.[34] As we advance, we make informed choices about how to present and share our contributions to the conversation. We acknowledge other people's ideas within our work. Copyright, ethics, and attribution have long been elements of information literacy. In digital scholarship, these can be more complex. It may be difficult to parse what intellectual property is protected and what is not within a single project. For example, the project Torn Apart/Separados combines maps, personal essays, data, government photos, and at least one Tweet.[35] An article or digital project could have multiple contributors in different countries.[36] Content is dynamic, and there may be no gatekeepers. ACRL describes how publishing is pervasive, how students and faculty "use electronic information tools to share aspects of their professional and educational works in a way that can be defined as publishing, even though it appears to be far removed from traditional publishing in the print world. . . . [They] are content creators and content users, shifting between those roles in many aspects of their work. Publishing is no longer the purview of specialists, and the traditional definitions are being challenged."[37]

In summary, new and dynamic forms of scholarship are flourishing, and their potential brings new responsibilities for creators and new teaching opportunities for librarians. Many of our teachable moments happen spontaneously. But if you can plan ahead, here are some things you might consider:

1. Know Your Context

Are you giving a workshop about text mining? Or are you a guest lecturer for a media studies class? When you are a guest lecturer, it is crucial to seek a dialogue with instructors prior to your visit. Ask about their aims for your visit. Do not be swayed by a terse response. ("Just tell them what they need to know about copyright.") Even if an instructor's goals for your presentation are unformed, you can deduce what would benefit students. Always request a syllabus to see where your visit falls in relation to the course content. What are students working on when you visit? What will they work on immediately following your visit? This information will help you to prepare your learning outcomes.

2. Read Your Audience

As a corollary, know your audience's learning styles. Here again, a dialog with the instructor is important. What year are the students? What are their majors and disciplinary norms? You could ask about their collective strengths and the overall group dynamics. Are they likely to be introverted or extroverted? Are they problem-solvers or creatives? How familiar are they with the subject of your presentation? Do they share attitudes and values?

3. Know Your Space and Time Constraints

Which room will you be in? Is it an odd shape? What kinds of furniture are there? How much time do you have? The University of Washington is on the quarter system, so class time is precious. I'm often asked to explain copyright and fair use to classes in twenty minutes. If I negotiate, I might receive forty. At my previous institution, I taught seventy-five-minute sessions. Either way, it's necessary to plan.

4. Create Learning Outcomes and Develop Your Lesson

What does your audience need to know or do as a result of your time with them? Wiggins and McTighe emphasize that the ability to transfer learning to new contexts is one of the chief aims of education.[38] They recommend the strategy of backward design: start with your desired results. Given your parameters, think about what would best benefit your audience. For instance, if class time is limited, learning the rights protected by copyright might be an achievable goal. Then consider the types of evidence that would demonstrate students' understanding. (As an added bonus, demonstrable evidence will help you with assessment later on!) Then create your exercise. Here are a few examples where everything's been brought together. The format follows this pattern:

> [Audience] will [active learning exercise displaying evidence of learning] in order to [learning outcome]

- Students will contrast the value of authority in various contexts in order to skeptically assess source materials during an investigation.
- Authors will compare rights clauses of three publishing contracts in order to negotiate their rights in future agreements.
- Students will rank five uses of copyright-protected works to develop a framework for which uses are fair use and which are not.
- Students will compare Creative Commons licenses in order to determine which license they will use in their own digital projects.

5. Experiment

What kinds of active learning exercises could you plan? Would your audience play games or role-play? Can you rearrange the furniture? Switching techniques will keep your teaching fresh and help you to accommodate different learning styles. I once asked dancers to move around a studio in response to questions. I've also asked introverted art students to draw ideas on a dry-erase board.

6. Recognize the Emotional Aspect of Learning

In my experience, copyright matters bring out strong and conflicting reactions. Creators can be fiercely protective of their work. Other stakeholders see copyright as a barrier manipulated by greedy powers; the word "evangelist" is not infrequently used to describe advocates of open access and open source technology. Faculty do not like to be told how to manage their life's work. Be prepared to encounter a spectrum of attitudes in any audience.

7. Meet Your Students Where They Are

Especially with undergraduates, avoid too much jargon and seek examples that are familiar to your audience. Many terms that academic librarians use daily are unclear to others on the same campus. "Scholarly communication," "impact factor," and "digital scholarship" are difficult to explain concisely. Students may not be familiar with the terms "tenure" and "disciplinary repository."

8. Assess

Assessment is yet another large topic. Yet you can include it even if you only have a short time with your audience. Measurable and demonstrable learning outcomes will help you. Do you have evidence to determine that your students achieved them? Here are a few assessment methods you could adapt:

> A straightforward technique is to ask questions that measure students' comprehension during your presentation. Clickers are designed for this, but I have never taught in a classroom that had them. So, I sometimes ask students to respond using discrete hand signals. That way, no single student dominates the conversation and other students do not have to admit any lack of understanding in front of their peers.

> A colleague has used another simple, nonverbal technique to monitor students' progress with in-class exercises. Post-it Notes in three different colors are handed out. Each color signifies a different message: green means "I'm working," pink means "I need help," and blue means "I am finished." Students affix the color that represents their status to the sides of their computers, and the instructor can tell at a glance how they are proceeding.

Two-minute papers at the end of a class are a common technique. They work best if you give students a specific prompt. For example, what was one thing you learned today? Or, is there anything from today's presentation that is still unclear to you?

A friend of mine recommends exit tickets for college-aged students. At the end of the lesson sheets of paper are handed out with quick questions. These could be in any form, for example, open-ended questions or Likert-scale surveys of students' confidence with the subject matter taught. All student must turn in their tickets prior to leaving the classroom.

Multiple-choice questions require preparation but are quick to administer. I once developed a set of questions that served as both a pre-test and a post-test for a course I taught about copyright.

Teachers also collect records of students' thought processes. For example, I have asked students to write or draw their responses to question prompts on a big dry-erase board. Then I photographed the results.

Teaching is challenging, but you are not alone.

AN AFRICAN PROVERB SAYS IT BEST: *TO GO FAST, GO ALONE. TO GO FAR, GO TOGETHER.*

Every library faces challenges in supporting scholarly communication and digital scholarship. In its Core Competencies for Scholarly Communication Librarians, NASIG identified these major areas of emphasis: copyright services, data management services, institutional repository management, publishing services, assessment, and impact metrics.[39] In a recent survey by the University of Cambridge, scholarly communications professionals identified skills necessary to their work. Their list corresponds closely with NASIG's and adds user experience and open access (content discovery). The Cambridge study predicts these two skills will be even more necessary in the future.[40] Is it reasonable to expect one person to be an expert on all of these evolving issues? NASIG thinks not.

> The specific duties of the scholarly communication librarian (SCL) . . . may be broad and amorphous. Variety is the only constant in the job duties of SCLs and responsibility for the full suite of competencies is beyond the reach of even the most accomplished librarian. Moreover, though a single librarian may be responsible for leading these efforts, scholarly communication impacts all librarians, and as such, specific duties are often diffused through an organization. The leadership exemplified by the SCL also may occur at different levels of an organization, from entry level to senior administration, and usually entails a specific focus within the broad scholarly communication space.[41]

Similarly, writers have described skills necessary for digital scholarship work. Among them, data management, copyright, and publishing overlap with scholarly communication librarians' knowledge base.[42] Because digital scholarship is such a vast umbrella, the Council on Library and Information Resources (CLIR) took a broader approach, grouping desired qualities into major competencies.[43] The ability to collaborate well is the most sought-after trait. Because digital scholarship is often done in interdisciplinary teams, good communication and interpersonal skills are vital. Second, CLIR identified a learning mindset that evinces flexibility, curiosity, and a willingness to fail. Disciplinary expertise (often in the humanities), methodological competencies (for example, data visualization, computational linguistics, and text encoding), technical skills, and managerial skills complete the list.

It is vital to underscore NASIG's three related points about scholarly communications work, which, I believe, apply equally to digital scholarship: no single librarian can master all aspects of it, it impacts all librarians, and all levels of organizations promote it.[44] So perhaps the most impactful thing that scholarly communication or digital scholarship librarians *can* do is to help colleagues see how they fit in the big picture. Librarians across functional roles must understand their vital roles in facilitating new forms of scholarship. Teaching librarians incorporate scholarly communication into their classes. Public service librarians explain copyright concepts to patrons. Catalogers help resources to be discoverable. Archivists preserve digital objects. Administrators structure organizations to advance all of this work.

Neither scholarly communication nor digital scholarship will reach a point when librarians can check them off of their to-do lists. Instructors will continue to reinforce information literacy concepts and consider forthcoming open resources that save students money. Researchers will communicate their outcomes to the public in creative ways. Content makers and users need to understand and leverage Creative Commons licenses. As new tools and models emerge along the way, librarians must help others take advantage of them. After all, every academic librarian is a teaching librarian.

In sum, scholarly communication and digital scholarship overlap in many foundational ways and require similar skills and mindsets. Both fields are entrepreneurial and interdisciplinary, and both will continue to change. And that change makes them interesting. Librarians, creators, administrators, and other stakeholders will use their combined expertise to ensure that developments in scholarly communication and digital scholarship shape the future of education. So, pack up your questions and bring them to the party.

Takeaways

- Librarians across departments play important roles in enabling new forms of scholarship to be created, shared, and preserved. Although terminology and sub-specialties vary ("data," "scholarly communication," "digital scholarship," "user experience," "metadata," "liaison"), we all work to achieve the common goal of publicly accessible scholarship.

- Many complex issues influence our paths forward with scholarly communications, outreach, and education.

- All librarians are teaching librarians.

NOTES

1. Grant Wiggins and Jay McTighe, *Understanding by Design: Guide to Creating High-Quality Units* (Alexandria: Association for Supervision and Curriculum Development, 2011), 15.
2. "ACRL Framework for Information Literacy for Higher Education," www.ala .org/acrl/standards/ilframework.
3. 17 U.S.C. §101 and Feist Publications, Inc. v. Rural Telephone Service Co., 499 U.S. 340 (1991).
4. Vincent Larivière, Stefanie Haustein, and Phillipe Mongeon, "The Oligopoly of Academic Publishers in the Digital Era," PLOS ONE 10, no. 6 (2015), https://doi.org/10.1371/journal.pone.0127502.
5. The American Chemical Society and Taylor and Francis comprise the remainder.
6. Together, the five most prolific publishers in these subjects (RELX Group, Springer, Wiley-Blackwell, Taylor and Francis, and Sage Publications) produced 15 percent of scholarly output in the mid-1990s. Their share rose to more than 51 percent by 2013.
7. Stephen Bosch, Barbara Albee, and Kittie Henderson, "Death by 1,000 Cuts: Flat Budgets, Price Increases, and a Reliance on Status Journals for Tenure and Promotion Keep Familiar Pressures on the Serials Marketplace," *Library Journal* 45, no. 7 (2018): 28–33.
8. "About Wiley-Blackwell," https://www.wiley.com/WileyCDA/Brand/id-35 .html.
9. "RELX Group," https://www.relx.com/.
10. UW's Law Library and Tacoma Library currently offer digital repository services through bepress.
11. Both are independent as of this writing.
12. "ResearchGate Privacy Policy," https://www.researchgate.net/privacy -policy; "Elsevier Privacy Policy," https://www.elsevier.com/legal/privacy -policy; "Academia.edu Privacy Policy," www.academia.edu/privacy.
13. "Elsevier Privacy Policy"; "Academia.edu Privacy Policy."

14. Members of Academia.edu grant a "worldwide, revocable, non-exclusive, transferable license to exercise any and all rights under copyright, in any medium, and to authorize others to do the same . . . provided that the Member Content is not sold for a profit," https://www.academia.edu/terms. Elsevier's terms state that "by posting, uploading, inputting, providing or submitting ('Posting') a Submission, you grant us (and those we work with) a royalty-free, perpetual, irrevocable, worldwide, non-exclusive right and license to publish, post, reformat, index, archive, make available and link to such Submission in all forms and media (whether now known or later developed), in connection with the operation of our respective businesses (including, without limitation, the Services) and to permit others to do so." See https://www.elsevier.com/legal/elsevier-website-terms-and-conditions.

15. "ACRL Framework."

16. For a good discussion from 2015, see University of California, "A Social Networking Site Is Not an Open Access Repository," http://osc.university ofcalifornia.edu/2015/12/a-social-networking-site-is-not-an-open-access -repository/.

17. "ACRL Framework."

18. American Library Association, "Core Values of Librarianship," www.ala.org/ advocacy/intfreedom/corevalues.

19. Council on Library and Information Resources, "Building Expertise to Support Digital Scholarship: A Global Perspective," https://www.clir.org/ wp-content/uploads/sites/6/2016/11/pub168.pdf.

20. NASIG, "Core Competencies for Scholarly Communication Librarians," www.nasig.org/site_page.cfm?pk_association_webpage_menu=310&pk _association_webpage=9435.

21. CNBC, "Here's Every iPhone Released, in Order, and What Changed Along the Way," https://www.cnbc.com/2017/06/29/every-iphone-released-in -order.html.

22. See Copyright Law of the United States (Title 17), https://www.copyright .gov/title17/.

23. For a comprehensive discussion of safe harbors for library activities, see Tomas Lipinsky, *The Complete Copyright Liability Handbook for Librarians and Educators* (New York: Neal-Schuman Publishers, 2006).

24. *Code of Best Practices in Fair Use for Academic Research Libraries* (Washington, DC: Association of Research Libraries, 2012), 5, www.arl.org/storage/ documents/publications/code-of-best-practices-fair-use.pdf.

25. Codes of best practices in a variety of fields are available through American University's Center for Media and Social Impact, http://cmsimpact.org/ program/fair-use/.

26. "Wix.com Terms of Use," https://www.wix.com/about/terms-of-use and "Wix.com Privacy Policy," https://www.wix.com/about/privacy.

27. The SPARC (Scholarly Publishing and Academic Resources Coalition) Author Addendum is one tool authors can use. See https://sparcopen.org/ our-work/author-rights/brochure-html.

28. Harvard University, "A Model Open Access Policy," https://osc.hul.harvard .edu/assets/files/model-policy-annotated_12_2015.pdf.

29. For a list of US federal agencies' article sharing requirements, see SPARC's "Article Sharing Requirements by Federal Agency," http://researchsharing. sparcopen.org/articles. See also Eugene McDermott Library, "Funder Mandates," University of Texas Dallas, https://www.utdallas.edu/library/ open-access/funder-mandates.html.

30. ACRL Working Group on Intersections of Scholarly Communication and Information Literacy, *Intersections of Scholarly Communication and Information Literacy: Creating Strategic Collaborations for a Changing Academic Environment* (Chicago: Association of College and Research Libraries, 2013).

31. Ibid., 6.

32. University of Nevada Las Vegas University Libraries has produced the engaging short video "Research Is a Conversation," which illustrates this point. See https://vimeo.com/175421812.

33. ACRL, *Intersections*.

34. ACRL, "Framework."

35. "Torn Apart/Separados," http://xpmethod.plaintext.in/torn-apart/ volume/2/index.

36. Just for fun, see "Combined Measurement of the Higgs Boson Mass in pp Collisions at √s=7 and 8 TeV with the ATLAS and CMS Experiments," *Physical Review Letters,* May 14, 2015, a physics article with hundreds of authors.

37. ACRL, *Intersections,* 6.

38. Wiggins and McTighe, *Understanding by Design*, 15.

39. NASIG, "Core Competencies."

40. University of Cambridge Office of Scholarly Communication, "Skills in Scholarly Communication: Needs and Development," *Unlocking Research,* March 23, 2018, https://unlockingresearch-blog.lib.cam.ac.uk/?p=1943.

41. NASIG, "Core Competencies."

42. For a review of the literature—and a long list of desired skills— see Margaret King, "Digital Scholarship Librarian: What Skills and Competencies are Needed to be a Collaborative Librarian," *International Information and Library Review* 50, no. 1 (2018): 40–46, DOI: 10.1080/10572317.2017.1422898. As the title suggests, "the capacity for partnership is at the core of the profile of the digital scholarship librarian."

43. Vivian Lewis et al., "Building Expertise to Support Digital Scholarship: A Global Perspective," (Washington, DC: Council on Library and Information Resources, 2015),https://www.clir.org/wp-content/uploads/ sites/6/2016/11/pub168.pdf.

44. NASIG, "Core Competencies."

PART II

Practices

VERLETTA KERN

4
Assessment at the University of Washington Libraries

As academic libraries struggle to understand their role in supporting digital scholarship, there is a clear desire to share needs assessment work broadly so that we can learn from each other. A 2018 discussion on the ACRL Digital Scholarship Section Listserv revealed relatively few such assessments have been performed or shared publicly.[1] Questions also remain across the profession on how to assess digital scholarship work given its nexus between traditional research and emerging technology.

At the University of Washington Libraries, where I work as the Libraries' first full-time digital scholarship librarian, we, too, are working to understand our role in a changing culture of digital scholarship. Fortunately, as an institution recognized nationally for its strong assessment program, an assessment of digital scholarship needs across campus was a natural starting point for determining our digital scholarship strategy. Our work has taken a series of forms: faculty and graduate student interviews/focus groups, Triennial Survey data, digital pedagogy assessment work, evaluation of questions and needs surfaced during two years of weekly Digital Scholarship Project Help Office Hours and teaching and research case studies. By sharing the details of these assessments—their goals and methods, collective findings, and some of the "next steps" taken following their completion—I hope to contribute to this emerging area of research and offer guidance to those pursuing their own digital scholarship needs assessment work.

BACKGROUND: DIGITAL SCHOLARSHIP AT THE UNIVERSITY OF WASHINGTON

Although the University of Washington (UW) has a long and established history of digital humanities work, the UW Libraries' formal Digital Scholarship Program remains in its infancy.[2] The role of digital scholarship librarian was created in January of 2016 as a 0.5 full-time equivalent (FTE) position designed to serve UW students, faculty, and staff in a concierge role, connecting those wishing to complete digital projects with people and resources to help realize their project objectives. The position has since evolved into a role overseeing digital scholarship strategy for the UW Libraries with a mandate to "conduct regular environmental scans of the campus in collaboration with subject librarians and other campus stakeholders to identify current and emerging digital scholarship projects, and recommend strategies to support the needs."[3] As a result, the position was made a 1.0 FTE position in July 2017 and was reorganized under the newly formed Scholarly Communication and Publishing department. Although the positioning of this role fits well in a department focused on emerging forms of scholarship, sharing research for the public good, and outreach, being the sole librarian responsible for not only carrying out digital scholarship work on a practical level but also advocating and visioning for the future of this work can be daunting! The success of our needs assessment work relied on careful collaboration with colleagues across the Libraries, support of UW iSchool students, and volunteers.[4]

As we will see, the five types of needs assessments ultimately conducted by the UW Libraries in relation to digital scholarship were largely spurred or shaped by the creation of this digital scholarship librarian position and contributed to the part of the ramp-up that resulted in the position's expansion and the UW Libraries' 2014–2017 Strategic Plan, which recognized providing expertise and support for digital scholarship as an area of focus. We will begin our needs assessment discussion with interviews and focus groups.

Focus Groups and Interviews

One of the earliest digital scholarship program goals was to discover what digital scholarship means to those working in the different disciplines.[5] It occurred to us, for example, that participants in certain fields might not see themselves or their work reflected in the term "digital scholarship," which could put the program at an initial marketing disadvantage. The Libraries was also curious to hear from researchers about the different types of digital scholarship work being done across campus—and where participants could use help in completing their work. To this end, the Libraries organized a series of digital scholarship focus groups, with UW faculty and graduate students.

Description

During the spring quarter of 2016, the Libraries, with support from two iSchool Capstone students, held focus groups with fourteen faculty and six graduate students from the humanities, social sciences, and sciences. These focus groups were organized by discipline and divided between faculty and graduate students. In cases where participants were unable to attend the designated time for the focus group, I arranged individual interviews. In order to solicit participants, subject librarians sent out email invitations to their departments, and I sent an invitation to researchers affiliated with the UW Walter Chapin Simpson Center for the Humanities. Once participants responded, the organizers sent them questions in advance of their scheduled focus groups/interviews (see appendix E), each of which ran for an hour and included light snacks and drinks. To help make note taking easier, two Libraries staff were present during each interview, one to lead the discussion and one to take notes.

Findings

1. The term "digital scholarship" doesn't resonate

It became quickly apparent when talking with participants that digital scholarship as a term is meaningless to those outside of a library context. Those in the sciences, for instance, heard the term digital scholarship and immediately jumped into discussions of electronic library article databases that support research. When asked why they equated digital scholarship with library article research, one participant responded, "Everything is digital. The term is meaningless, so when you take away the digital, you're left with scholarship. To me, scholarship means research through traditional library tools." In the humanities, those working with digital tools and methods or doing what would be considered digital scholarship work in a general context did not see themselves as digital scholars. On the flip side, humanists who have been working in the area of digital humanities for several years also did not see themselves as digital humanists or digital scholars; one responded, "This is humanities scholarship. We've moved past the need to include digital in the definition."

Digital scholarship's lack of appeal as a description for a suite of services is confirmed in the literature. Although planning support for digital scholarship work, the University of Houston's Digital Scholarship Team notes, "Identifying a term that both describes digital scholarship services and resonates with students, faculty, and staff is an imperative step in this phase."[6] A 2014 OCLC Report confirms the statement of our humanities and science participants: "No matter which approaches to supporting the digital humanities you opt to take, keep in mind that what we call 'The Digital Humanities' today will soon be considered 'The Humanities.' Supporting DH scholarship is not much different than supporting digital scholarship in any discipline. Increasingly, digital scholarship is simply scholarship."[7]

It is clear that if libraries want to establish successful digital scholarship services or centers on campus, we must give thought and pay careful attention to how researchers describe their work in order for them to see themselves in the library services and spaces provided. We continued to explore the question of "what do people call this work" as our assessment project moved forward.

2. Technical skills are difficult to acquire

Across the board, all disciplines represented in the focus groups voiced frustrations in the lack of clear opportunities to systematically learn new technical skills. Desired skills and tools ranged from getting help with web design to learning GitHub to learning programming languages like Python or C++, to learning R. Those who wished to learn programming languages expressed frustration that they could not take computer science courses without being enrolled in the School of Computer Science and Engineering. Faculty and students alike also expressed a strong desire to create a web presence that effectively showcases their work but lacked the skills or expertise to do so. This mirrors Jennifer Vinopal and Monica McCormick's findings, as expressed in their 2013 work on supporting digital scholarship in research libraries. They write, "Scholars want help developing, using, and maintaining Web sites for storing and presenting their digital research content."[8]

UW student participants also described taking courses that required them to use technical tools without formal training, leaving them scrambling to get help from peers and online sites like Stack Overflow to fill in knowledge gaps. On the flip side, instructors who participated in the focus groups complained that UW's quarter system limited their availability to teach the use of tools in addition to course content. Consequently, when forced to choose where to focus class time, faculty often chose to focus on content over tool instruction.

3. Multidisciplinary collaborations are challenging

Faculty and students alike were excited by the possibility of cross-disciplinary collaborations on projects but felt they did not have a clear path to identifying and establishing such collaborations, which they considered an overwhelming barrier to performing cross-disciplinary work. For example, one faculty member in the sciences hoped to identify a philosophy researcher who could collaborate on a project examining race and gender in machine learning algorithms but had no idea who in other departments might be interested in this work. With a full research and teaching load, the faculty member had little time to explore potential collaborators. Another researcher was fortunate enough to identify an international collaborator but institutional restrictions on resource sharing (e.g., you must be affiliated with the UW to access and contribute materials to a UW server) left the duo without a sound infrastructure to support their work. As research collaborations expand beyond institutional silos to global collaborations, more efforts will need to be taken to create secure, safe, and accessible infrastructures for researchers to perform and share their work.

The challenges of building communities of practice are one of the major barriers to furthering a culture of digital scholarship. The 2017 Educause Center for Analysis and Research (ECAR) report, *Building Capacity for Digital Humanities,* reflects this point even as it envisions a strong future for cross-disciplinary collaborations: "Matching a scholar's research with corresponding methods from other disciplines and finding like-minded and open-minded collaborators is a common dilemma because it is rare to find somebody with all the skills required."[9] It is our aspiration that the UW Libraries, as a discipline-gnostic space, can help foster community around digital scholarship and, in turn, help foster desired cross-disciplinary connections.

4. Opportunities to showcase work are needed

Study participants expressed frustration that there was not a central place on campus to showcase digital scholarship work happening across the UW. This topic came up both from the perspective of wanting a place or opportunity to share the work that researchers had done and as an opportunity to get new and fresh ideas from other researchers. A 2014 University of Pittsburgh needs assessment of digital scholarship reported a similar finding: "There is a need for centralized spaces available on campus where faculty and students can exhibit the products of their digital scholarship."[10]

5. The standing of digital scholarship work in the professional community

Faculty and graduate students dedicated to doing digital scholarship work are often forced to do double the work based on traditional promotion and tenure processes or thesis and dissertation requirements. Junior faculty participants in particular expressed that if they dared to take on a digital project, they needed to continue to work just as hard on producing a traditional monograph or publishing in academic journals to meet tenure and promotion guidelines for their departments. A 2010 report by Diane Harley et al. that includes interviews with faculty succinctly captures some of the same faculty concerns about embracing new forms of scholarship, especially early in one's career: "The fact remains, however, that: (1) new forms of scholarship must be perceived as having undergone rigorous peer review, (2) few untenured scholars are presenting such publications as part of their tenure packages, and

(3) the mechanisms for evaluating new genres (e.g., nonlinear narratives and multimedia publications) may be prohibitive for reviewers in terms of time and inclination.[11]

Although numerous groups are experimenting with peer review of digital projects, until promotion and tenure systems become more accepting of new methods of scholarly publishing, untenured faculty will remain skeptical about digital scholarship, will need to go above and beyond to perform both types of publishing, or will wait until after tenure to engage in digital scholarship work.

Graduate students were also in a difficult position because many faculty positions request digital scholarship skills in job postings, yet traditional thesis and dissertation requirements are still print-centric. As a result, graduate students, who wish to succeed on the future job market, found themselves both writing a traditional thesis or dissertation alongside creating digital components of the thesis or dissertation that will not count toward graduation requirements at UW. Although there are trends shifting away from the traditional print thesis and dissertations, these have yet to be fully recognized by most UW departments and the UW Graduate School.[12]

6. The UW Libraries remains a natural home for digital scholarship

The UW Libraries was mentioned time and time again as a natural home for digital scholarship services. Participants spoke favorably about the UW Libraries as a discipline-neutral space with the ability to serve the needs of all disciplines, and to provide equipment and services that could be used by anyone from across the University.[13] The UW Libraries was also suggested by participants as a natural place for cross-disciplinary connections to occur. This finding was encouraging as we moved forward in assessing digital scholarship needs.

Limitations

Although the cross-disciplinary information provided by the focus group assessment was useful, the usefulness of the results may be limited by the fact that only four of the participants were from the social sciences (three faculty and one graduate student). Additionally, questions posed to those in the science/social sciences focus groups differed from those asked in the humanities groups, as a sample run of the questions with the former group revealed a need for additional context, which was corrected in the latter groups. In the future, the deployment of broader and more open-ended questions might yield a results set that maps more equally across the disciplines.

Triennial Survey

Although focus groups are extremely useful for gathering deep information about the faculty and graduate students on the subject of digital scholarship, they obviously lack the broad perspective of certain large-scale assessments like campus-wide surveys, which the UW Libraries is also experienced at deploying. As the digital scholarship librarian, I recognized an opportunity to address the large-scale view of digital scholarship across the university in the UW Libraries' Triennial Survey, which we administer to faculty, graduate students, and a sample of undergraduate students on all three UW campuses every three years. By incorporating questions related to digital scholarship into the 2016 version of the survey, I hoped to gain a better understanding of (1) what types of digital tools and methods were being used by faculty and graduate students across campus, and (2) which departments were doing this work.

Description

The UW Libraries' Triennial Survey is sent out by email to faculty, graduate students, and a sample of undergraduate students on all three campuses every three years since 2004.[14] Questions in the survey are far-ranging, and cover everything from a user's experience with UW Libraries' services to the use of library spaces. In spring 2016, I worked with the UW Libraries' Assessment Team to add a specific question to the survey pertaining to digital scholarship:

> Does your research and teaching involve any of the following digital activities/tools? Please check all that apply.
>
> ☐ My work does not involve any of these
> ☐ Text/data mining
> ☐ Data visualization (using tools such as Tableau)
> ☐ Web authoring or publishing (using tools such as Scalar or Omeka)
> ☐ Digital mapping/digital map making (using tools such as ArcGIS, Neatline, Google My Maps)
> ☐ Digital annotation (using tools such as hypothes.is and Lacuna)
> ☐ Other (please specify)

All told, 1,527 faculty across all three campuses received the survey, with a 35 percent response rate, and 2,780 Seattle campus graduate and professional students received the survey, yielding a 22 percent response rate.[15]

Findings

The 2016 survey results indicated that 40 percent of UW faculty and 40 percent of graduate students said their work involved at least one of the listed digital activities/tools.[16] The students and faculty of the College of the Environment and the College of Built Environments ranked the highest for UW schools and colleges for using one or more digital activity or tool. Text/data mining and data visualization ranked the highest for faculty at 24 percent and 23 percent, respectively. Graduate students ranked data visualization and text/data mining the highest at 26 percent and 24 percent. These results varied slightly from college to college. For example, the College of the Environment ranked use of digital mapping/digital map-making tools at a higher rate. These results have been incredibly useful in identifying which schools and colleges to target as we continue to plan for digital scholarship services and provide a starting point to plan for larger scale digital scholarship support.

Limitations

Based on the comments received in the survey, we noted that a few respondents were slightly confused by some of the digital scholarship question multiple-choice options. Although we gave examples of specific tools that could relate to a digital scholarship activity, for example "data visualization (using tools such as Tableau)," it was clear that some respondents answered "no" to question options when they engaged in the underlying activity but used a different tool than the one(s) mentioned in the option parenthetically. This confusion may have impacted some of the survey results and will be addressed in future iterations of the survey. Likewise, given the high number of respondents who indicated they used text/data mining techniques, in the 2019 survey this activity will be separated into two response options, one for text mining and one for data mining. In doing so, I hope to reveal a more accurate representation of the digital scholarship work happening on campus, and to offer more guidance in developing targeted services. With limited resources to pilot new services, this information will help us decide whether to experiment with text mining or data mining first. It will further conversations with potential campus partners who may be interested to work with us in piloting future services.

Digital Scholarship Project Help Office Hours

As many public services liaisons can attest, consultations with researchers are valuable opportunities for better understanding the needs and activities of a given academic population. In order to learn more about the UW digital scholarship community, and to help encourage scholars engaged in digital scholarship projects, I began collaborating in spring 2016 with staff in

UW's centralized Learning Technologies unit to offer Digital Scholarship Project Help Office Hours. From the very start, these hours were another formal method for the Libraries to gather data related to digital scholarship needs, including which UW populations require assistance with digital projects (e.g., departments, as well as degree classes), what types of projects researchers are working on, and what types of difficulties those researchers are running into.

Description

Digital Scholarship Project Help Office Hours are held weekly for an hour and a half in the UW Libraries' Research Commons Consultation Space, a small room with semi-private cubicles that is located in one of the Libraries' main campus buildings. Office Hours are co-staffed by me, the digital scholarship librarian, and Beth Lytle, an information technologist from UW Learning Technologies.[17] Together, the two of us help Office Hours participants get started with digital projects, or to complete particular aspects of projects on which they are stuck. For each drop-in, we record information about which department the participant is from, their UW status (e.g., faculty, graduate student, undergraduate student), and where they are stuck (e.g., scoping a project, looking for storage and hosting for materials).

Findings

1. Who attends office hours?

In the first year of Office Hours, attendees included mainly UW faculty members and a few graduate students. More undergraduates began using the service in year two, thanks to faculty encouragement. Office Hours are the busiest during the summer months when certain UW faculty and graduate students begin work on their Walter Chapin Simpson Center Digital Humanities Summer Fellowships.[18] There has also been strong diversity in the departmental affiliations of Office Hours attendees. Some of the departments represented have included Architecture; Comparative History of Ideas; Comparative Literature and Cinema Studies; English, French and Italian Studies; Gender, Women, and Sexuality Studies; Geography; History; and Music.

2. What work is happening?

Our findings suggest that UW researchers are engaged in a wide range of digital scholarship projects, from creating Omeka sites to interest in story mapping projects to data visualization to text encoding and stylometry. Additionally, many faculty members have come to Office Hours with questions about effectively incorporating digital technology into their courses—which suggests an opportunity for the Libraries or Learning Technologies to step into the pedagogical components of digital scholarship.

3. Where do participants get stuck?

Another finding was that many Office Hours participants have trouble knowing how to start a digital project. For instance, both Beth and I spend significant time helping participants scope their research questions into more manageable projects.[19] Help is also frequently requested from attendees to decide which digital tool will best represent a participants' work, (e.g., from offering multilingual access to digitized texts and images to sharing the lived experience of an African American family member's journey from the southern United States to the Pacific Northwest during the 1950s).

Those wishing to use Omeka and related plug-ins come to Office Hours for advice on how to install Omeka on the UW server. Other questions range from locating software on campus to completing text encoding projects to creating content in Wikipedia to assistance with metadata construction.

However, the number one question we receive during Office Hours centers around where to host and store digital projects for free or at low cost. This finding mirrors a 2016 Jisc report finding, which states: "From the researchers' point of view, the infrastructure, and the ways in which different systems interoperate, should be invisible in much the same way that most people rarely give a second thought to how power, water and telephony services are provided to the home or office."[20]

The issue of limited storage space is particularly problematic for instructors who teach digital tools or methods as part of a class, and thus fill their allotted departmental server space quickly with student projects. Instructors often express their frustration at having to pay additional storage fees when they are trying to teach students practical and marketable digital skills. For those creating research projects, it is clear that more work needs to be done to help researchers develop a better understanding of the long-term costs of not only storage and hosting of projects but also the costs to update software and migrate content to new platforms as older platforms lose support over time alongside the long-term costs of digital preservation. We have begun to incorporate conversations about planning for costs, planning for metadata integration into projects, and long-term preservation into library workshops focused on digital project creation but still have much work ahead in expanding knowledge in this new realm of digital publishing.

Limitations

The information gathered during Digital Scholarship Project Help Office Hours has provided me personally and the UW Libraries in general with a good start for understanding the range of needs and barriers the campus community faces when completing digital projects. That said, there is still likely a set of needs yet to be discovered, such as those faced by researchers who cannot currently attend scheduled Office Hours, or who lack the time to make a consultation appointment.

Omeka Case Studies

With a variety of questions surfacing during Office Hours surrounding the digital scholarship tool Omeka, we focused the next portion of our assessment work on one-on-one interviews, walking step-by-step through the experience using Omeka from both the research and the teaching perspectives. Our goals for this assessment included developing a better understanding of objectives for digital work in teaching and research, what steps were taken to complete the work, and what pain points surfaced in completing digital projects from the teaching and research perspective.

Description

I interviewed two faculty instructors regarding their experiences integrating Omeka into their courses and one faculty member who used Omeka to create a hybrid publication published with a University Press was interviewed. Our interviews lasted an hour and notes from the interview were shared with the instructors to confirm accuracy. All three faculty members represented different departments within the UW College of Arts and Sciences and did not know details of one another's work prior to the case study interviews.

Findings

1. Teaching case studies

Though the teaching examples represented two different departments, similar themes emerged. For example, instructor 1 used Omeka with lower division undergraduate course and instructor 2 used Omeka with an upper division undergraduate course. Both instructors wished to offer students an opportunity to learn and incorporate skills beyond those of simply writing a term paper. As Omeka holds a strong focus on metadata integration, the instructors used this opportunity to teach critical thinking skills by developing metadata for objects they collected and integrated into their assignments. Both instructors emphasized the importance of describing items and the ramifications of how they are found (or not found) online as result, developing multiple keywords to describe objects, and asking students to think more critically about metadata attached to items they search for in the future as they interact with materials on the web. Surprisingly, when asked if they had invited a librarian to speak with their classes on the topic of metadata construction, the instructors expressed that they had not realized librarians would talk to classes about this topic. Library expertise did not immediately come to mind when thinking of metadata construction. As a result of these conversations, I look forward to working more closely with our metadata librarian and the Libraries' larger Teaching and Learning Group to think about ways to incorporate and scale metadata conversations directly into classroom settings. These instructors represent a growing shift in digital literacy education. As the 2017 Horizon Report on Digital Literacy notes, "most of the digital literacy training in higher education is directed toward consumption and evaluation of information and media, and not on the creation of products using digital resources. Additionally, postgraduates expressed that they had minimal or no training in the use of digital artifacts to communicate ideas or stories (51.1%), and they indicated they were given minimal guidance around the laws, rights and responsibilities, and security for using technology and media (58.1%). These responses mirror the limited experiences undergraduates have to practice with these digital tools."[21]

Libraries have an opportunity to partner with faculty and share expertise in metadata construction, rights training, preservation, and new modes to communicate research more broadly. As we move from a model of students as consumers of information to creators of information sources, we need to adapt library instructional methods to meet these needs. This will involve more communication and collaboration among public services staff, technical services staff, and IT staff to create a successful transition. The role of digital scholarship librarian seems like a perfect bridge to begin these conversations based on the public-facing work performed by digital scholarship librarians and the need for coordination with technical services and IT colleagues to move digital scholarship projects from idea to reality.

These Omeka case studies also helped the UW Libraries to identify a broader need for guidance on integrating technology into course assignments. Libraries have traditionally offered assignment design services to faculty, assisting them with the integration of research skills into course assignments based on course goals. Faculty would like to see a similar service offered that focuses on integrating digital tools and methods into course assignments. Instructor 1 described a willingness to learn digital tools and methods but with heavy teaching loads, research agendas, and the compact nature of the quarter system, limited time was left to investigate which tools would be most appropriate for classroom purposes. This problem is compounded because new tools are coming out all the time, leaving instructor 1 feeling overwhelmed when trying to identify which tools to focus on when teaching. Both instructors expressed a strong desire for a single point to find for support in identifying the best tools and gain assistance with tool setup. This is a current gap on the UW campus—UW librarians are still focused on creating traditional research assignments, UW's Center for Teaching and Learning does not yet offer support in this area, and UW Learning Technologies only offers support for a specific set of University-supported tools. As a result, both instructors used teaching assistants (TAs) to run a broad investigation of available digital tools and used TAs to help set up Omeka on the UW server. One can imagine the number of resources wasted if each department is hiring TAs to duplicate this work time and time again. Unfortunately, UW is not unique in this situation. As ECAR reports, "In the absence of institutional support, grass-roots initiatives tend to be siloed. Multiple individuals or groups in different departments or divisions may work with the assumption that they are the only people doing digital humanities on campus because they have never seen other DH work in their local context."[22]

The case studies highlighted limitations in UW's infrastructure to support digital work. Because Omeka is not a centrally supported tool at UW, instructors who wish to install it on UW server space must tackle installation on their own. Instructor 2 estimated that, along with a teaching assistant, around forty hours was spent trying to get Omeka installed and running properly on the UW server. Both instructors complained that hosting the course Omeka sites on the UW server resulted in sluggish response times when multiple students were working on the Omeka site at the same time during class sessions. Running an unsupported tool also means that there is no centrally supported assistance when the tool breaks. Indeed, Instructor 1 reported that the site once crashed the night before a major assignment was due when all of the students logged in at the same time to upload their assignments. This resulted in the course TA having to pull away from assisting with course content and grading in order to bring the site back up. Instructor 2 reported similarly that a UW server upgrade once broke the Omeka course site a few days before the beginning of the quarter. Because the instructor was busy trying to make final preparations for courses, there was little time to investigate the source of the problem, and the instructor ended up paying a fee out of pocket to have University IT make the needed repairs to get the site running in time for the first day of classes. It is clear that a single point of entry and a robust digital infrastructure are key in helping faculty integrate new modes of scholarship into the classroom at low cost.

2. Research case study

The faculty member involved in this case study was under contract with a university press to publish a book. In order to keep costs down (it can be expensive to publish image-heavy books) and to provide open access to foreign contributors to the publication, the faculty member created a hybrid publication using Omeka. The Omeka site would contain additional images and offer an opportunity to incorporate discussions of media materials not possible in a typical print publication. Unfortunately, many university presses in the United States are not able to commit to long-term storage and hosting of digital companions to print work, leaving researchers to identify their own hosting and storage solutions should they choose to go the hybrid publication route.

Similar to the teaching case studies, this faculty member had to decide on whether to select a UW-supported tool or a non-supported tool. The faculty member began their hybrid publication journey with selection of a UW-supported tool, WordPress. Unfortunately, this site was hacked, leading to an immediate site shut down by campus IT and the loss of all project data. The faculty member next selected a non-UW-supported tool, Omeka, to host the content, and hired a programmer to support the project with the help of additional grant funding. As with the teaching case studies, Omeka was painstakingly installed on the UW servers where it was sluggish due to the amount of image and media files contained within the site. Lack of clarity in how to set up a custom URL for the UW-hosted site also led to additional stress and unnecessary work on the part of the faculty member. Eventually it became clear that the site needed to be moved to a non-UW server to avoid these slowdowns and hassles.

At this point, the faculty member approached the UW Libraries in search of a hosting solution. However, without infrastructure and long-term digital preservation policies in place to support this type of hosting, the Libraries was unable to take the project. Instead, I worked with the faculty member to identify a low-cost hosting solution and helped to negotiate the transition of the site to that space. Still, questions remain as to why faculty member's personal funds must be spent on an ongoing basis to support scholarship that is ostensibly required to advance one's career, or to support UW classroom instruction. For faculty who receive grant funding from which the university takes a cut, the question is why funds from awarded grants aren't reinvested to support infrastructure necessary to share work publicly, particularly when public dissemination of research is a requirement from more and more grant funding agencies.

All case studies presented in this section would have benefited greatly if there was a single place to go early in the digital project planning process to get answers on how best to support the work as well as a robust digital infrastructure to support the work. My hope is that this assessment data will create an urgent need for the Libraries to begin experimenting with digital infrastructure to support student and faculty work. It also opens up the ability to begin conversations around funding opportunities to develop space on campus in support of digital scholarship work.

Limitations

The focus of these case studies on the singular tool Omeka is a clear limitation. A fuller case study assessment might have included the examination of additional tools, although such a project would be significantly more time-intensive Additionally, this study was limited to only the cases of three faculty, all of whom come from the same UW college, the College of Arts and Sciences. For a future study, it would be useful to look at faculty cases from different colleges that reported greater digital tools and methods integration.

Digital Pedagogy Assessment

Description

Based on our teaching case studies and focus group conversations, we wanted to take a deeper dive into what digital scholarship looks like in the classroom. Our goals for this portion of the assessment work were to determine who is teaching digital tools and methods in the classrooms (e.g., tenured faculty, untenured faculty, TAs, lecturers), to determine which departments and schools are incorporating digital skills and methods into the classroom, to determine at what level this work is being done (e.g., graduate versus undergraduate), and examine how various disciplines refer to digital scholarship work.

For this portion of the assessment study, the course descriptions in the UW course catalog were reviewed for mentions of digital tools and methods used as part of the course. Lists of courses were compiled by discipline and sent to subject liaisons for review, asking if, to their knowledge, the list of potential courses involving digital tools and methods was complete (see appendix F for email request templates and course selection criteria). Liaisons were then asked if they would be willing to send a request to their departmental administrative assistant to request a copy of the course syllabus. If the library liaison was unable to send the request, I did so. Requests were sent to departments over the summer months when departmental activity was quieter overall, leading to success in acquiring many of the requested syllabi. Of the 154 syllabi requested, 86 syllabi were received and reviewed of which 63 were determined to fit our initial criteria of incorporating digital tools or methods into the classroom.

Findings

1. Who is teaching these courses?

Instructors listed as the instructor of record on the syllabus, or in the course catalog if no instructor was indicated on the syllabus, were searched to determine their tenure status. Tenured faculty were found to be teaching most of these courses, followed by graduate students, and then nontenure-track faculty. Courses were taught at the lowest rate by nontenured, tenure-track faculty. These findings mirror those found during our focus groups/interviews where junior faculty expressed nervousness about how nontraditional forms of publication would be received during tenure and promotion processes, whereas graduate students expressed a strong need to show evidence of work with digital tools and methods in order to be marketable for future academic positions. Results may also be coupled with concerns that lack of a robust infrastructure to support digital work make it less desirable for untenured faculty to pursue full teaching schedules and tight research time lines for tenure and promotion processes. Unfortunately, it seems this trend is not unique to UW. A recent Ithaka study notes, "Although a little over a third of full professors and assistant professors who answered our survey indicated that they have created or managed digital resources, almost half of the associate professors who responded have done so."[23]

2. Which departments are incorporating digital tools and methods into classes?

Similar to findings from the Triennial Survey data, the departments doing the most work incorporating digital tools and methods into the classroom included the College of Arts and Sciences, the College of Built Environments, and the College of the Environment. It is clear that as digital scholarship services are planned, the UW Libraries will want to keep a close eye on what is happening in these colleges.

3. Where is the work happening?

Perhaps not surprising given the large number of undergraduates at UW, digital tools and methods are being taught at a higher rate in undergraduate courses. This may be tied to our finding from the focus group/interviews assessment that graduate students feel the need to demonstrate their ability to use digital tools and methods to be marketable and thus are more likely to experiment with digital tools and methods in the undergraduate courses they teach. It is clear we must think critically how to scale additional support for undergraduates performing digital scholarship work.

4. How is digital work described?

Given the focus groups/interviews assessment findings that digital scholarship as a term does not resonate with the campus community, we were curious to see how instructors were describing this work in the various disciplines. English Studies instructors described all work, from digital story making to creating archives to story map production, as multimodal work. The largest discrepancies seemed to arise when looking at how disciplines described incorporation of tools or methods to create maps or perform geographical analysis. Terms used included GIS, spatial analysis, mapping, visualization, online maps, digital geographies, multimedia maps, digital spatial technology, critical cartography, and geovisualization. It is clear that to get cross-departmental buy-in for digital scholarship services and spaces, the UW Libraries will need to develop discipline-targeted messages or find another term, perhaps open scholarship, that allows all disciplines to see themselves in the services, programs, and spaces developed by the UW Libraries.

Limitations

Although the data gathered from this portion of our assessment process was informative, it should be noted that there are likely courses we missed in our assessment process due to limited course descriptions in the course catalog and subject liaisons' limitations because they did not have full knowledge of every course taught in their departments. It should also be noted that two departments refused to share their syllabi for the purposes of this study, because they did not want to share intellectual property created by the instructors. The College of Engineering was largely left out of this study because its largest department, the department of Computer Science and Engineering, is well-funded and therefore can pursue its own solutions to many of the issues expressed by our assessment participants. Were it included, the College of Engineering would likely be a leader in the incorporation of digital tools and methods into the classroom.

WHAT'S NEXT

Although the assessment work we've gathered thus far has been informative in establishing a baseline picture of the culture of digital scholarship and in beginning to form relationships with digital scholars across campus, it is time to move from assessment to action! Next steps we will be taking (or have already taken) in this process are outlined below.

Sharing Assessment Data. Assessment data has been shared widely in the UW Libraries, particularly as the strategic planning process is underway. Results have also been shared with the campus IT directors and the vice provost for Academic and Student Affairs in hopes of raising awareness and codeveloping solutions to these emerging needs.

Partnerships. We are identifying potential campus partnerships in hopes of filling in some of the gaps in the systematic learning of tools or programming languages. For example, it is hoped that a closer partnership with UW's eScience Institute may lead to a greater set of solutions for those undertaking digital projects in the future.[24]

Programs. In partnership with the UW Libraries' Research Commons unit, a collaborative space focusing on support for all steps of the research process along with opportunities to share research, I am experimenting with a new program series called Hacking the Academy.[25] The series takes a closer look at the new ways scholarship is produced, shared, archived, and reused through series of panel discussions and workshops. Now in its second year, the series' most highly attended programs fall into the category of workshops where participants are able to actively gain new skills or find funding opportunities for new modes of scholarship.

WICKED PROBLEMS
FOR CONTINUED EXPLORATION

Of course, some problems surfaced by these assessments are more difficult than others to address and point to larger areas of exploration for UW's digital scholarship community. Many of our most wicked problems are tied to issues of funding, space, and limited personnel in an already resource-constrained environment. This leaves us in an uncomfortable, institutional soul-searching space. Wicked problems lacking simple solutions include:

Role of the library. What is the Libraries' role in supporting digital scholarship? What responsibilities lie solely with the Libraries and which should be picked up by or shared with campus partners?

Priorities. With limited institutional resources, how do we shift resources and priorities to support this new movement of students as creators of information? Do we stop doing some things in order to shift funding and resources to new areas? How do we make these decisions and communicate them to the broader campus community?

Platforms. Which digital scholarship platforms do we invest in? How do we balance the desire to self-host infrastructure and the realities of the competition for tech positions in the Seattle area with the risks of investing in hosted services that may be swallowed up by for-profit entities down the road?

Access versus preservation. How do we juggle the need for opportunities to share work openly through digital scholarship platforms with the need for long-term preservation?

Funding. How do we fund digital scholarship infrastructure when collection budgets are already limited? How do we estimate an ongoing budget for storage and hosting of digital scholarship work that maintains certain projects completed by the UW community over time and includes opportunities to grow the collection down the road?

Policies. What role can the Libraries play in helping faculty and students change promotion and tenure requirements or theses and dissertation requirements to include digital work?

We have recently established a Tri-Campus Digital Scholarship group, charged by three associate deans in the UW Libraries and including both UW Libraries' staff and stakeholders across the campus community. This group is a good step forward not only in establishing deeper partnerships across the three campuses but also with the campus at large. The group will come together with a shared vision and work toward a solution to these wicked problems.

CONCLUSION:
A WORD OF CAUTION

Whereas some libraries have significant digital scholarship programs already in operation, the UW Libraries is still making strides in understanding the underlying culture of digital scholarship at UW. The assessment work completed thus far offers a window into that culture and the microcosms of digital scholarship bubbling up throughout campus. Sharing assessment data is helping to raise awareness of growth opportunities across campus to support digital scholarship. Openly sharing digital scholarship assessments has also surfaced patterns of need across institutional boundaries.

That said, although assessment data collection can be useful in determining next steps and creating library buy-in for moving a digital scholarship program forward, it should be noted that the mere act of assessment creates an expectation that participants' perceived digital scholarship problems will be solved. Consequently, unless one is in a position to make changes and create such solutions, one risks leaving digital scholars with a sense of frustration, feeling like they are contributing their time and goodwill to a cause that isn't producing results. Assessment is the beginning of creating long-lasting relationships with digital scholars. These relationships must be nurtured through continual check-ins with those involved in assessment and with status updates on how data shared is being used to move interests forward.

Librarians should also exhibit caution by limiting themselves to acting only on the needs gathered during the assessment process without considering the future of the field. As one focus group interviewee put it, "needs assessments only represent what is being attempted at this time at the University. Who knows what faculty or students could achieve by being opened up to a larger world of possibilities they don't even know exist?" As Brian Matthews, the associate dean for Learning and Outreach at Virginia Tech, writes in *Think Like a Startup: A White Paper to Inspire Library Entrepreneurialism*, "Assessment isn't about developing breakthrough ideas. In short: we focus on service sustainability rather than revolutionary or evolutionary new services."[26] The 2014 OCLC Report *Does Every Research Library Need a Digital Humanities Center?* concurs with Matthews on the importance of keeping an eye towards the future of the Libraries partnering with researchers as creators of new knowledge, "It has been argued that the digital revolution is reconnecting scholars and memory institutions. Ignoring this trend could sever those relationships and position the library more as a museum than as an integral contributor to scholarship."[27] Although solutions to these problems are difficult to mediate and resolve, inaction in supporting the changing role of how scholarship is produced will result in serious consequences for a library's standing across campus and in higher education as a whole. Between the work you'll read about in this book and the newly formed Tri-Campus Digital

Scholarship Group, the UW Libraries stands ready to take on the challenges of building a robust digital scholarship program to meet the needs of today's researchers and those yet to come.

Takeaways

■ Limitations of traditional publication systems (tenure and promotion or thesis and dissertation requirements) have serious implications on a scholar's opportunity to engage in this work and/or a scholar's workload, feeling the need to produce both types of scholarship to move forward.

■ Above all, digital scholars want a single point of entry where all of their digital project questions can be addressed coupled with a reliable digital infrastructure with which to perform this work.

■ Libraries need to work with faculty to incorporate new forms of scholarship into the classroom through codeveloping research assignments putting students at the center as content producers rather than content consumers, engaging in active training and conversations in metadata construction, talking through the lifecycle of digital work, offering hands on rights training, and incorporating discussions of reproducibility best practices into the classroom.

NOTES

1. Association of College and Research Libraries, "Digital Scholarship Section Listserv," March 26–27, 2018.
2. Digital humanities work began at the University of Washington in the late 1970s with faculty members Walter Andrews (Near Eastern Languages and Civilizations) and Leroy Searle (English). Two separate campus entities have also been around since the 1980s: The Center for the Humanities (now the Walter Chapin Simpson Center for the Humanities) and the Humanities Arts and Computing Center (now the Center for Digital Arts and Experimental Media).
3. University of Washington Libraries, "Digital Scholarship Librarian Position Description," May 17, 2018.
4. I would like to acknowledge those who contributed to the assessment process ,including Jackie Belanger and Maggie Faber of the UW Libraries Assessment Team; UW iSchool students Abigail Darling and Becky Ramsey Leoparti; Michelle Urberg, Liz Bedford, Jenny Muilenburg, Khue Duong, Beth Lytle, and the Libraries' Teaching and Learning Group's Assessment Subcommittee. This assessment work is possible thanks to their feedback on assessment design and their assistance collecting and analyzing assessment data.
5. UW has taken the approach to include the arts, humanities, social sciences, and sciences when developing services for digital scholarship.

6. Josh Been et.al., *Digital Scholarship Road Map: A Report from UH Libraries' Digital Scholarship Team* (Houston: University of Houston Libraries, 2016), 6, http://hdl.handle.net/10657/1623.

7. Jennifer Schaffner and Ricky Erway, *Does Every Research Library Need a Digital Humanities Center?* (Dublin, Ohio: OCLC Research, 2014), 16, www.oclc.org/content/dam/research/publications/library/2014/oclcresearch-digital-humanities-center-2014.pdf.

8. Jennifer Vinopal and Monica McCormick, "Supporting Digital Scholarship in Research Libraries: Scalability and Sustainability," *Journal of Library Administration* 53 (2013): 29, doi: 10.1080/01930826.2013.756689.

9. Kirk Anne et al., *Building Capacity for Digital Humanities: A Framework for Institutional Planning* (Washington DC: Educause Center for Analysis and Research, 2017), 9, https://library.educause.edu/resources/2017/5/building-capacity-for-digital-humanities-a-framework-for-institutional-planning.

10. Aaron Brenner, *Audit of ULS Support for Digital Scholarship* (Pittsburgh: University of Pittsburgh, 2014), 16, http://d-scholarship.pitt.edu/id/eprint/25034.

11. Diane Harley et al., *Accessing the Future Landscape of Scholarly Communication: An Exploration of Faculty Values and Needs in Seven Disciplines* (Berkeley: Center for Studies in Higher Education, 2010), 9, https://escholarship.org/uc/item/15x7385g.

12. Digital dissertations are starting to gain traction at some institutions including George Mason University, which has developed guidelines for digital dissertation work in the Department of History and Art History; see https://historyarthistory.gmu.edu/graduate/phd-history/digital-dissertation-guidelines. The Modern Language Association's Committee on Information Technology has also developed a list of various Guidelines for Evaluating Digital Work. To date, UW's Center for Digital Arts and Experimental Media (DXARTS) is the only campus entity to fully support digital dissertation work.

13. Participants acknowledged that some of the equipment they were interested in using was available in various departmental labs on the UW campus; however, usage of this equipment was restricted to those enrolled in the department housing the lab. Rather than the costly endeavor of each department trying to spin up labs duplicating resources, the UW Libraries was suggested as an opportune place to house all potential equipment for use by any UW student, faculty, or staff.

14. University of Washington Libraries, "Triennial Survey," www.lib.washington.edu/assessment/surveys/triennial.

15. University of Washington Libraries, "Triennial Survey Results: Digital Scholarship Discussion," July 20, 2016, 1.

16. Ibid.

17. Chapter 7 provides additional information on the history of these Office Hours.

18. Each year, UW's Walter Chapin Simpson Center for the Humanities funds a select number of graduate students and faculty to pursue a digital humanities research project. Information on this program and funded projects may be found at https://simpsoncenter.org/programs/digital-humanities-summer-fellowships.

19. See chapter 7 for a broader discussion of DS consultations.

20. Sheridan Brown et al., *International Advances in Digital Scholarship* (Oxford: Jisc and CNI, 2016), 6, https://www.jisc.ac.uk/reports/international-advances-in-digital-scholarship.

21. B. Alexander et al., *Digital Literacy: An NMC Horizon Project Strategic Brief,* 3.3 (Austin, X: The New Media Consortium, 2016), 6–7, http://cdn.nmc.org/media/2016-nmc-horizon-strategic-brief-digital-literacy.pdf.

22. Anne et al., *Building Capacity for Digital Humanities,* 17–18.

23. Nancy L. Maron and Sarah Pickle, *Sustaining the Digital Humanities: Host Institution Support beyond the Start-up Phase* (New York: Ithaka S + R, 2014), 15, www.sr.ithaka.org/wp-content/mig/SR_Supporting_Digital_Humanities_20140618f.pdf.

24. Although "science" is the title, the eScience Institute aims to serve all of campus through support of data science. The Institute offers hours and serves in data visualization, cloud computing, and more. Additional information on the eScience Institute may be found at https://escience.washington.edu/about-us/.

25. Sample programs for Hacking the Academy may be found at www.lib.washington.edu/digitalscholarship/hacking-the-academy-programming-series. Special thanks to Dan Cohen and Tom Scheinfeldt for their willingness to let us use the title of their book as the title of our program series.

26. Brian Matthews, *Think Like a Startup: A White Paper to Inspire Library Entrepreneurism* (Blacksburg: Virginia Tech, 2012), 9, http://hdl.handle.net/10919/18649.

27. Jennifer Schaffner and Ricky Erway, *Does Every Research Library Need a Digital Humanities Center?* (Dublin, Ohio: OCLC Research, 2014), 16, www.oclc.org/content/dam/research/publications/library/2014/oclcresearch-digital-humanities-center-2014.pdf.

PERRY YEE and
ELLIOTT STEVENS

5

Digital Storytelling

You, the reader, have clearly picked up this book because you are interested in digital scholarship and the ways that academic libraries can best support it. With this chapter, we are here to argue that you should commit yourself to digital storytelling when you develop or grow a culture of digital scholarship at your own college or university. We base this on a few different reasons, which we'll touch on in the coming pages: that an online digital storytelling workshop is relatively easy to establish, it builds the bedrock of goodwill with graduate students, and it has an alchemical way of leading teachers and students alike to more complex projects. We will also discuss our history and process as codevelopers and instructors of a digital storytelling workshop at the University of Washington (UW) Libraries.

WHAT IS DIGITAL STORYTELLING?

Digital storytelling can be a hard concept to define. Does any story produced with computers, devices, digital media, or the internet qualify as a digital story? Take Jim Dwyer's "Scenes Unseen: The Summer of '78" piece for the

New York Times.[1] In it, Dwyer combines long-lost, analog color photographs from New York City parks and his own text—which users have to scroll through online, creating a lovely effect of unfolding—to evoke a sense of place and people. Contrast this with examples of born-online texts, such as Prezi presentations,[2] and completely nonvisual outputs, such as audio-based podcasts. Do these projects count as digital stories? Is one more authentic than another? We hear these questions often when co-teaching digital storytelling workshops to graduate students at the UW Libraries. They reveal that digital storytelling is impossible to define. Or, rather, it's very possible to define, but its definition relies on the technology the definers are using, not to mention the stories they want to tell. In this chapter, we have chosen to define a digital story as a short video that includes a combination of images, recorded narratives, video, music, sound design, and captions. We base this definition on our own work teaching a specific style of digital storytelling to UW graduate students—an approach adapted from the workshops offered since 1993 by Joe Lambert's Center for Digital Storytelling.[3]

HOW IS DIGITAL STORYTELLING RELATED TO DIGITAL SCHOLARSHIP?

For one thing, digital storytelling can be used to explain what in the world digital scholarship even *is*. In academia, it's hard to pick a word vaguer than "scholarship," and to smoosh on another general word, like "digital," only compounds the problem. By contrast, with "digital storytelling," university researchers—faculty, graduate students, and librarians—can more easily imagine short videos and other practical projects with applications to their own work. They can also use it as a tool to highlight projects in digital scholarship that they are already working so other academics can understand what "digital scholarship" means to themselves or how it is defined at a particular institution. Admittedly, at UW, we have not done this kind of digital storytelling in the service of digital scholarship, but as our program develops and grows, it's something we predict researchers will want to do. For example, UW faculty members Walter Andrews and Sarah Ketchley have worked with colleagues to build Newbook Digital Texts, "an innovative digital humanities publishing house reimagining and restructuring traditional academic research, publication, and publishing."[4] Within Newbook, Ketchley has created the Emma B. Andrews Diary Project, which features unpublished journal excerpts from the eponymous Emma, a British traveler who was often in the vicinity of archaeological sites in Egypt in the late 1800s to early 1900s.[5] Ketchley has transcribed and edited these texts using the open text format TEI, pinned the rarely seen journal bits into layered digital maps, and included images from the time period. This is innovative, engrossing scholarship, but even here, we feel challenged to describe it simply. To communicate the importance of the Emma B. Andrews Diary Project, it would be far easier, and far more direct and effective, if it was possible to share a digital story about it with you instead of this jumbled chain of phrases and clauses.

Another way that digital storytelling is linked to digital scholarship is that researchers might choose to include short video stories in larger works of digital scholarship. An astonishing example of this is the website Seoul of Los Angeles, which was created by Kristy H. A. Kang, an assistant professor at Nanyang Technological University in Singapore.[6] In this site, Kang delves into the history of Los Angeles's Koreatown through images, writing, interviews—and yes, digital stories. When we first started putting together plans to teach a workshop in digital storytelling at UW, we imagined our students eventually making websites similar to Kang's. Although this level of complexity has yet to happen, we have built up a much better understanding of what it means for a library to invest in digital storytelling and how such an investment ultimately improves and diversifies the digital scholarship taking place at a university.

ORIGINS OF THE DIGITAL STORYTELLING PROJECT AT UW LIBRARIES

Digital storytelling at UW began after co-author Perry's unit, UW Libraries Instruction Design and Outreach Services (LibID), conducted some revealing interviews with graduate students at the University. LibID consists of a team of four librarians and staff members who serve graduate students in dozens of online and hybrid degree programs collectively housed in UW's professional and continuing education (PCE) wing, the UW Continuum College. In 2016, Perry and his team conducted interviews with these graduate students to investigate their needs and how they differed from students in traditional, on-campus programs. Because these students are often online, at a distance, or work full-time, LibID wanted to know if PCE students also felt excluded from on-campus events or felt connected to the University outside of their studies.

Results from this assessment made it clear that students wanted more opportunities to meet and learn from others outside of their programs:

> I don't know anyone outside of my program . . . I wish there were more opportunities for getting together.

> I would like to see more collaboration for research. If we could work with other majors and have more of a social structure, that would be valuable. It's a missing element of working with others.

PCE students also wanted to find workshops or trainings that would help to develop presentation skills and facility with multimedia in order to be more competitive on the job market and in workplaces. Finally, these students revealed themselves to be an underserved community with limited or no access to the events and programming available to their on-campus counterparts. This quote resonated with LibID:

> Because of the nature of our program, a lot of us are working full-time adults and we don't have a lot of time on campus. If I had more time, I could have felt more connected [to the University].

Thinking further about these interviews, Perry and his team entertained the idea of a fully online workshop in digital storytelling as a way to address some of these student needs. The workshop would be offered online to create a comparable experience for both distance and local student participation. LibID believed that the needs of these students were neither isolated nor unique and decided to partner with librarians in the Research Commons, the unit where co-author Elliott works, to create a pilot workshop in online digital storytelling that would appeal to all students. The Research Commons proved the perfect partner in this project as the space is teeming with graduate-student activity, and it acts as the UW Libraries' interdisciplinary hub of support for researchers. It is a space where graduate students can get experience presenting their research to interdisciplinary and diverse audiences and a place that provides one-on-one consultation for people working on digital scholarship projects. With the existing relationships that LibID and the Research Commons already had with graduate students—and with our interdisciplinary connections and interest in digital scholarship—it made perfect sense for us to collaborate on this experimental venture together. Although no one was specifically requesting online digital storytelling workshops, we felt that if we put something together, there was a good chance it would be successful.

DIGITAL STORYTELLING FELLOWS

Together the two of us have experience in teaching, instructional design, video production, and fiction writing, but neither of us was familiar with online storytelling. Before we began designing the pilot workshop, which we would come to call Digital Storytelling Fellows, we assembled a team to develop it. We reached out to a couple of the UW Libraries' graduate student employees enrolled in the University's iSchool to see if they'd like to join us on our project. These students came with rich experiences as teachers as well as an interest in instructional design. As a newly formed teaching team, we set out to explore existing online digital storytelling programs and locate trusted models to refer to and perhaps emulate. We looked to others in higher education for guidance and scanned the field to find the big players in academic digital storytelling. We identified four specific resources to guide us on the journey of launching our pilot program.

One of these helpful sites was the Educational Uses of Digital Storytelling website, developed by Bernard Robin of the University of Houston's College of Education Department.[7] One of the goals of this website is "to serve as a useful resource for educators and students who are interested in how digital storytelling can be integrated into a variety of educational activities." The site includes materials on digital storytelling lesson plans, rubrics, outlines for evaluating and assessing digital works, and information on copyright and fair use. We used three videos from Educational Uses of Digital Storytelling as examples of stories that could be told through the visual medium. The site also highlights content from Samantha Morra, an educator and practitioner of digital storytelling. Her blog, *Transform Learning,* outlines an eight-step process for digital storytelling that guides storytellers from ideation of a project to putting it together and reflecting on the work.[8] The compendium of knowledge curated on Educational Uses of Digital Storytelling helped us wrap our heads around the concept of digital storytelling in an academic context. We also looked at the video portal—the format in which stories are collected, curated, and shared—as a model for hosting our own digital content online.

The next valuable resource we examined was *ds106,* a website dedicated to digital storytelling that also serves as an open and online course through the University of Mary Washington.[9] The course, initially offered by educator Jim Groom and later by Martha Burtis, is free for anyone to join. It allows participants to develop, create, and share digital stories in a variety of formats. We incorporated several ideas from *ds106,* particularly in the area of building online community around a single assignment. How the instructors defined digital storytelling through having an open and broad acceptance of various methods—imagery, audio, video, coding, and more—remains to be one of our most influential takeaways from *ds106.* We adopted this mindset by actively encouraging participants to enter into the digital storytelling process at any stage depending on individual context. For example, one student may have a series of photographs that highlights research in unique ways, while another has already recorded an oral history interview. Because *ds106* modeled variety, individualism, and creativity in digital storytelling, we developed our assignments, feedback, and reflection activities with these ideas in mind.

In addition, we reached out to a local expert, practitioner, and digital storytelling instructor, Jane Van Galen, a professor at UW Bothell's School of Educational Studies. Van Galen uses digital media in the classroom to "enable the inclusion of more voices in deliberations about civic and cultural life."[10] We met with Van Galen to discuss her work and to determine the feasibility of a completely voluntary online workshop focused on digital storytelling in the visual medium. With her help, we were able to incorporate inclusive teaching practices that provided a safe space for vulnerable students to tell incredibly personal stories. Utility was another prominent theme in these discussions, meaning that each assignment, discussion, and interaction should be in service to the overall goal of helping participants complete a video narrative. Van Galen suggested that we include specificity in our project scope in contrast to *ds106*'s method of project acceptance. These conversations helped us to solidify and scaffold our assignments appropriately within our estimated time allotted for project work.

StoryCenter, an organization started in the early 1990s by Joe Lambert, an arts activist from the Bay Area, was the final source of inspiration when developing our workshop.[11] StoryCenter's trainings are led by facilitators who coach aspiring storytellers to create short, personal, and meaningful digital stories based on their lived experiences. Of the two of us, Elliott was able to experience StoryCenter's methods firsthand through participating in the workshop for three consecutive seven-hour days. The workshop began with an ideation activity called the Story Circle, a group activity led by the facilitator where workshoppers talked through their ideas aloud and received feedback. Additional stages of development included scriptwriting and training on the use of WeVideo. Participants shared their work with each other and with the facilitator, Rob Kershaw, director of public workshops for StoryCenter. The facilitator's role included moving about the classroom, testing, challenging, and helping all with their work. In the last hours of the last day, the participants screened their work in a final event. Elliott was deeply affected by the Story Circle activity and felt that it helped participants develop their ideas and also established the community sharing, trust, and synchronicity that made the workshop meaningful. Towards the end of the workshop, Elliott pulled Kershaw aside to ask about the feasibility of bringing the StoryCenter method into a completely online environment. Kershaw replied that it could work, but that he'd never tried it before, nor seen it done at StoryCenter.

These resources, like many others, provided insight into the number of digital storytelling practitioners in the educational landscape who are developing, innovating, delivering instruction, and looking for others to build and grow their digital storytelling community. They served as our source of inspiration. Although none of them were exactly what we were looking for, we concluded that if we wanted to offer an online workshop centered on synchronous instruction, engagement, and sharing, we'd have to create it ourselves.

All told, this exploratory process of identifying and vetting resources filled the entirety of the summer and fall quarters—a total of seven months between July and December. We were fortunate to have ample free time in our schedules to meet with Dr. Van Galen and for Elliott to enroll in the Story-Center workshop, but curating the resources in which we would base our initial course development took a majority of our available working hours. As we could not identify any existing online digital storytelling workshops at the time, we developed our best practices alongside our instructional design practices while building the course and the workshop content. Using our knowledge of the UW graduate student community and our familiarity with elements of each of these resources, we began constructing our online digital storytelling pilot workshop.

THE PILOT SEASON

Pre-Production

With graduate students as our target audience, we chose "Digital Storytelling Fellows" as our program's title because we wanted to emphasize both the academic nature of the workshop as well as the hope that participants would come together as friends and peers—a community of people committed to helping one another and united in the desire to tell stories. With respect to those stories, we decided to focus the theme of the workshop on those that highlight graduate-student research. Early on, we thought a tagline could be "Tell the story of your research—or your relationship to it." We decided we'd accept up to ten students into the workshop and that we'd ask them to make two-to-three-minute digital stories.

We knew Digital Storytelling Fellows would also have to include a schedule that would meet the needs of the busy online graduate students we worked with. We had to find the sweet spot of a time line for participants to ideate, design, develop, and produce a digital project without being too overwhelming and without overcommitting the time of our teaching team members to this single endeavor. Through many discussions, we settled on a three-week workshop with five to six of those hours devoted to synchronous working meetings.

To be inclusive of the underserved populations who are not usually afforded these types of high-touchpoint interactions with Libraries staff, we chose not to charge a fee to students to participate in the program, even though similar professional development opportunities can cost in the hundreds, if not thousands, of dollars. Deviating from traditional norms such as high registration costs was just another way we thought our program would differ from existing physical storytelling workshops, and we believed this would work in our favor because students are unlikely to attend such a workshop if a fee is involved.

With these design decisions in mind, we began developing the online learning environment for students. We chose Canvas as our content hub for all workshop resources. To facilitate our synchronous meetings, we settled on Adobe Connect, a popular web-conferencing tool. We also needed a platform to develop and produce our digital stories, so we created concept pieces using a variety of them, including Microsoft Sway and Adobe Spark. Ultimately, however, we decided to use the platform-agnostic option of WeVideo, the same tool introduced to Elliott at StoryCenter. Familiarity and access to UW students and staff were the driving factors behind our tool selection.

For lesson planning, we identified benchmarks and milestones outlined for the course. In the first week, we planned to hold the first synchronous meeting and start the session by encouraging students to generate a community agreement. This idea came from one of the graduate students on our teaching team who had experience as a talented, compassionate educator as well as a graduate student in an online program. A community agreement isn't a list of ground rules checked off by a facilitator nor is it a catch-all boilerplate policy. It is an opportunity for everyone in the workshop to speak about permission, consent, and respect together and without preference for whoever is a facilitator or storyteller. In our review of online digital storytelling materials—and in our participation in StoryCenter's program—we had never encountered community agreements, so we were excited to include this practice in our new design. After coming to a consensus on a community agreement, we thought it would be good to have participants work through a modified Story Circle activity, based on StoryCenter's model, in which they would think aloud about their ideas, propose stories to tell, and invite feedback. Unlike other digital storytelling workshops, we chose to be far less prescriptive about what people should do, trusting instead that the community agreement would serve as a guide in the event of strong emotions, difficult memories, or conflicts.

In weeks two and three, we imagined participants would draft stories in WeVideo and bring them to the next synchronous session. At this session, students would receive feedback from peers, although the teaching team would hold an open forum for technical assistance with video editing. We thought we would ask that scripts be completed by this session and media planned for incorporation into the project be collected and uploaded to WeVideo. Teaching team members would provide script feedback through Canvas and via email, assist with media gathering, and field general questions throughout weeks two and three.

By the final synchronous session, participants would have completed their video compositions. We thought this last live session should be optional and serve as a celebratory engagement for all involved to wrap the workshop. We would air digital stories and ask students to reflect on their experiences.

Implementation: Here We Go!

Our initial goal was to entice up to ten students to join the inaugural cohort of Digital Storytelling Fellows. However, in the three days after the pilot was announced, we received a whopping forty-six applications and had to close registration to stem the overwhelming demand. These workshop applicants represented over twenty different departments such as Museology, Anthropology, Nursing, International Studies, Education, Geography, and Electrical Engineering. Participants were in various stages of their graduate careers, and the group's overall makeup consisted of students from all three UW campuses as well as a number of students in PCE managed programs. With difficulty, we winnowed this group down to just ten participants, chosen with respect to their diversity as well as the order in which their applications were received.

This inaugural group of Digital Storytelling Fellows created an array of video projects that ranged from heart-wrenching, thought-provoking pieces to informative, persuasive calls to action. Participants enrolled in the workshop with varying degrees of technical expertise. Some had developed previous video projects using commonly available editors, whereas others had zero experience with creating or editing video or story development. This highlighted the need to share knowledge among group members so that those who were savvier could help the technologically anxious. More important than technical skill and prowess, the workshop allowed participants to truly hone in on their stories. They were able to identify, with great specificity, an audience for their projects. Sometimes, the focus shifted from participants' initial perceptions of who their audience was or what stories they wanted to tell.

One student from an Interdisciplinary Arts and Sciences program pitched an idea for a story on Attention Deficit Hyperactivity Disorder (ADHD) that the student had hoped to share with colleagues. The project provided details on a story wherein an anthropomorphized ADHD cartoon character would guide a narrative about warning signs of ADHD and how to manage daily activities for children. Through the Story Circle activity, we discussed an idea to refocus the narrative and change the audience from departmental colleagues to children afflicted with ADHD. This idea proved to be a revelation to the student, and the final product portrayed a character managing life with ADHD. This character discussed how to identify triggers and warnings of oncoming ADHD panic attacks for children and how kids with ADHD could interact with others.

Another personal experience was related by a student in the Museology program, who told a story about working in a "big important museum" and how gay, lesbian, bisexual, transgender, and queer experiences were not represented in any of the exhibits or displays. The student, who self-identified as a queer woman in the video, mentioned that museums are perceived as authoritative purveyors of history and knowledge. Despite bringing this issue to museum leadership, the student intimated that inclusivity was not a top priority at this particular organization. During a workshop feedback activity, another participant acknowledged a lack of thought about representation in museums. This student then posed a question, "Who else isn't being represented in museums?" This triggered an ah ha! moment for everyone in the workshop and the storyteller decided to cover the racial and ethnic demographics of museum curators, conservators, and educators in leadership roles (spoiler alert: they're overwhelmingly white). The student argued that museum curation should be a community-driven process and that diversity among museum staff and museology graduate programs needs to be a priority.

Renewed and Revised

Overall, the initial launch of the workshop was a success. It was relatively easy to set up and establish. We were able to build the workshop with platforms already available to us (e.g., Canvas and Adobe Connect) or that were inexpensive, like a fifty-user WeVideo license. We had support from our supervisors, who saw the value in this project and were understanding about the time we devoted to it. Of the ten students we accepted into the inaugural Digital Storytelling Fellows program, half completed the workshop by producing and publishing the final drafts of their videos.

Since the pilot, we've offered the workshop four additional times, and graduate students continue to show great interest in it and apply in droves. Typically, we see forty to fifty students apply for each workshop; overall, we have accepted fifty-nine students from over 190 total applicants, the latter pool representing over fifty UW departments. Though the excitement about the workshop has remained constant, that doesn't mean that the workshop itself has remained unchanged. Whenever we bring Digital Storytelling Fellows to a close, we always meet as a teaching team to reflect on how things went; to review our materials, practices, and assignments; and to look for areas of improvement and revision. In one of these meetings, Perry described our priorities as a teaching team to be "process over format," and since then that phrase has proven to be the most honest and aspirational summation of how we work and what we value. To us, "process over format" means the *what* doesn't matter nearly as much as the *why*. Ask yourself, *why* is this content relevant to my learners? *Why* am I teaching this way? *Why* do we select the tools and platforms used in our workshop? *Why* do we choose our instructional strategies? *Why* do we incorporate reflection, interaction, and assessment as part of our workshop process? Ultimately, *it doesn't matter* what tools we use. They are means to an end.

Process over format provides a way to think like an instructional designer and evaluate the efficacy of your online or offline pedagogy. As digital scholarship practitioners, it's important to remember that products, platforms, and formats are all rooted in a specific place and time. They change rapidly and without warning. Ensuring that your own practices of instruction, your pedagogy, and your methods of evaluation originate from places of discovery, curiosity, experimentation, and critique will help your processes remain evergreen and timeless.

To illustrate process over format in action, let's talk tools and platforms. We learned early in the workshop that the tools we use must be evaluated before each workshop and reevaluated immediately after a workshop. Whether it's due to software or platform updates or better available options, or because the spirit of a workshop is moving in a different direction, we always make sure not to become too attached to any of our tools. Rather, we enter with this mindset: *it doesn't matter what tool you use, as long as students benefit from it.*

Content: The main criteria for our content hub is that students needed to have some familiarity with the platform. Canvas acts as our repository of learning objects and is the main portal for asynchronous learning in the workshop. With its pervasive nature on campus and in departments, Canvas seemed like the best and easiest choice for hosting content. At UW, Canvas like other LMS platforms, is restricted by default to UW students, staff, and faculty. Although we benefit by being able to experiment in this private space, we would like to eventually move to other platforms on the open web for increased transparency, openness, and reuse of workshop materials. Ultimately, it is *you*—not the institution—who must decide what tool or platform is best to host content for your participants. *It doesn't matter what platform you use, as long as students have access to it at their convenience.*

Communication: The platform for workshop communication needed to meet a few specific criteria: we needed a platform that could (1) provide teaching team members with shared governance of all workshop-related communications, (2) facilitate collaborative chats ranging from one-on-one direct message style conversations to full team (ten+) channels, (3) be easy to use, (4) be available in a variety of formats, and (5) be 100 percent free for students.

The criteria were established following our pilot workshop (after which Elliott served as the primary point of contact for all workshop-related communication). All messages were routed through Elliott, which was ultimately unsustainable, put a huge strain on our resources, and closed off communication to all but a single teaching team member. In subsequent workshops, we moved communications from email to Slack, a collaborative online chat tool that supports multiple administrators or owners for a single channel. Slack fits our needs perfectly. It is well-enough known that many students have heard of it in passing, and some students had used it in other contexts. The change of platform reduced the number of messages to students, provided real-time and asynchronous communication in a single platform, and promoted open group communication. We also removed discussion threads from the Canvas course and shifted student interactivity and engagement entirely to Slack. *It doesn't matter what platform you use, as long as students have access to you and your messages.*

Conferencing: Our video conferencing tool also needed to meet three specific criteria: it needed to be (1) easy to use, (2) allow for webcams and microphones, and (3) enable teaching team members to host meetings at no cost. Adobe Connect fulfilled two of our three requirements, but the main criteria—ease of use—was missing. Each session required twenty minutes of technical support just to begin a discussion. We switched to Zoom, a web conferencing tool that serves as a hybrid of video conferencing, online meetings, and chat, and found that it met and exceeded all of our expectations. We are able to cover Zoom basics in less than a minute's time. As a practitioner, you could incorporate similar tools such as Google Hangouts or Skype. You could also consider having students record responses to prompts or presentations via tools like Flipgrid or VoiceThread. Ultimately, you should think about the user experience, how you want to engage with students, and how they will engage with each other. *It doesn't matter what platform you use, as long as students have access to you and each other.*

Project Development: When choosing a project development tool for video editing, we needed an editor that was (1) platform-agnostic, (2) cloud-based, and (3) easy for most people to use.[12] WeVideo fits these needs. However, the service isn't perfect and subsequent evaluations have identified accessibility and usability issues with the software. We-Video is also a paid subscription service. We pay for fifty seats on an annual basis, though other payment options including individual plans are available. *It doesn't matter what platform or device you use, as long as students have the ability to tell their stories in their own voice.*

DIGITAL STORYTELLING LEADS TO MORE DIGITAL STORYTELLING

By describing how we developed Digital Storytelling Fellows, ran its pilot workshop, and revised it through iteration and our guiding phrase "process over format," we hope you feel motivated to start an online workshop like ours. Or, if you're already offering digital storytelling workshops to graduate students or other audiences, perhaps what we've shared here gives you something new to consider.

And though we've put substantial time and effort into Digital Storytelling Fellows, we still believe it has been much easier to establish than many more general digital scholarship programs. For all of us on the teaching team—librarians, staff, and graduate students alike—the workload has never been onerous. We've been able to incorporate it into our jobs, and in some ways, because many of our responsibilities are concerned with graduate student life and research, Digital Storytelling Fellows has led to new and valuable connections to individuals, programs, departments, and disciplines. We have never needed a new physical space or expensive digital infrastructure for this program, we didn't have to hire new staff or apply for a grant, and we haven't had to purchase expensive gear that would quickly become obsolete. Aside from our time, the only budgetary expense has been a yearly fifty-seat license for WeVideo, which has become something of a multi-tool in the Libraries. For example, librarians in other units are using it to make marketing or tutorial videos. We've also used it to teach digital storytelling to high school interns in a summer program.

We've found that Digital Storytelling Fellows has helped us build good-will with graduate students. After all, this work is done for the benefit of our students. They were happy that it was offered, and we were pleased that Digital Storytelling Fellows met their needs.

Our respect for students highlights the importance of program evaluation and assessment. In our general workshop workflow, we weave assessment, evaluation, and reflection throughout the course. Assignments are given feedback from multiple members of the teaching team to account for different perspective and viewpoints. Additionally, cohort members are able to provide feedback on specific assignments during our live synchronous sessions. At the end of the workshop, we ask participants to evaluate the program via a workshop survey.

Because we also wanted to assess the efficacy of this program through a long-term evaluation, we checked in with students long after their workshop had concluded. Of the twenty-five students who completed the workshop, nine responded to a request for a sit-down interview to talk about their experiences in the workshop and what, if any, digital storytelling projects they had worked on since their time as Digital Storytelling Fellows.

Interviews were conducted with students from the inaugural workshop offering in winter 2017 up to the most recent workshop in Winter 2018 to generate a broad range of perspectives. Students recounted a wide array of experiences such as incorporating digital storytelling into their teaching as graduate students, using their work to enhance their resumes, and adapting existing projects in their portfolios to include more storytelling and video elements.

Students from the earlier cohorts found it challenging to incorporate digital storytelling into their day-to-day work because it is often seen as a "novel" approach, but we see that students from more recent cohorts are incorporating more digital scholarship into the classroom. From the assessment process, we learned the importance of providing inspiration to participants and modeling instruction for future teachers and practitioners was a key takeaway. The results are illuminating when looking at the comments given on the evaluations from a long-term perspective:

> Expectations were clear . . . but it seemed really fast-paced. Everything was good and [the instructors] were supportive, but what didn't work well was that there should have been more time, not meetings, but more time to do the work.

> I thought the amount of tech support and staff and instruction and how available everyone was amazing. I've never had an online class with that amazing, immediate feedback. Helped bridge the gap between online and in-person.

> The teaching was really well ramped up. It was great to get our feet wet before the training. The pedagogical choice was amazing, as was the tech help. A lot of people can be turned off by scary video software, but there was so much scaffolding and support, so it wasn't scary for me.

> I liked the accessibility of it. That you could stay in contact with the teaching team pretty easily through email, [Z]oom, etc. I also liked that the schedule was very . . . really loose. It was easy to fit into everything else that I was doing, work, other classes. I put forth a lot of effort ...., but it wasn't very time-consuming. I could put forth energy, but it was not too demanding.

Positive and constructive comments like these illustrate how there is a kind of alchemy that can happen in these workshops. What we teach may be challenging, but it also could have been taught in 1993 or even 1923 (absent the digital component). And, amazingly enough, despite all that graduate students do—all the research, the writing, and the teaching—they consider their time in Digital Storytelling Fellows not only memorable, but meaningful.

We have enjoyed teaching digital storytelling because we've seen how it's used more and more, and how it results in even more ambitious and complex projects in digital scholarship. One way we can prove this—as demonstrated by both the long-term assessment we've been doing and our continuing relationships with graduate students—is by looking at how participants have incorporated it into their teaching.

Former Digital Storytelling Fellows, most of whom have been from the English Department, have gone on to teach digital storytelling in their classes. Sometimes we've worked with them in one-shot sessions to provide assistance. It's been fascinating to see how these former Fellows have brought digital storytelling to their students. One instructor teaches a course with a service-learning component in which students are matched up with local organizations. As a culminating assignment, the students make digital stories related to the work of these organizations. Students are asked to consider if their story is *about, for,* or *with* the people in the organization—a question that prompts them to think deeply about the rhetorical uses (and misuses) of digital media. One former Fellow teaches a class that focuses on J. K. Rowling's *Harry Potter* series, the research that informs it, and the scholarship that currently surrounds it. The students in this class write a heavily researched academic article for a scholarly audience during the first two-thirds of the quarter. At the end of the quarter, they make a short digital story in which they explain their research to a general audience. In both of these instances, we've assisted by providing students with guidance and discussed activities related to script-writing and video-editing. We have also delved into exploring copyright, fair use, citation, and metadata with them. We've found this instruction to be a wonderful mashup of media creation, information literacy, critical information literacy, and digital-project management. At the moment, we have been able to field the requests we've gotten for these one-shot instruction sessions, but if the use of digital storytelling continues to grow exponentially, we might have to reconsider how to build capacity for classroom support.

DIGITAL STORYTELLING LEADS TO MORE DIGITAL SCHOLARSHIP

We firmly believe that a solid digital storytelling program leads to more, and better, digital scholarship. We have seen this phenomenon happen not only with graduate-student teaching, but also with their research interests.

Previously, we mentioned a graduate student who, after having taken our workshop, started to assign digital storytelling projects to students who were working with community organizations. This graduate student's research interests are in access and inclusion, African-American history and literature, and kinesthetics and automobility. In our workshop, he made a digital story about Tory Sanford, an African-American man who got lost driving in Missouri and who, for unknown reasons, police officers captured and booked. Under muddy circumstances, Tory Sanford died in jail, and the student from our workshop made connections among this underreported case, the dangers of driving while Black, and the history of the *Negro Motorist Green Book*, which is a reference resource published from the 1930s to 1960s that Black people used to navigate racist places. When we did our long-term assessment and got in touch with this student again, we learned that he had applied for and gotten into another competitive fellowship program on our campus—the Mellon Summer Fellows for Public Projects in the Humanities. Now, instead of making a three-minute video, this student is working to shoot and compose a full-length documentary about the history of redlining policies and the uses of the *Negro Motorist Green Book* in Seattle. What's more, this student wasn't the only Digital Storytelling Fellows graduate to later become a Mellon Summer Fellow. Another student, this time from the geography department, was accepted to the same program. The student was able to develop an existing digital story about the first gay bar in Seattle into an app-based walking tour of queer history in the historic Seattle neighborhood of Pioneer Square.

The distance learning component of Digital Storytelling Fellows helped to cultivate digital scholarship interests in UW graduate students. For instance, while conducting our long-term assessment, we learned of a third former Digital Storytelling Fellow who had taken the workshop while living in Zimbabwe.

The student often called into our Zoom meetings from a wildlife park that had a strong WiFi connection and once left a session early, saying "I am told there are lions nearby and I have to go immediately."

This ethnomusicology student was in Africa to learn about matepe music and produced a digital story about one specific group of matepe musicians. After the workshop, we learned that the same student applied for and was accepted into a prestigious UW program called the Simpson Center Digital Humanities Summer Fellows. In this fellowship, four graduate students spend eight summer weeks learning new media skills in specialized seminars and developing a project in digital scholarship. Our former student chose to make more short videos about her research in matepe music in Zimbabwe, but this time for a more specific audience: people in southeast Africa who might be curious about her research. With this audience in mind, the student focused on creating digital stories that play particularly well on phones and social media. Such a progression from basic digital storytelling to more complex digital scholarship is one more example of how a program like Digital Storytelling Fellows can catalyze and encourage student researchers to become active and successful digital scholars.

SPINOFFS AND SYNDICATION

The experience of developing and offering UW Libraries' Digital Storytelling Fellows workshop highlights the fact that digital storytelling is an evolving process that requires reflection and iteration. It is also a scholarly activity that uses unique and innovative methods of presenting research. It is digitally born, technology-based, and represents a shift from traditional storytelling methodology and is part and parcel of the larger endeavor of digital scholarship. Indeed, we truly believe that online digital storytelling will improve an institution's culture of digital scholarship. Just as a good story will captivate its audience, digital storytelling has the power to inspire and ignite a passion for digital scholarship across a campus. And, because digital storytelling is becoming a distinct genre, its growth can spark interest in academic staff, faculty, and students alike.

Digital Storytelling Fellows has made a lasting impact on both students and the teaching team. We have been able to foster a spirit of creativity and discovery for our students and staff through its development. Our students have gone on to teach digital storytelling as instructors and use their newfound skills and knowledge to chase other digital scholarship pursuits. It completely shifted the trajectory of one student's academic career:

> I have had a major academic lane change [after completing the workshop]. I am going more towards cinematography and film. This class was a really big part of me realizing this [is] my passion. It was literally

through this class that I realized how much I love video editing and photography. That got me on the path to cinematography.

Although we can't promise that an equally profound moment will come from your own digital storytelling endeavors, we *can* promise that launching some type of digital storytelling program or workshop in your library is achievable. In the meantime, we plan to continue developing additional long-term assessment, to institute this assessment process more regularly, and to broaden our outreach to additional departments. We also are exploring new genres of digital storytelling by delving into the world of audio storytelling and podcasting. Our goal is to continue inspiring students and faculty to see digital storytelling as a viable option for course assignments, perhaps by making our workshop's instructional materials and course content free and open in the future. We also hope that what we've presented in this chapter has helped you to see the value of digital storytelling, and to understand that it leads to continued digital scholarship in a myriad of ways. Perhaps the next story we read will be of your own adventure into digital storytelling.

Takeaways

- Digital storytelling leads to more digital scholarship, thus seeding and growing the culture of digital scholarship on campus.

- When designing a digital storytelling workshop, everything needs to be done in service of the student. Our philosophy of "process over format" guides in continually improving our workshop, and also in enhancing the student experience.

- Give students the space necessary to learn from you *and* to teach you about their work and their processes. Ensure that you are both serving the role of student *and* teacher; sage on the stage *and* guide on the side; mentor *and* mentee.

NOTES

1. Jim Dwyer, "Scenes Unseen: The Summer of '78," *The New York Times,* April 27, 2018, https://www.nytimes.com/interactive/2018/04/27/nyregion/newyork-parks-photos.html.
2. For future technology archaeologists: This was an online presentation program that human beings started using in 2009. It made many people motion sick with its animations. You can find it at https://prezi.com/.
3. The Center for Digital Storytelling is now called StoryCenter. You can find it at https://www.storycenter.org/.
4. Newbook Digital Texts, "Welcome to Newbook Digital Texts," www.newbookdigitaltexts.org/.

5. "Emma B. Andrews Diary Project," www.emmabandrews.org/project/emma-b-andrews-diary-project.

6. Kristy H. A. Kang, "Seoul of Los Angeles," http://seoulofla.com/.

7. Bernard Robin, "Educational Uses of Digital Storytelling," University of Houston, http://digitalstorytelling.coe.uh.edu/.

8. Samantha Morra, "8 Steps to Great Digital Storytelling," *Transform Learning* (blog), June 5, 2013, https://samanthamorra.com/2013/06/05/edudemic-article-on-digital-storytelling/.

9. *ds106*, http://ds106.us/.

10. "Jane Van Galen, Ph.D.," University of Washington Bothell, https://www.uwb.edu/education/faculty/janevangalen.

11. StoryCenter, https://www.storycenter.org/.

12. The term "platform-agnostic" refers to something that can be used regardless of operating system.

ELIZABETH BEDFORD

6

Stewardship

Academic libraries have always taken their duty to preserve traditional collections very seriously. But there is an increasing sense of urgency around our additional responsibility to steward the research output of our institutions—especially as digital scholarship transforms those outputs, and forces libraries to wrestle with new questions and new challenges. Stewardship is in many ways a Sisyphean task, requiring the ability to accept that "perfect" preservation is both a useful aspiration and an unattainable goal; we will never be "done" preserving an object, physical or digital. Faced with this potentially overwhelming reality, the question becomes how to identify what *is* attainable, what decisions can be made, and what actions can be taken.

This chapter will address three areas of uncertainty that provide framing for decision-making—or lack thereof—around taking digital materials under library stewardship. I have borrowed these areas from Janet Gertz's (director of preservation, Columbia University Libraries) excellent article "Should You? May You? Can You?," which was originally introduced to me through the work of the UW Libraries' Digital Workflows Task Force.[1] Broadly, Gertz differentiates among three kinds of decision-making in digitization projects: *should* concerns selection, *may* refers to legality, and *can* encompasses technical and financial resources. Although the article focuses these questions on the challenge of choosing physical materials to be digitized and made available online, the framework is much more widely applicable than this one mode of digital collections. In each of the following sections, I give background on the ways the three questions manifest when thinking about stewardship of digital scholarship in its many forms, providing illustration from University of Washington (UW) Libraries' experience in developing a new research data repository, DRUW (Data Repository at University of Washington). Our services at UW are a work in progress, and although some of our experiences with DRUW provide useful lessons learned, others reveal the questions that remain unanswered.

But first, let's establish some context for the challenges we face in stewarding the products of digital scholarship.

CHANGING ENVIRONMENTS FOR PRESERVATION AND ACCESS

Traditional journal articles and monographs offer significant advantages when considering whether libraries should, may, and can preserve the materials. For the most part, they are self-contained units of scholarship, produced by an established workflow of submission, review, and publication. They are widely recognized by academia as being fundamental to scholarly discourse, and their long-term value, either for the advances they contain or the record of scholarly thinking they represent, is usually uncontested. In the paper era, the preservation of these materials was widely understood to be libraries' responsibility. Crucially, these activities are explicitly supported by United States federal law; the doctrine of first sale (17 U.S.C. § 109) allows libraries to distribute single purchased copies of a work of intellectual property, and the libraries' and archives' exceptions to copyright law (17 U.S.C. § 108) allow libraries to make a limited number of copies of a work for the purposes of preservation and access. The shift in academic collections in the early 2000s from paper to digital did have significant repercussions for both preservation and access, because the move from purchasing to licensing and the US Copyright Office's clarification that digital display was protected under copyright meant that libraries' activities were no longer protected by the doctrine of first sale. However, traditional scholarly publishers, libraries, and other cultural heritage institutions have been able to take advantage of their long-standing relationships and workflows to create large-scale preservation partnerships. The journal preservation network LOCKSS (created and managed by Stanford University Libraries) and the nonprofit organization Portico (a service of Ithaka) are examples of this trend, as is the monograph-focused HathiTrust partnership.

The outputs of digital scholarship, in contrast, have none of these advantages. Unlike traditional articles and monographs, they usually do not have centralized publishing workflows that can be tapped as the basis for a preservation workflow. They are rarely "finished," but rather can be living works that are added to and edited over time. Their long-term value can also be ambiguous; some digital scholars may fight for their work to be recognized as perpetually valuable by the academic establishment, whereas others may feel that their outputs lose inherent value over time as techniques improve and new questions emerge. And they often incorporate potentially proprietary materials as objects of study in a manner and at a scale that introduces complex intellectual property considerations to their preservation. For libraries, the result is that the selection of digital research outputs for long-term retention is often unclear, legality is often questionable, and appropriate workflows are often opaque.

The Digital Challenge

If I want to figure out what's on a bunch of 3.5-inch floppy disks that were in a shoebox I pulled out of a closet, I need a computer with a disk drive and an operating system that can run the software designed to render the files. For most people, this would be a nonstarter—the current technical context has shifted so drastically from that of twenty years ago that this kind of setup would be extremely rare at home. In practice, all digital objects are created and used within a specific technological context, and as the technology landscape changes, our ability to preserve those objects for future use is therefore dependent on whether we can reconcile these different contexts. As advocates for future users, we face the further complication that we have no way of knowing precisely what those future landscapes will look like.

This is the puzzle that digital preservationists attempt to solve—how do you ensure this kind of reconciliation between contexts? To start, it's helpful to have a framework for what it means to have successfully preserved a digital object. Priscilla Caplan, former assistant director for Digital Library Services at the Florida Center for Library Automation, gives us an excellent breakdown of the elements of preservation, describing a fully preserved object as *available* (you have it), *identifiable* (you know what it is), *understandable* (you can interpret what's inside), *fixed* (it hasn't changed over time), *viable* (it's on media that hasn't degraded), *renderable* (you have software that can open it), and *authentic* (you know its provenance).[2] The preservation community has put a great deal of thought into the conceptual framework, individual pieces of information, and systematic workflows required for this kind of comprehensive stewardship.[3]

Unfortunately, the products of digital scholarship represent an extreme example of the challenges that can arise in the preservation process. Let's say a project takes the form of an Omeka website embedding a Twitter feed with Tweets that include a specific hashtag. Technically, this represents a complex interaction between a sophisticated web platform (Omeka) and a database owned and hosted by a for-profit company (Twitter). We have techniques that can save and render the HTML and CSS code that underlies the website at a moment in time, but we can't just grab a copy of the entire Twitter database, which is what that code is designed to interact with. (The Library of Congress, in fact, made the decision in 2017 to vastly reduce its Twitter preservation program because the volume of data was overwhelming its resources.)[4] And even if we could, that copy would not reflect the changing nature of the database itself, with Tweets continually being added and deleted. Preservation works most easily with static snapshots, and the dynamic interactions that form the heart of many digital scholarship projects are extremely resistant to this kind of freezing-in-time. This is in fact one of the most significant and widely researched challenges currently facing the preservation community: how to wrestle with the logistical and technical questions of new kinds of output.[5]

Curation: Beyond Preservation

The concept of curation will be familiar to many in the archives and museums worlds, but it is also increasingly part of the conversation in the library world—particularly among data librarians.

Some libraries provide services to make sure researchers' data are well-documented and well-organized; rather than solely preserving a static file, these librarians work with the researcher to make sure that the file itself represents the most useful version of the data. This kind of service goes even further than Caplan's definition of understandability and is a growing area of interest for many information professionals. The UW iSchool associate dean for research Carole Palmer and colleagues describe this distinction as one between "data stewardship," which I would argue is much more aligned with the kind of preservation I described in the previous section, and "curation," which involves a more active interplay with the data itself: "Data stewardship is about management of a shared resource . . . but it is a function of 'managing data' that implies a less active, fixed maintenance of data over time. Curation, on the other hand, is concerned with availability and future use of data, including the enhancement, extension, and improvement of data products for reuse beyond a single scholarly community."[6]

The kind of service Palmer describes requires both a deep understanding of the disciplinary particulars of a data set and a deep investment of time for doing the work of curation. Think about a database of flu genome sequences on the one hand, and a set of images representing the output of materials science experiments on the other. The kind of description and organization required to make the two data sets understandable and useable is quite different, requiring adherence to different disciplinary metadata schema and experience with different tools and software. In fact, the breadth of knowledge that would be required to service all of the potential kinds of data coming in to a domain-neutral repository would be extremely difficult to develop in a meaningfully comprehensive way.

Stewardship in the Real World

So, what happens when we simply don't have the time, energy, and resources to ensure all of Caplan's preservation elements, or to curate all of the data? One option is to throw our hands up in despair; the other is to take a deep breath and figure out what we can do with the resources in front of us. No heritage professional has ever said "I have too much time and too much money," and so the preservation community has in fact spent a lot of time thinking about what "good enough" preservation also looks like. The National Digital Stewardship Alliance Levels of Digital Preservation, for example, provide an excellent framework for those of us starting programs in less-than-ideal circumstances.[7] Shared infrastructure is another strategy; in the curation realm the Data Curation Network is an effort to address the issue of domain-specific curation needs by developing disciplinary understanding within one institution, while simultaneously creating a network to share curation duties with other institutions with different disciplinary expertise.[8] Stewardship exists along a continuum, and although we all aspire to the highest standards, it's important to remember that good work can be accomplished even if it doesn't perfectly address all of the existing needs.

From a practical perspective, the concept of *bit-level preservation* is incredibly important in resource-tight environments. The idea here is that if we keep the material as healthy as possible, preservationists and curators can have some expectation of success, if and when resources appear down the road. In Caplan's terms, we are attempting to make sure files are available, identifiable, fixed, and viable. Bit-level preservation involves a system that keeps track of the files and makes sure they aren't lost or degraded. This includes putting an automatic back-up process in place, and ideally it also incorporates hashing each file and carrying out periodic checksums to make sure that bit rot hasn't made the files unusable. This kind of preservation is significantly less labor-intensive, but make no mistake—stewardship in any form takes significant time and effort. In a world of finite resources, libraries must identify priorities for their research support services. The alternative—setting a goal of stewarding the research output of a university in its entirety—is a recipe for failure and waste.

This brings us to the first of our three questions for the stewardship of digital scholarship. Namely: should libraries take responsibility to address these vulnerabilities in the products of digital scholarship? And if so, where do we start?

1. SHOULD WE? LENSES FOR PRIORITIZATION

Historically, libraries have been in the business of building and stewarding collections. At academic libraries, those collections are meant to support, enable, and enrich the teaching and research carried out at individual institutions. And indeed, collections-related activities still form the bulk of the work and the majority of the expenditure at UW Libraries.

Yet there has always been an understanding that the line between collections materials and the scholarly output of a university can be blurred. Research is cyclical; the products of scholarship of one researcher form the basis for new work by another. Some of these products have long histories of explicitly being a part of the UW Libraries' collections policies. For example, our university archivist has long collected materials from faculty that include the notes, data, and objects that informed their published research. And in some ways, our traditional collection strategy of subscribing to departmentally relevant journals and monographs has already had the side effect of capturing many of the outputs of researchers on campus who choose to share their work in those formats. Nevertheless, the idea that UW Libraries has an explicit goal of collecting the research and scholarship produced by members of the University—in essence, that archival practices should be brought out of Special Collections and integrated into the work of public services at libraries—is quite a cultural shift.

An increasing community-wide interest in the idea of libraries as online publishing platform providers is supporting this shift. OCLC vice-president and chief strategist Lorcan Dempsey introduced the idea of the Inside Out library in 2010 and has subsequently developed the model into an extremely useful way of thinking about the purpose of a library.[9] Dempsey's viewpoint is that libraries should no longer solely focus on bringing external resources into a central accessible point—bringing the outside in—as was the strategy of traditional librarianship. Rather, he argues that libraries are in an excellent position to make sure that the resources that are currently under library stewardship are made as broadly accessible as possible—pushing the inside out.

The initial understanding of this strategy focused on unique collections and involved digitizing rare materials and making them available to a wider audience online. But over time, this understanding has morphed into a broader aim of providing stewardship services for the incredible unique resources produced by a university as a whole. The fact that materials produced outside of the traditional scholarly publishing workflow are particularly vulnerable make them prime candidates for library stewardship, which Clifford Lynch, executive director of the Coalition for Networked Information, articulates thusly: "the evidence suggests that the traditional commercial scholarly journals are pretty safe from a stewardship perspective, but the new components of scholarly communication . . . are typically very much at risk. These belong in institutional, disciplinary, and stewardship community repositories."[10]

Collections, Data, and the UW Libraries

But again, what does this mean from a practical perspective? As is the case with many large collections-driven research libraries, the UW Libraries' transition from "inward" stewardship and traditional collections to "outward" steward-ship and online digital repositories has been shaped by a combination of inspi-rational values and challenging on-the-ground practicalities. For example, in 2014, the UW Libraries announced a three-year strategic plan that explicitly embraced both the idea of sharing collections with the world and the goal of making UW-produced scholarship accessible stating "we partner with faculty and students at the University to support not only discovery of and access to our collections, but we also aid in the management of scholarship and making accessible the exceptional work accomplished."[11] This strategic language is sig-nificant, but it is only the first step on the road to a functional and sustainable program.

Consequently, a number of our new projects have come about because of service-oriented librarians who see a need and then put in the legwork to determine if that hunch has broad enough implications to sway decision-mak-ers in administration toward programmatic support. This was the case with our data repository project, which was given the green light based on the tireless advocacy of our former data services librarian, Stephanie Wright. Over the course of her time at UW, Wright developed close relationships with many scientists around campus. These interactions convinced her that a data-focused institutional repository, providing long-term archiving and access to data produced by UW faculty and researchers, would fill a pressing need.

Wright was responding to campus advocates of the worldwide open sci-ence and reproducibility movement, which has changed the conversation around sharing and archiving research data that underlie scholarly works. Broadly, the debate centers around two issues: scientists' ability to (1) repur-pose others' data for their own, potentially radically different research, and (2) check others' claims by looking at the underlying data. This can be quite controversial for scientists who feel threatened by additional scrutiny of their research or who fear being "scooped" on potential publications by others tak-ing advantage of their hard work. Interestingly, attitudes for and against are largely disciplinary based. The Inter-University Consortium of Political and Social Research, for example, has served the social science community as a centralized data archive since 1962. But many other disciplines are attempt-ing to catch up, and individuals in those disciplines who are ahead of their peers in promoting those values need significant support.

A major driver for data sharing and archiving has been new funder requirements that explicitly address data management practices. A 2013 Office of Science and Technology Policy memo called on federal funders to cre-ate plans for promoting better data management practices among grantees, which has resulted in many funders now strongly encouraging open access to the data underlying research results.[12] But this requires a platform for providing easy access to the data, and researchers whose disciplines do not have this infrastructure in place are left scrambling. This has led to a rise in interest for libraries-based institutional data repositories.

DRUW: Making the Case

Although Wright's intuition was important, launching a new initiative would require significant evidence of a broad need on campus. The UW Libraries has a strong culture of both assessment and user-focused services, and so one of the first projects Wright spearheaded after the creation of UW's Data Services program in 2012 was a Research Data Management Needs Assessment.[13] This work found "a significant need for research data storage solutions." Respondents designated the following as their top five priorities for libraries data-related services:

1. Ensuring that data is secure
2. Backing data up
3. Short-term storage (five years or less)
4. Long-term storage
5. Controlling and providing access to data

All of these services are well within the purview of an institutional data repository.

On the basis of this and other assessment projects, the UW Libraries decided to embark on creating a disciplinary-agnostic, campus-wide data repository service. Ultimate responsibility for the project fell to the Digital Repository Working Group (DRWG), recently renamed the Repositories Steering Committee (RSC), which is comprised of a team of librarians and staff members representing expertise in IT, scholarly publishing, metadata, preservation, and collections.

Setting the Boundaries

User assessments have been useful in gathering a broad baseline of information about the populations at UW who desire specific support for research data and were crucial in spurring and maintaining administrative support for the development of a data repository. However, their usefulness was more limited when it came to setting specific boundaries on the scope and priorities for DRUW. The Blue Ribbon Task Force on Sustainable Digital Preservation and Access, a seminal project investigating the economic factors that affect cultural heritage institutions' ability to steward digital materials for the long-term, declares that one of the most important factors for ensuring sustainability is "a process for selecting digital materials for long-term retention"—in essence, creating a collections policy.[14] Without setting boundaries on a preservation effort's scope, it is extremely easy to become overwhelmed by the breadth of possible needs, and scarce funding and effort are in danger of being spent in ways that are ultimately less impactful.

As a scholarly publishing outreach librarian, I built off of the work of our former repository librarian, Mahria Lebow, and our current preservation librarian, Moriah Caruso, to lead RSC's latest efforts to create and confirm DRUW's policies. Developing an initial collections policy was extremely difficult, especially because the definition of data is so broad, and the long-term value of data is seen as wildly different among different disciplines. Complicating matters further, the UW Libraries does not have a central collections policy, but rather a template for individual liaison librarians to follow in creating their collections strategy documentation. As such, collections strategies at the UW Libraries are for the most part highly tailored and dependent on the expertise of individual liaison librarians. By contrast, for a disciplinary-neutral repository like DRUW to succeed, it must maintain a balance between the broad swath of user needs across the institution and the practical boundaries that ensure the repository's sustainability. It is a task that we have found extremely difficult, especially without the benefit of an internal collections precedent.

And so, RSC focused on the definitions we felt comfortable articulating. One boundary RSC was able to set has been around a very basic definition of "data:" DRUW's focus is on the objects of research rather than the products of research. One way of thinking about this is the distinction between scholarly claims (products) and the materials that allowed a scholar to come to and support that claim and their subsequent conclusions (object). In the heritage community, this split is often described as primary source (object) versus secondary source (product). In our collections policy we have therefore articulated the major qualifiers as the following:

1. DRUW is an archive for data that is an output of research conducted by University of Washington faculty, staff, or researchers. DRUW imposes no disciplinary restrictions.
2. If the research produces software and algorithms used to process data, or other protocols surrounding data collection and analysis, this may be contributed alongside any UW-produced or -modified data.

Our feeling was that we will have a better sense of whether we need to tighten our scope only after we begin to see what kind of use the repository is getting. Essentially, we are embracing iteration; to this end, we have set up a schedule for policy review that will force us to revisit the collections policy in two years, by which point we hope to have much more information about how the repository is being used. In the interim, we have written a withdrawal policy, which leaves the UW Libraries the wiggle room to deaccession data sets if their inclusion negatively impacts the sustainability of the repository. Our question of "should we" steward the research data of the University prompts a broad response of "yes!," but we feel that we must gather more information before refining the practical details.

2. MAY WE? LEGAL AND POLICY IMPLICATIONS

Determining whether materials' content and value place them under the umbrella of libraries' collections policies is of course only the first step in making a determination about a stewardship workflow. We also need to be aware of the legal and policy context within which our programs operate, and whether those constraints affect the range of activities in which they can engage—particularly regarding intellectual property and privacy laws.[15] Digital scholarship materials often introduce specific legal challenges, having to do with an increased tendency for scholars to incorporate others' intellectual property into their own works, either linked or directly incorporated, and with the challenges that research data bring in terms of human subjects data and the tendency of many data scientists to recombine and reuse each other's data sets.

In the context of stewardship, distribution, or providing access, is extremely important when it comes to determining whether permission from the rights holder is needed or whether existing exceptions to copyright law cover libraries' activities. At UW Libraries, our preservation replacement program, for example, sends deteriorating physical books to vendors to scan and print new hard copies, which is covered in the exception to copyright protections detailed in section 108 of U.S. Code. In this process, the vendor also creates a digital file, which it returns to us alongside the physical book. We send this file to HathiTrust, which limits access for files that are still under copyright. Only if the copyright of these books lapses will Hathi add the digital files to its broad access program; we in the UW Libraries do not attempt to get explicit permission from the copyright holder to make the books available immediately. The end result of a workflow—whether it is solely for preservation or includes an aspect of providing access—is therefore a critical determinant in the kinds of legal and technical protections that must be put in place when designing a program.

For all digital products that libraries take into their collections with the aim of providing both preservation and access, there are a number of basic needs that must be met:

Permissions suitability. First, it is imperative that donors have the right to give us the material for the purposes of making it available openly. This means that they have all of the appropriate intellectual property rights to enter into licensing agreements, and that the content itself is suitable for wide distribution—meaning the donors have explicit permission from human subjects and have excluded sensitive information and material restricted by intellectual property issues.

Library license. Second, there needs to be a mechanism for the donor to license the appropriate copyrights so that we are able to carry out the distribution and preservation of the materials.

End-use license. Third, whenever possible it is highly desirable for an end-user license to be attached to the material, to promote open scholarship.

Unfortunately, there are numerous complexities that libraries face in addressing these three requirements in the context of digital scholarship. Our experience at UW Libraries developing the DRUW Terms of Deposit illustrates this problem clearly.

DRUW: Getting the Rights

Data ownership and copyright is an ambiguous area in United States and worldwide intellectual property law. Facts, for instance, cannot be copyrighted, but the organization of facts (such as database structures) and the protocols for the collection and analysis of facts are potentially copyrightable and would likely be covered by intellectual property law. At UW, University policy states that under most normal research circumstances, copyrightable material is owned by the producer. However, when it comes to research data, the University asserts all ownership, a fact that would certainly surprise most UW researchers. In addition, our office of technology transfer asserts that commercial software is an exception to the copyrightable materials policy. Because DRUW is envisioned as a resource that will accept a wide variety of data—not only straightforward facts, but also copyrightable materials like software and images—UW's policies present a confusing mix of ownership issues that our repository's Terms of Deposit needed to address.

As I said earlier, it is crucial that materials in the repository are deposited by persons with the appropriate rights to do so, and that the library has the appropriate rights to distribute the materials if they are not already owned by the University. At UW, the *Grants Information Memorandum 37: Research Data* (GIM 37) provides the most direct insight into our University's current thinking on how data should be treated.[16] While drafting the DRUW Terms of Deposit, we initially attempted a blanket license from the University to the researchers that allowed them to deposit data into the repository. This was incredibly unwieldy, however, and we weren't sure it was absolutely necessary. GIM 37 explicitly differentiates among a number of roles when it comes to the treatment of research data: "Owner," "Stewardship," and "Access." UW designates itself the owner of all research data, but the other two roles are delegated either to the Principal Investigator (PI) or to the PI's department. After consulting with UW's Attorney General's Office, we made the executive decision that by retaining the right to take custody of data, the memorandum explicitly gives UW, and by extension, the UW Libraries, the right to host data in the service of accessibility. By assigning a stewardship role to the PIs themselves, the memorandum gives researchers the right to deposit that data if they deem it appropriate. We therefore wrote the final Terms of Deposit to begin with a simple assertion that the PI's rights under GIM 37 allow PIs to deposit their research data.

This strategy does not, however, address materials owned by the researchers, and so the heart of the DRUW Terms of Deposit is a Grant of License from the Depositor to the University. Again, because we anticipate that future DRUW deposits will include copyrightable material that is owned by the researchers themselves, there needs to be a mechanism for the UW Libraries to get the rights necessary to distribute the materials. We therefore carefully crafted language to incorporate both researcher-owned materials and UW-owned materials:

> For all copyrightable materials in which the depositor has personal ownership, depositor grants UW a non-exclusive, irrevocable, world-wide license to exercise any and all rights under copyright related to the deposited materials and to their associated metadata, for the purposes of preserving them and making them freely and widely available in DRUW.[17]

Encouraging Open End-User Licenses

As a proponent and enabler of open scholarship, we at the UW Libraries are committed to encouraging depositors to license their materials using common open source licenses. Unfortunately, current UW policy did not make this licensing straightforward. We needed to first make sure that all stakeholders were on board with the idea of open licensing, and then figure out the mechanics of how to legally assign those licenses.

UW Executive Order (EO) 36 provides the basis for our university's policy on materials produced by staff or faculty that come under copyright or other intellectual property law.[18] The basic tenets of the policy are that under most circumstances copyright stays with the researcher, but that any patentable inventions must be assigned to the University or one of its appointees, and that licensing fees must be split between the inventor and the University in some proportion. The office that supervises these transactions is the University's Office of Intellectual Property and Technology Transfer, which is now called CoMotion.

The idea of openly sharing intellectual property was rather new to Co-Motion, because they are primarily focused on helping researchers patent their inventions. In prior years, UW librarians had come up against some hostility to this idea, but the growing conversation among faculty in favor of openness has made CoMotion realize that having an option to share openly is extremely important. E036 as it is currently written is vastly too broad and does not lay out explicit instructions for materials intended to be distributed with an open source license. That said, a common sense reading of policy dictates that in a situation where monetization is not the goal, the only issue is whether any of the University's monetized materials would be in danger because of the license. In recent years, CoMotion has thankfully shifted its thinking to encourage more open source software licensing and has created both a guide for licensing open source software and a custom noncommercial use license for software. However, because CoMotion remains worried about UW-patented software, it explicitly forbids "Apache, GPLv3, other licenses that include a grant of patent rights which can impact the IP rights of the authors and other researchers at the University even if not involved in the project."[19]

Having established CoMotion's willingness to allow open source licensing, we then needed to determine the mechanism for applying that license. The question of who the licensor is for materials in a DRUW deposit, and which licenses will be offered, was nontrivial, because under US copyright law, only a copyright holder can license materials. Again, we know that materials deposited in DRUW may have complex ownership. Originally our strategy was for the PI/depositor to be the licensor, selecting from a predetermined list of possible licenses. But if that strategy were to be pursued, UW would somehow need to grant the depositor sub-licensing rights for materials that UW owned. Because GIM 37 does not mention sub-licensing as a responsibility with research data, and there are ambiguities about licensing in E036, we determined that it would be much more straightforward to have UW serve as the licensor, and have depositors grant the Libraries explicit sub-licensing rights for those materials subject to copyright. Consequently, we added a section to the Terms of Deposit that grants UW the right to sub-license any materials owned by the depositor based on the selection they make: "Depositor also grants UW a non-exclusive, irrevocable, worldwide license to allow others to exercise rights in accordance with a license selected by the depositor during the deposit process."[20]

Ultimately, we chose to offer depositors a broad range of open licenses to cover the broad range of potential content: Creative Commons licenses (https://creativecommons.org), an Open Data Commons license (https://opendatacommons.org/), the MIT license (https://opensource.org/licenses/MIT), and the BSD license (https://opensource.org/licenses/BSD-3-Clause). We set the Creative Commons Zero license (CC0) as our default setting because it is applicable for all content types.

Open Licenses

Creative works, software, and many kinds of data are protected under intellectual property (IP) law, which means that others who want to use those materials often need explicit permission from the IP holder to do so. A license is the mechanism that the IP holder uses to tell others what they can and cannot do with their work; open licenses allow the IP holder to preemptively grant permissions to others.

Open Source Software Licenses

The nonprofit organization Open Source Initiative (https://opensource.org/) keeps a list of licenses, which generally fall into two categories: those that are "viral," that is, require others to use the same license for derivative works, and those that are not. MIT and BSD are part of the latter category.

- ■ SUITABLE FOR: software

Creative Commons "Zero" (CC0) License

The legal equivalent of designating something in the public domain—users may do whatever they want with the work, without crediting the author.

- ■ SUITABLE FOR: software, data, creative works

Open Data Commons Licenses

A suite of licenses designed to accommodate the IP complexity that can arise with data sets.

- ■ SUITABLE FOR: databases

Creative Commons Attribution Licenses

A suite of licenses designed to give IP holders a wide range of options for allowing and limiting reuse of their materials.

- ■ SUITABLE FOR: creative works, some data

Settling on the mechanisms to answer the "may we?" question was a shockingly complicated and mind-bogglingly slow process. However, after two years and three rounds of negotiations, we now have confidence that our deposit agreement has the right balance of legal protection and encouragement for open sharing.

3. CAN WE? TOOLS, WORKFLOWS, AND STAFFING

The "can we?" question is where the rubber hits the road in terms of establishing a stewardship program. Ultimately, it doesn't matter if a library has decided that material is within its collections purview and that there are legal avenues for its collection and preservation, unless practical workflows for the ingest and stewardship of that material can be established and sustained. To do this, libraries must first define and articulate their responsibility toward these materials, and then explore the software and staffing necessary to put that responsibility into practice.

UW Libraries has explored a number of combinations of local or remote hosting and open or licensed software as part of its strategy to protect and provide access to its collections. Our existing platforms are:

- dSpace for our institutional repository, ResearchWorks—hosted locally, based on open source software
- CONTENTdm for our Digital Collections—hosted remotely as a service, based on proprietary software
- bepress for UW Tacoma's Digital Commons and the UW Law Library—hosted remotely as a service, based on proprietary software[21]

There is a robust body of literature around platform selection, particularly focusing on the trade-off between flexibility and effort required for maintenance of proprietary and open source software.[22] But a new and intriguing consideration is what role institutional values should play in selection. Bepress, for example, is an incredible platform, but its recent acquisition by Elsevier in 2017 has raised serious concerns about the trustworthiness of the company. The UW Libraries is still wrestling with the decision of whether to continue the relationship with bepress, in light of the challenges the alternatives would present.

The fundamental question of how much open source software costs is unfortunately tremendously opaque to most librarians. Libraries and archives have spent centuries honing the skills necessary to preserve and safely provide access to physical materials, and these skills are seen as firmly within the purview of LIS training programs. Digital archivists have been developing frameworks and strategies for their work since the 1980s, but only recently have the programming skills necessary to build and maintain digital preservation and access tools been conscientiously integrated into library curricula. Deteriorating relationships with for-profit vendors have made homegrown solutions extremely attractive. However, the IT skills gap has meant that it is easy for decision-makers to fundamentally miscalculate the time and effort such infrastructure represents. Open source software presents major challenges for development, and the UW Libraries' IT department was unprepared for what a difficult project it would be. Although our IT team was able to overcome substantial hurdles to launch a pilot version of the repository, we are unsure about its long-term sustainability.

DRUW: Bit-Level Preservation with Hyrax

The DRUW project does not have assigned staffing for comprehensive preservation or curation, and so we made the decision that the service we could offer would simply be bit-level preservation. Still, this level of service requires the UW Libraries to create and maintain a platform to store and make accessible the deposited material, which in itself is no small task.

In the end, the Libraries decided to build the DRUW data repository with Hyrax software, an open source platform developed by the Samvera community that relies on Fedora as its underlying database.[23] We were excited about Hyrax partly because the Samvera community is engaged and enthusiastic, and partly because the kind of features that are being built into the program are direct reactions to issues that other repository software has surfaced. Online repositories essentially have three layers; they are a combination of (1) a web-based access platform, (2) an underlying database where the information is stored, and (3) a program that allows these two entities to talk to each other (often called the API layer). Fedora is an extremely robust database, and the initial vision for Hyrax was that the focus would be on making sure the middle layer could interact with multiple access layers that would be tailored to the content. Think about two repositories: one for student films, and one for traditional, PDF-based theses and dissertations. It would be useful for the film access platform to have streaming capabilities, but that would be redundant for the PDF-based content. Similarly, the kind of metadata that would be recorded for the two different content types would be considerably different. The idea is that Hyrax would allow separate access platforms for different repositories but only a single underlying database, which streamlines the technical architecture considerably.

Hyrax in Practice

Over the course of this project, as many libraries active in digital stewardship have discovered, we have learned that installing and configuring open source software can be remarkably difficult. Modern users of commercial software often don't understand that installation and configuration wizards are actually a miracle of development effort. In the same way, it is borderline magic that commercial software will send an automated notification that an update has been released, have you double-click on that notification, automatically make the update, and allow you to go on using the software without any decrease in functionality. It represents the fact that many, many developers did a tremendous amount of testing behind the scenes to make sure that every potential feature still works properly after the update.

This kind of extensive testing doesn't happen with open source software, which means that every Hyrax upgrade comes with a high probability that some functionality elsewhere in the program will break. Furthermore, any customizations that our developers make on the local instance of Hyrax may or may not play well with the upgrade. So, every upgrade involves a significant amount of testing, tweaking, and potentially rewriting of previous customizations. As of writing this chapter, UW Libraries is able to devote the equivalent of approximately 1.5 full-time employees to its Hyrax development and maintenance (divided among at least five different real-life people). This number gives a clue as to why development of DRUW has been slow, and why we decided that our IT department cannot support customization. Instead, we will be focusing on maintaining a "vanilla" Hyrax instance and are trying to actively engage with the Samvera community so that our concerns can have a chance to be incorporated into the community development road map.

DRUW Development Skill Sets

Few people outside of IT departments have a deep understanding of the incredible breadth of skill sets required to develop and maintain an institutional repository hosted locally and based on open source software. The following five "roles" do not necessarily need to be played by separate people (although it certainly helps!); rather, they represent the kind of work that needs to be done, and for DRUW, the particular knowledge base that was required to create a Hyrax instance that would interact with UW's broader systems.

Information Architect

Decides how the system's schema should be configured to create an environment where deposited materials are organized and have appropriate descriptive information to be most useful in the future.

- SKILLS: Data modeling, metadata, workflow optimization

Developer

Customizes and configures the repository, including figuring out how to interact with other software and services.

- SKILLS: Ruby/Rails, Rake, Omniauth gem, Fedora, Solr, database management, CSS

(cont.)

Operations

Ensures that all of the software dependencies that comprise a functional repository environment are able to be installed and configured correctly.

- SKILLS: Vagrant or Ansible, Fedora, virtual machines, configuration management

Systems Administrator

Makes sure that the repository environment can be successfully deployed in the real world on existing hardware systems.

- SKILLS: Fedora, Solr, database management, Apache configuration, Shibboleth authentication, high availability server configuration, backup and security

User Experience

Tests that the repository functions correctly and identifies ways to make sure users' needs are being met and appropriate information is given to them.

- SKILLS: Quality assurance testing, user assessment, documentation development

Establishing Strategies for Risk Mitigation and Indemnification

Beyond the work needed to create the platform, RSC also needed to figure out how to make sure that no inappropriate materials get into the repository. Data collected through research on human subjects has the potential to contain sensitive information, which would be illegal to share openly. We also know that many UW researchers who reuse data often don't pay attention to the intellectual property status of existing data. If the data repository were to host such data, our technical infrastructure and quality control workflows would need to ensure compliance with both federal laws, such as HIPAA and FERPA, and university mandates.[24] DRUW was envisioned as a platform for completely open access, and so providing secure storage and controlled access to sensitive data would not only impose a significant burden on the system, it would also run contrary to the primary mission. And as I said earlier, current Libraries staffing isn't sufficient to review the data for compliance. So how do we address and attempt to mitigate the level of risk that our system unfortunately invites?

The Terms of Deposit ends with a section of warranties that do cover these issues; however, conversations with UW's Attorney General's (AG) office revealed its opinion that relying on these warranties would not be enough to indemnify UW in case of a legal action. The risk is that in a lawsuit, depositors could argue that they hadn't read the Terms of Deposit and therefore didn't realize that they were not supposed to upload the materials. In order to combat this risk, the AG suggested that we implement workflows that would bolster the concept of *constructive assent,* whereby it would be difficult for a depositor to argue that they did not know or understand the limitations that were described in the Terms of Deposit Warranties section. As previously indicated, UW Libraries does not have the staffing capacity to create, implement, and sustain a new Hyrax feature that would pop up to remind users about sensitive data and intellectual property upon each deposit event, as the AG suggested. Some other workflow needs to be established, and we are actively exploring our options.

Ultimately, for DRUW, the answer to "can we"—and thus the answer to "will we"—is "we don't know." We have hard choices to make around whether the level of service we have been able to put together is in fact worth the effort it takes to maintain it. However, we have learned a tremendous amount throughout the policy and technical development of the project, and those lessons will be invaluable as we continue to develop our broader stewardship program.

CONCLUSION

I use the term "stewardship" throughout this chapter intentionally, partly because it has fewer connotations for heritage professionals than the relatively well-defined activities of preservation and access provision, and partly because it is something of an umbrella term that encompasses the full lifecycle of digital assets.[25] At UW Libraries, we are in fact wrestling with a lack of practical workflows and defined outcomes for our programs related to the preservation and access provision of nontraditional scholarly outputs. The term stewardship, for me, embraces this uncertainty while honoring a deeply felt belief that we have a responsibility to care for these materials and make them available to the world for the long term.

In this new and changing landscape, the trick is to make sure that we communicate our activities accurately and completely—that users have faith that we say what we mean and mean what we say. In particular, it's extremely important to remember that although librarians and other heritage professionals use terms like "archiving," "preservation," and "curation" as a shorthand among ourselves to designate a set of activities, these terms don't necessarily resonate with our patrons. In fact, they may have entirely different connotations depending on the circumstance. For heritage professionals, the term "archive" invokes a process of selection, description, arrangement, and preservation of materials, but for anyone using the Mac Mail app, the Archive is the folder where users put emails they don't want to deal with but don't want to delete. And that's fine—most words have multiple definitions in the dictionary. We just need to make sure that we're clear to our users about which definitions we're using. Stewardship is a continuum, and part of our job is to help users understand and appreciate the steps we successfully take toward that long-term goal.

Takeaways

- A hallmark of digital scholarship is its evolving nature, and living resources present tremendous challenges in selection and workflows for preservation. Libraries must encourage disciplinary communities to develop norms around selection and retention and must also set and communicate explicit boundaries for themselves around stewardship responsibilities.

- Both the objects and products of digital scholarship are usually covered by intellectual property law, and therefore libraries must be extremely careful to make sure that they have the proper rights in place to steward the materials. Libraries should also encourage intellectual property holders to make their works available under an appropriate open license.

- Open source software development takes tremendous staff resources and requires extremely specialized skill sets. Libraries must be fully aware of these costs and have plans in place to fully support them in order to be successful in developing software-based services. If resources are unavailable, libraries have difficult decisions to make about how and whether to involve outside vendors in service provision.

NOTES

1. Janet Gertz, "Should You? May You? Can You?: Factors in Selecting Rare Books and Special Collections for Digitization," *Computers in Libraries* 33, no. 2 (March 2013), www.infotoday.com/cilmag/mar13/Gertz—Factors-in -Selecting-for-Digitization.shtml; Moriah Caruso et al., *Digital Workflows Task Force Final Report* (Seattle, WA: University of Washington Libraries, 2017).

2. Priscilla Caplan, "What Is Digital Preservation?," *Library Technology Reports*, no. 2 (February-March 2008) https://journals.ala.org/index.php/ltr/article/ view/4224/.

3. The gold standard is the OAIS model, an incredibly useful and incredibly detailed examination of the activities that should go into a preservation program; see Consultative Committee for Space Data Systems Secretariat,

Reference model for an open archival information system (OAIS): Recommended practice (Washington, DC: CCSDS, 2012), http://public.ccsds.org/publications/archive/650x0m2.pdf.

4. Library of Congress, *Update on the Twitter Archive at the Library of Congress* (Washington, DC: Library of Congress, 2017), https://blogs.loc.gov/loc/files/2017/12/2017dec_twitter_white-paper.pdf.

5. Those interested in digging into these questions have a huge body of literature to explore. Some good starting points are the journals *Code4Lib,* the *International Journal of Digital Curation,* the back issues of *D-Lib Magazine,* and *Journal of the International Association of Sound and Audiovisual Archives.* Relevant conferences include iPres, the International Digital Curation Conference, and the National Digital Stewardship Alliance's Digital Preservation Conference.

6. Carole Palmer et al., "Foundations of Data Curation: The Pedagogy and Practice of 'Purposeful Work' with Research Data." *Archive Journal* 3 (2013), www.archivejournal.net/essays/foundations-of-data-curation-the-pedagogy-and-practice-of-purposeful-work-with-research-data/.

7. National Digital Stewardship Alliance, "Levels of Digital Preservation," https://ndsa.org//activities/levels-of-digital-preservation/.

8. Data Curation Network, https://sites.google.com/site/datacurationnetwork/home.

9. Lorcan Dempsey, "Outside In and Inside Out," *Lorcan Dempsey's Weblog,* January 11, 2010, http://orweblog.oclc.org/outside-in-and-inside-out/.

10. Clifford Lynch, "Updating the Agenda for Academic Libraries and Scholarly Communications," *College and Research Libraries* 78, no. 2 (2017), https://crl.acrl.org/index.php/crl/article/view/16577.

11. University of Washington Libraries Strategic Planning Committee, *Delivering Success: 2014–2017 Strategic Plan* (Seattle: University of Washington Libraries, 2014), www.lib.washington.edu/about/strategicplan/2014/directions/research-scholarship.

12. Executive Office of the President, Office of Science and Technology Policy, *Increasing Access to the Results of Federally Funded Scientific Research* (Washington, DC: Executive Office of the President, 2013), https://obamawhitehouse.archives.gov/sites/default/files/microsites/ostp/ostp_public_access_memo_2013.pdf.

13. Stephanie Wright et al., *Fall 2012 Research Data Management Needs Assessment Results* (Seattle: University of Washington Libraries, 2013). See also chapter 8.

14. Blue Ribbon Task Force on Sustainable Digital Preservation and Access, *Sustaining the Digital Investment: Issues and Challenges of Economically Sustainable Digital Preservation* (2008), http://brtf.sdsc.edu/biblio/BRTF_Interim_Report.pdf.

15. See chapter 3 on copyright.

16. University of Washington Office of Research, *Grants Information Memorandum 37: Research Data* (Seattle: University of Washington), https://www.washington.edu/research/policies/gim-37-research-data/.

17. University of Washington Libraries, *DRUW Terms of Deposit* (Seattle: University of Washington).

18. University of Washington Office of the President, *Executive Order 36: Patent, Invention, and Copyright Policy* (Seattle: University of Washington), www.washington.edu/admin/rules/policies/PO/EO36.html.

19. University of Washington CoMotion, "Open Source: Releasing Software Under Open Source Licenses," https://comotion.uw.edu/what-we-do/intellectual-property-licensing/open-source/#section-1-0.

20. University of Washington Libraries, *DRUW Terms of Deposit.*

21. See chapter 10 for more about UW Tacoma's bepress work.

22. Two great starting points are Oya Y. Rieger, "Select for Success: Key Principles in Assessing Repository Models," *D-Lib Magazine* 13, no. 7–8 (2007), http://dx.doi.org/10.1045/july2007-rieger and Hillary Corbett and Jimmy Ghaphery, "Choosing a Repository Platform: Open Source vs. Hosted Solutions," in *Making Institutional Repositories Work*, ed. Burton B. Callicott, David Scherer, and Andrew Wesolek (West Lafayette, IN: Purdue University Press, 2015), https://crl.acrl.org/index.php/crl/article/view/16549.

23. More information on Hyrax may be found at https://github.com/samvera/hyrax/wiki. For more information on the Samvera community, see http://samvera.org/samvera-flexible-extensible/the-samvera-community/, and for more information about Fedora, see https://duraspace.org/fedora/.

24. The Health Insurance Portability and Accountability Act of 1996 and the Family Educational Rights and Privacy Act, respectively.

25. See the National Digital Stewardship Residency's stated mission of training professionals "in managing, preserving, and making accessible the digital record of human achievement." Library of Congress, "National Digital Stewardship Residency," www.digitalpreservation.gov/ndsr/.

PART III

Environments

BETH LYTLE

7

Learning Technologies

The intersection between technology and scholarship is a fascinating one, particularly in the context of digital scholarship. Access to technology is an important pillar of any campus's digital scholarship culture, and along with it comes support for that technology, whether in the form of documentation, trainings, consultations, office hours, or something else entirely. This chapter will outline how my experience as an instructional technologist at the University of Washington (UW) has informed my approach to the culture of digital scholarship and how the UW Libraries and my home department of Learning Technologies have fostered a growing relationship in support of digital scholarship on the UW campus.

BACKGROUND: WHAT IS UW LEARNING TECHNOLOGIES?

UW Learning Technologies (LT) is a centralized campus unit focused on teaching and learning with technology that offers support and training for several centrally supported tools. LT reports to the Provost's Office as part of

Academic and Student Affairs (ASA) and more specifically as part of Academic Technologies, which also includes Classroom Technology and Events (CTE). This placement prioritizes our focus on teaching and learning instead of solely technology and helps to clarify our priorities to our clients. ASA also includes the UW Center for Teaching and Learning (CTL), of which LT and the Libraries are both partners.[1] The Libraries also reports to the Provost's Office, bringing our units closer together in reporting structure and creating opportunities for future collaborations. LT is collocated with librarians and library staff in UW's Odegaard Undergraduate Library, a conveniently accessible physical location for students and faculty, but we are not otherwise formally integrated into the structure of the UW Libraries.

Learning Technologies' primary services include:

Walk-in software and computer support. The LT department staffs the Computer Vet desk found in Odegaard Undergraduate Library, which provides walk-in, phone, and email support for software issues with computers on a free, best-effort basis.

Computer lab operation and maintenance. The department has a systems team consisting of four student staff and one full-time supervisor to maintain the Student Technology Fee (STF) supported computer labs in Odegaard Library for student and teaching use.[2]

Centralized learning technology support. Our Learning Management System (LMS) and Multimedia teams, which include approximately twenty-five student staff, support our designated centrally supported tools, including Canvas (LMS), Panopto Lecture Capture, Poll Everywhere (classroom response), Zoom web conferencing, and the video and sound studios in Odegaard Library through in-person consultations, phone, and email.

Technology-focused workshops. Finally, we have a team of around five student instructors who teach workshops on audio and video production, use of the Adobe tools, and productivity software.

Most of our teams are staffed by students, approximately fifty throughout the year, who are trained in customer service and support as well as the use of the particular tools that they support. Our full-time team, as of summer 2018, consists of instructional designers, instructional technologists, a training and operations lead, a multimedia consulting lead, the systems team supervisor, and the help desk manager.

As an instructional technologist, I work with LT's student staff to support and troubleshoot the centrally supported teaching and learning resources previously mentioned. I also work on questions of instructional design, teach workshops, and consult with students, staff, and faculty on questions about teaching and learning technologies and questions around digital pedagogy. This role, combined with my MLIS, fits well with digital scholarship support as I can leverage my knowledge of central IT resources, libraries, consultation skills, and familiarity with technology used for teaching and learning.

GETTING INVOLVED WITH DIGITAL SCHOLARSHIP

Although my current responsibilities with teaching and learning technologies provide a natural segue into the world of digital scholarship, my relationship with digital scholarship began much earlier, during my time as an MLIS student at the UW iSchool. During that time, not only did I started participating actively in academic digital scholarship conversations, but I also began working for LT as a Graduate Staff Assistant (GSA). These graduate student experiences fundamentally shaped my understanding of the UW community's technology needs, and by extension the services and support that LT offers in relation to digital scholarship and digital humanities (DH). The following examples help illuminate these connections and the lessons learned along the way.

EXAMPLE 1
Demystifying the Digital Humanities

The Demystifying Digital Humanities (DMDH) workshop series, a jointly funded venture of UW's Walter Chapin Simpson Center for the Humanities and the UW Textual Studies program, began in 2012 and ran for three consecutive academic years. It was created by two English Studies doctoral students, Paige Morgan and Sarah Kremen-Hicks, and consisted of a series of six workshops designed to provide curious graduate students with "a guided introduction to the points of intersection between traditional and digital humanities (DH), including how traditional humanities approaches and questions are used or translated in DH studies, and identifying major DH subfields and their goals."[3] The DMDH series provided me with a thoughtful introduction to many DH topics, including the essential fact that many of the tools used in DH work are not centrally supported. For example, alpha (i.e., early) stage software is not usually available for public use when it is proprietary but may be available for open source software. Alpha software releases can also be unstable and buggy, whereas beta-stage software usually has complete features and a smaller set of bugs, either known or unknown. Development stages can also help to indicate the level of support available to users running the software. In contrast to production releases, which are usually stable and supported, alpha and beta releases may have minimal support, which means the performance of the software may change irregularly. It is thus important to understand development stages before selecting a platform to host a DH project.

The DMDH series also highlighted that software support can take many forms. For DH tools that are supported centrally on a campus, for instance, there is often a help desk offering some combination of phone, email, and in-person support. For individually licensed software, however, support may depend on your plan and how much you are paying. There may be a user community where users can consult with one another about issues that are occurring with a tool, as is the case with most free open source software. Before signing up for a tool, it is critical to ask questions about what support is available, especially if you are paying for a particular plan. Which issues will the vendor help address, and which are the user's presumed responsibility? It is also good to clarify whether this support will be available via email, chat, phone, or documentation. Today, as an instructional technologist, I carry on the tradition of DMDH in trying to make these issues more transparent and accessible to those interested in the digital humanities.[4]

EXAMPLE 2

Digital Humanities Coursework

In 2014, while attending the DMDH workshop series, I enrolled in a humanities reference course that included a focus on DH. The course appealed to my main interests in how DH work is hosted in libraries, and how librarians can support scholars using DH methods in their research and teaching. For instance, as part of one assignment, students created their own DH projects in teams. Although virtually all of these projects have since been taken down due to lack of maintenance (a common issue with DH projects), the assignment yielded valuable knowledge around how to collaborate on a digital project—and in my case, around how to apply some of the principles I gleaned from the DMDH workshops. Indeed, later that same year, the organizers of the DMDH series hosted a DH showcase at which my collaborator and I presented our project and reviewed projects others had been working on across campus. In LT, we continue to see demand from DH researchers for opportunities to foster these sorts of collaborations and to build additional DH skills.

EXAMPLE 3

Digital Humanities Summer Institute

During the summer of 2017, I was part of a group that was awarded a local grant to attend the Digital Humanities Summer Institute (DHSI), a popular professional development experience hosted annually by the University of Victoria in British Columbia. Our group's goal was to gain familiarity with key DH topics from a practitioner perspective in order to better support DH/DS needs on the UW campus. I selected the DHSI course Critical Pedagogy and Digital Praxis in the Humanities, taught by Robin DeRosa, director of Interdisciplinary Studies at Plymouth State University, and Chris Friend, assistant professor of English at Saint Leo University. The course was described as "an exploration of pedagogy," and challenged attendees to rethink their approaches to teaching by discussing how students can "define, control, and take responsibility for, their learning environment."[5] The course tied in nicely with many aspects of my work with LT, including how to teach technical programs to others, and how to integrate technology into pedagogy. However, it also forced me to think in new ways about how pedagogy can be constrained by the types of technology I work with daily. The instructors and participants in my session were very direct in discussing the failings of the educational technologies available to them, such as Learning Management Systems, and their views of the role instructional technologists should play when working with faculty.

Overall, the workshop provided me with valuable insight into the types of tools digital scholars are looking for and the types of projects they are envisioning. It also jump-started my interest in student-directed content and learning, which allows members of a class to work with the instructor to find areas within the class topic that they are interested in focusing on. It is a concept that offers many potential learning benefits, but is also challenging from an assessment perspective, which is part of my work as an instructional technologist. For example, how do you evaluate students who have met their learning goals for a course and improved their knowledge of the subject material during a term but may or may not have learned enough to succeed in the next course in a sequence? The question of how to assess the knowledge contained within a project as opposed to the technical skills that went into building a project is one that appears regularly in discussions of digital scholarship projects, both in the classroom and in more complex tenure and promotion cases. Suffice to say, there is no single recommendation or criteria for DS project evaluation, although there are a number of guides from the Modern Language Association, the University of Nebraska Center for Digital Research in the Humanities, the Middle East Studies Association, and professor Todd Presner's article in the *Journal of Digital Humanities*.[6]

My experiences as a graduate student have thus deeply shaped my understanding of the needs, opportunities, and learning processes of researchers who are new to digital scholarship, as well as those who are experienced digital scholars. In the rest of this chapter, I will discuss the current services that Learning Technologies offers, many of which I believe can be used as a model for other universities' technology-focused units in terms of how to support digital scholarship work in partnership with campus libraries and librarians.

LEARNING TECHNOLOGIES AND DIGITAL SCHOLARSHIP PROJECT OFFICE HOURS

Digital Scholarship Project Office Hours originally started as a collaboration between the DMDH graduate student coordinators and a colleague in LT. Together, these parties offered weekly drop-in office hours to anyone on campus seeking assistance with a digital humanities project, until the DMDH workshops ended in 2015. However, in 2016, the new digital scholarship librarian approached me about resuming these office hours offerings. Ever since, the two of us have worked collaboratively to offer help for students and faculty across campus who are working on digital projects. As part of these new Digital Scholarship Project Help Office Hours, we are available for walk-in help for 1.5 hours once a week during academic terms (figure 7.1), although we schedule consultations outside of that time as needed. Through these consultations, we have expanded our knowledge around the challenges of DS/DH work at UW, have developed an understanding of the types of projects that are being accomplished and envisioned, and learned about the software that scholars would like to use. This information has allowed us to improve our efforts to further the culture of DS at UW, and to help other DH advocates on campus as well. For instance, we recently collaborated with other UW librarians to create a Digital Scholarship Research Guide aimed at providing first-line support to researchers who are getting started on digital projects, or who are looking for software that will help them with specific projects, such as story mapping or time line building.[7]

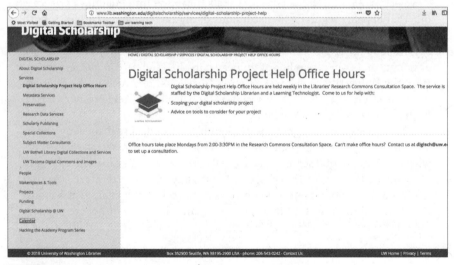

FIGURE 7.1
Screenshot of DS Project Help Office Hours Page

Performing the Digital Scholarship Consultation

Consultations can be challenging as faculty and students come to them with projects in every possible state and stage imaginable. Some are still trying to scope out their projects; often they are coming from a workshop or intensive training and are trying to translate what they have just learned to UW's infrastructure and resources. Others have had a grant proposal approved and need to determine the available campus resources. At UW, we frequently see students working on independent research or course projects with innovative ideas but struggle to scope their projects to the time available. There are also cases of established digital projects that need to be moved from their original location to a new location for a variety of reasons, or authors who would like to incorporate media resources into traditional text-based publications. Whatever their level or question, the important thing to keep in mind when approaching a consultation is that there is no one-size-fits-all answer, and that each consultation will therefore inevitably involve creative thinking about how to get a client from point A to a relative point B.

Thus, as varied as digital scholarship projects can be, all of our consultations start in essentially the same place. We begin by having the client describe their project, the inspirations behind it (this could be a research question, a particular resource, or another DH/DS project), and their vision for what the final product may be, or whether they are experimenting. Think of this as a sort of reference interview but for a digital project rather than a straight-up research project. It is also helpful to inquire toward the start about any available resources, which could be anything from grants to partnerships with other organizations to proposed and current collaborators. Establishing a client's intended audience early is likewise extremely helpful when assisting with project development. Although the explicit question of audience can be challenging for scholars, encouraging them to consider it ultimately helps to make better design and marketing choices. For the same reason, initial conversations about digital projects are a good time to inquire about any other constraints that clients may have, such as grant requirements, data sharing permissions, course project guidelines, or guidelines from a sponsor.

Once we have an idea of the desired scope and available resources, our next step is to discuss the project's time frame, which is often one of the most restrictive constraints for digital projects. When the client is in a time crunch, we tend to recommend an iterative design approach, and encourage the concept of a minimum viable product (MVP). The idea is that you do not have to be perfect on the first attempt and create a completed full-scale digital project. Iterative design can also be beneficial as scholars and researchers can also try things out and see if they work for their intended audience without having to design and build something that would be a massive undertaking. It serves as a reminder that much can be learned from things that do not go as planned during a first run of a project. Such an approach lines up well with the idea of a first draft and gives busy scholars the necessary data to improve later sections of the project. Having an MVP and a better sense of the amount of time and money involved in a full-scale project could also help when applying for grant funding for later stages of the project.

After the basic description and time frame, we ask about the components of a client's digital project. Components are hard to generalize, but could include someone's wish to have a stable archive that is not publicly accessible, or a public-facing searchable website. Scholars could also have different types of content ranging from text to multimedia. Whenever discussing content, it is important to bring up the topic of copyright. Have clients secured the rights to use the content in their project and in the specific ways that they are considering? Are they required to use a repository to store their data, and are they required to make the data or project available for reuse? If they wish to store these materials in a repository, have they met any requirements that the repository may have for accepting materials?

Reproducibility and making data available to other scholars for reuse are an important part of a highly collaborative field. This may differ from traditional humanities methods and draw more from the scientific tradition, which has much to offer but may feel unsettling for those who are new to these methodologies. Nonetheless, reproducibility can offer other researchers needed insight into project construction that will affect their own work. Data retention requirements, which can include questions of how long the data must remain available, as well as when it must be discarded, if required, may be a requirement for research grants. Happily, the UW Libraries offers assistance with resources for data management—but not necessarily at the level that researchers desire. Additionally, clients may face licensing questions. During consultations, we tend to ask whether clients want or need to consider a Creative Commons license. Creative Commons licenses help users clearly state how they are sharing their data, and what others may do with it.[8]

Once we have broached the issue of content, the consultation often turns toward more detailed project issues, such as metadata and storage. For instance, when working with clients interested in metadata, we recommend identifying up front whether they are using a standard file format, such as an open nonproprietary format, a format commonly used in the discipline, and one that is not encrypted or compressed.[9] It is also worth encouraging scholars to consider whether that is a format that is amenable to preservation, such as one on the ResearchWorks Archive List of Preferred File Formats.[10] We cover the value of naming conventions, which are important to standardize at the beginning of a project, especially for projects that will be long-running or involve a large number of collaborators. As for storage, we recommend that clients keep multiple (usually three) copies of their data in different places, one of which is in a different geographic area. We also recommend including a master and working copies. Storage is an especially complex issue to discuss with clients, as it can mean so many different things and is open to interpretation. For example, there is the question of where things are stored while being worked on, where content will be stored long-term, and, in the end, how much space is needed for project storage. The file types employed in the project also make a difference, as text files do not take large amounts of storage, but audio and video do. Any time a client expresses long-term storage plans, the digital scholarship librarian and I must ask these type of preservation questions and evaluate whether to refer them to documentation or UW subject area experts for further assistance.

Another common entry point for the DS/DH work that we see in Office Hours is specific platforms and tools. Virtually any consultation session that involves digital scholarship will include some discussion of the pros and cons of the platforms or tools that are being considered or are familiar to the user for various reasons, as well as whether their initial solution is the platform or tool that will work best for them in the long run. As consultants, it is important to remember that scholars' needs change over the course of their projects, and that these fluctuations may shift the value of a specific tool or platform. We always suggest that scholars check to see how easy or challenging it will be to get their content and metadata out of their chosen digital project platform should they need to migrate platforms in the future; after all, platforms and programs do not last forever. If it is not possible to export their content from a platform, clients are advised to approach it with extreme caution and utilize it only for experimentation.

For those clients who are still in the process of selecting a platform, there are several other items that are important to review during the selection and evaluation process. As discussed in the DMDH workshop, the first is determining which stage of development the platform is in (e.g., alpha, beta, or production), and what each of these stages means for them as users. Knowing whether a platform is new and shiny or older and reliable will help clients decide how much of their time they are willing to dedicate to any troubleshooting and development that may come up when using a newer platform. Overall, we try and counsel the clients we meet with to consider flexibility, visibility, and portability when choosing their tools and platform, and when dealing with related issues, such as data. The result is the following key points, which we address through careful questions and follow-up inquiries.

Data export. Can you export and extract your data? If data can be exported, is it in a proprietary file format (a file type that requires a specific program to read it) or a format that will allow you to use your data in another platform?[11]

Platform. Does the platform allow you to prepare their data elsewhere and import it? Is the platform open source? If you have selected a platform that you are paying for, is this a one-time payment or an annual fee? If there is an annual fee, do you get a reminder to renew?

How much storage space is offered as part of the fee and how do fees change if more storage is needed? What other file storage options are available to users at free or low cost, such as institutional Google Drive and Microsoft OneDrive accounts or Critical Commons?

License agreement. What is in the license agreement that you are agreeing to in order to use the tool? Are there any deal breakers in the license agreement?

Web hosting. Where is the project being built? Who owns the space where it is being built? If this is institutional space, what happens to it when you are no longer affiliated with that institution? Is the content of the project easily exportable?

Preservation. How long do you expect the project to last? This could include time while a graduate student, use in a career portfolio, and pieces that are companions to published print works.

Projects We See

We see a wide range of digital scholarship projects during our Office Hours, from student efforts to faculty research to course-integrated projects. Some walk-in clients are instructors teaching about digital scholarship or digital humanities with concerns about student research projects. Others are independent scholars exploring the field in response to job postings or larger trends in digital humanities.

During Office Hours consultations, we try to identify needs related to scholars' projects and assess what resources clients have tried to access. Not surprisingly, given the diversity of our clientele, we see a wide range of needs, from simple to complex. However, one recurring need that both students and faculty express is for help with website creation and design, particularly because there are very few central resources for digital scholarship, and most resources that do exist are static websites rather than robust consulting services. Depending on needs, some support may be provided by the UW Libraries' Design Help Desk, also located in the Research Commons, which offers free help to students, staff, and faculty with a focus on visuals for presentations or publications.[12] There is also some limited help available to UW community members who are looking for User Experience (UX) help—via a mailing list, a community of practice, and limited UW consulting, in addition to some static online UX information.[13] We frequently see people who are interested in learning more about both website and UX design (although they usually do not ask for or know to ask for UX help specifically), as well as people hoping to hire students with UX expertise. Often these requests come in the form of asking how to design for a specific audience such as K–12. Other regular requests include help identifying grant opportunities and assistance constructing and applying metadata to the various objects that arise in digital projects, including images and video. Unfortunately, there are limited resources available in this area, because there few metadata specialists in the Libraries. Although they can be scheduled to consult with individuals on projects, they do not currently have the capacity to support classroom instruction on metadata integration into student projects.

Coding help represents another area of growing demand from Office Hours clients. This help can include anything from wanting to learn how to do basic work with R or Python, to specific troubleshooting on existing code. Learning to code within the walls of the UW presents its own set of challenges to students, because the computer science department at UW is highly competitive and its resources are not readily accessible to students who are not in the department. Software Carpentry workshops designed to teach researchers the computing skills that they need to do their research are a good alternative but are offered infrequently, fill up quickly, do not support on-demand learning, and don't always meet individuals' needs in part due to differing definitions of "no prior experience necessary" and the ways in which humanities participants' needs differ from science users or social scientists.[14] Usually, Software Carpentry is offered as a two-day intensive workshop where participants sign up to focus on either Python or R. The eScience Institute offers instructor training once a year and workshops on a quarterly basis throughout the academic year, with the limitation that these workshops are run by volunteers and require an instructor and several assistants to run the sessions.[15] We have begun conversations with eScience to see if there is potential in the future for their Office Hours to offer some troubleshooting help with coding questions. We are also exploring whether eScience would be able to help digital scholars determine the costs associated with coding projects for grants. This potential collaboration is still in the early stages of discussion. As is the case with UX expertise, faculty and graduate students who have grant funds often come to Office Hours wanting to hire students with expertise in coding or website design. This is something that we are not currently able to assist with, but we hope there will be an opportunity to partner with eScience to support.

A third area of high demand is storage for multimedia projects. This area is complicated by issues such as volume of material, types of access desired, and the estimated length of project life. For example, many clients would like to be able to publish media to accompany a physical text, but few publishers have the ability or interest in publishing multimedia companions to traditional academic texts. Storing this content therefore takes extra space, which costs money and requires decisions about how long such a resource can continue to be available.

Finally, there is the area of web hosting, which brings unique challenges to clients engaged in digital scholarship. We see a consistent need for opportunities to experiment with different digital publishing platforms, particularly Scalar and Omeka, despite the fact that UW does not currently support these hosting platforms. Free versions of such third-party tools do not offer enough storage space for experimentation, or the full set of features that clients need. UW users get 1 GB of free web hosting space from UW-IT, but often this does not meet the needs of scholars with large video collections or long-running projects.[16] Consequently, UW digital scholars frequently have many questions specifically about installing or using Omeka, a popular open source web-publishing platform. Whereas outside services such as Reclaim Hosting offer one-click installs of Omeka, it is more complicated to install Omeka on a UW-provided web space. Installing Omeka on an individual's personal Shared Web Hosting at UW means activating web hosting, installing MySQL, downloading and installing Omeka, and configuring Omeka as well as any plug-ins. Maintaining Omeka individually requires running regular updates and ensuring that any infrastructure updates from UW-IT do not conflict with the installation. Practically speaking, many clients are not interested in investing the time to learn how to do this sort of manual install and upkeep, or do not have the funding to pay for a separate service such as Reclaim Hosting.

Reverse Engineering DH Projects

One final topic that arises often during digital scholarship consultations is that of reverse engineering existing digital projects. Often, we see individuals inspired by other DH/DS projects that they have seen determined to replicate that project's setup within the bounds of their personal research topic. The problem with these requests is that there is a wide variety of experience and funding behind some digital projects, but the details of this variance are not often clear to casual observers of their results. Miriam Posner, assistant professor for Information Studies and Digital Studies at UCLA, gives an illustrative overview of the technical skills needed to recreate the selected projects on her blog and also described the process of deconstructing projects as looking for the sources, examining how they have been processed, and determining how they are presented.[17] She includes a description of each project, and reviews the accompanying skills needed to build it. Miriam's transparency is the exception to the rule for digital scholarship even though this is encouraged, particularly from a reproducibility standpoint. It is not usually easy to deconstruct a project, and not even all of her projects have easily accessible overviews of their process and tools. Thus, for those who come in to our Office Hours with "inspiration projects," we usually start by walking through the original project site with them and asking them a gentle series of questions. These questions include:

- Can you tell how many people were involved in this project and what roles they played in project construction?

- How much time did it take to build the project?
- Is the project still a work in progress?
- When was it last updated?
- Is this project affiliated with any institutions?
- Is it receiving support (financial, technical, etc.) from anywhere?
- What software is being used?
- Is this custom-built project (e.g., specifically designed to meet a predefined set of criteria by a specific company rather than utilizing a common platform)?

Another good resource for these cases is the recently published worksheet from the ACRL Digital Scholarship Section's "Deconstructing Digital Scholarship Consultations in the Library."[18] In it, the authors suggest several other points to consider in deconstructing projects. Some of these questions focus on the purpose of the project or draw parallels between similar academic or research projects. Other questions are related to audience, methods, standards, data sets, methodology, and documentation. Creating documentation is not everyone's idea of fun, but it can make a good project even better, and also serves an important function by explaining rationales and processes for later viewers of the project—including those who might wish to reconstruct the project for their own research purposes.

Marketing Office Hours

One of the biggest challenges in offering Digital Scholarship Project Help Office Hours has been marketing. Earlier iterations of Office Hours were offered in combination with the DMDH workshop series, which increased their visibility. By contrast, our current Office Hours are listed generally as part of the consultation offerings in the UW Libraries' Research Commons unit, along with the Graduate Funding Information Service (GFIS), Writing Help Desk, and Design Help Desk. The Office Hours take place in a consultation room just off the main Research Commons space, which is itself located in one of the UW Libraries' main branches. Information about the Office Hours, along with all the other Research Commons consultation services, is sent out regularly via the UW Graduate School's general mailing list, the Research Commons online newsletter, and the Walter Chapin Simpson Center for the Humanities list. Although our Research Commons partnership has been excellent in terms of placing Office Hours in a central campus location, we have realized over time that the Research Commons' general marketing tactics may not be ideal for reaching our target audience of digital scholars. It has been challenging to figure out where, when, and how to publicize our Digital Scholarship service without pairing it with other services or including it as part of special workshops or other one-off event series.

Special Considerations: Consulting with Graduate Students

Although all digital scholars have unique and valuable needs when it comes to support for their projects, graduate students arguably face additional challenges when it comes to entering the world of DS/DH. A 2014 blog post by Paige Morgan, one of the creators of the DMDH workshops, touches on how to get started with digital humanities projects as a graduate student based on her experience as a UW grad student.[19] We have incorporated many of these ideas into our digital scholarship consultations.

First, and most importantly, Morgan points out that doctoral-seeking graduate students may not want to make their DH project part of their dissertation. In fact, it may be better for graduate students not to make completion of their degrees dependent on successfully acquiring new skills. By keeping their digital projects "unofficial," graduate students can have more fun, while at the same time learning lessons that will supplement their degree. Morgan also highlights that the sooner students can learn about legal, copyright, and IP issues, the better for their careers. She adds that these topics can shift during the course of a digital project.

Morgan also highlights the importance of background research. Graduate students must make sure that they are not pursuing a project that someone else has already done. This can be challenging to determine because there is not a standard repository or location of all DS projects. Her advice is to "scour the internet" for anything related to the chosen research area or topic. Of course, as with other academic work, students could choose to build on the work of other scholars who have already tackled part of a topic, or who have approached the same topic with different methods or based on different data. Although many solutions exist, the takeaway for students is that they may discover a need to rethink their approach to a given digital project in the same ways they would for non-digital projects where there is prior work. This is a good reminder to everyone involved in DS/DH work that, at the most basic level, digital projects are still scholarly projects, and function just like any other research project—but with the addition of new tools for analysis, or methods, or both.

One of Morgan's final points is that experimentation is a core part of many digital projects. As I mentioned earlier, the humanities do not have the same tradition of experimentation as the sciences do, but this is a major part of DS work. One of the ways to approach experimentation is through documentation. Track and record all discussions about the work, things that succeeded and things that failed, and the reasons why decisions were made. This will help in documenting a project for the future, for other scholars, for tenure committees, and for grant applications. Finding a good way to convey this to students without sounding negative is critical for successful consulting.

Our experiences working with students and faculty during digital scholarship consultations led us to explore additional options to meet some of the recurring needs that we see. To address faculty and graduate student concerns, we have experimented with developing workshops and program opportunities in hopes of expanding the culture of digital scholarship at UW.

LIBRARIES AND LEARNING TECHNOLOGIES DIGITAL SCHOLARSHIP WORKSHOPS

Some of the questions that have come up during Digital Scholarship Project Help Office Hours have encouraged LT and the Libraries to develop digital scholarship friendly workshops and events. For the past two years, the UW Libraries has hosted one such event, Going Public, which was designed to connect individuals who are already doing community-involved research as well as to offer workshops to expand skills for those who are interested in public and community scholarship but are not sure where to start.[20] It is a half-day symposium that addresses topics relating to communicating research and public scholarship to a wide audience, and includes workshops on data visualization, digital storytelling, and altmetrics.

When fostering digital scholarship culture, the importance of events should not be underestimated. Indeed, many Office Hours clients wish to learn more about what DS/DH work is happening on campus. Another complication is the lack of opportunities to see what people outside of specific disciplines are doing. This lack of awareness impacts the formation of cross-disciplinary collaborations. It is not uncommon to hear from digital scholars who would like to form collaborative project groups but struggle with finding others to work with, or who run into difficulties transitioning from the role of solo researcher to member of a team. To address some of these needs, select members of the Libraries and Learning Technologies teamed up to offer "Hacking the Academy," a program series based on Daniel J. Cohen and Tom Scheinfeldt's open access book by the same title. Together, we designed Hacking the Academy to be a multidisciplinary exploration of the ways in which scholarship is changing into a more open, collaborative, and iterative process.[21] Another event inspired by the Digital Scholarship Project Help Office Hours was the Digital Scholarship: Planning for Success workshop, first offered in spring 2017. When planning for Office Hours, the digital scholarship librarian and I noticed an increase in the number of academic job postings for faculty and staff that mentioned desired knowledge of DS/DH. Students told us that introductions to digital scholarship and to people or projects would help them gain what they saw as the required experience necessary to be competitive on the job market. To meet this need, a group of UW librarians and instructional technologists developed Digital Scholarship: Planning for Success as an introductory graduate workshop with the following goals: have participants understand the basics of digital project management, understand considerations for working with digital objects, learn how to collaborate and share work, and identify guidelines and considerations for choosing tools. We covered topics ranging from copyright and metadata basics, including a brief overview of Creative Commons licenses. We also touched on digital preservation and storage and presented case studies that allowed participants to dig in to some basic digital project deconstruction. This was an ambitious set of goals and consequently a large amount of information for one ninety-minute workshop!

In the end, there were several challenges in offering the Planning for Success workshop. First, although all the content we covered was crucial to the execution of a successful digital project, we realized after the fact it was too much information to cover in the time allotted, and that the result was not necessarily the introduction to DH that many participants had been expecting. Rather, through our workshop assessment, we discovered that much of the information presented was overwhelming for people new to the field, particularly graduate students who were just trying to expand their knowledge in order to be competitive in the academic job market. The second challenge we ran into was the scope of the information presented in the workshop. We chose to cover a collection of the issues that would help make a digital project successful in the long run (e.g., questions of storage and platform transitions), but not issues that tend to arise early in a digital project's time line, such as selection of tools, or fun ways to engage with digital projects. As we later learned, tools are one of the main ways that new scholars approach the fields of DH and DS. It is more approachable to consider learning a platform that does something specifically useful than to have to reimagine an entire research process to account for technology and data management. It is also more exciting to consider a new project without being constrained to the parameters of digital infrastructure. Learning how to balance the long-term necessities of project maintenance with ways of thinking about and engaging with digital projects has been a challenge we have encountered when offering consulting and instructional services to support UW's digital scholars.

CONCLUSION

Digital Scholarship consultations live at the intersection of pedagogy and technology and thus fit well with my job as an instructional technologist. At the same time, it is this intersection that represents one of the challenging aspects of supporting a healthy digital scholarship culture. This is because scholars are still trained only to develop deep knowledge of their specific fields; although they may use technology, they do not usually conceptualize it in the same way that technologists and librarians do. By contrast, we in the academic information field are used to thinking in terms of project management, documentation, reproducibility, acceptance of failure, and the intricate dance of collaborative work, especially with others who are not in our fields. What's more, as an instructional technologist who has a working partnership with a librarian for DS consultations, I have found that we each know different parts of the University and different types of resources and are able to help direct clients to more resources than either of us would be able to on our own. Personally, I have found collaboration with librarians and other support partners to be one of the most enjoyable and productive parts of working in digital scholarship. In the future, I hope to see more of these types of collaborations, not only at UW but at other universities. By working together across such units, we can expand the resources available to digital scholars, resulting in more innovative teaching and research methods for higher education communities as a whole.

Takeaways

Planning and Experimentation. Planning is critical to a successful project, particularly a successful digital project. Digital project management skills and a willingness to experiment are helpful although can be unfamiliar to digital scholars.

Infrastructure. Digital projects require centralized infrastructure such as web hosting, larger amounts of storage space, and easy access to varied platforms.

Community. People involved in digital projects need a central, nondepartmental space to gather for networking and access centralized resources and consultations.

NOTES

1. The CTL supports the UW teaching community though collaborative, innovative, and research-based consultations and workshops. See "Center for Teaching and Learning," https://www.washington.edu/teaching/.
2. The STF is a student-run committee that accepts proposals for use of the money generated by the Student Technology Fee based upon the needs to students outside of classrooms (https://uwstf.org).
3. Walter Chapin Simpson Center for the Humanities, "Demystifying Digital Humanities Simpson Center for Humanities," https://simpsoncenter.org/programs/initiatives/digital-humanities/demystifying-dh.
4. Ibid.
5. Chris Friend and Robin DeRosa, "Critical Pedagogy and Digital Praxis in the Humanities," *Digital Humanities Summer Institute,* http://

dhsi.org/content/2017Curriculum/10.%20Critical%20Pedagogy%20 and%20Digital%20Praxis%20in%20the%20Humanities.pdf.

6. Modern Language Association, "Guidelines for Evaluating Work in Digital Humanities and Digital Media," https://www.mla.org/About-Us/ Governance/Committees/Committee-Listings/Professional-Issues/ Committee-on-Information-Technology/Guidelines-for-Evaluating-Work -in-Digital-Humanities-and-Digital-Media; Center for Digital Research in the Humanities Nebraska, "Promotion and Tenure Criteria for Assessing Digital Research in the Humanities," https://cdrh.unl.edu/articles/ promotion; "Middle East Studies Association," https://mesana.org/ resources-and-opportunities/guidelines-for-evaluating-digital-scholarship; Todd Presner, "How to Evaluate Digital Scholarship," *Journal of Digital Humanities,* December 19, 2012, http://journalofdigitalhumanities. org/1–4/how-to-evaluate-digital-scholarship-by-todd-presner/.

7. Verletta Kern, "Digital Scholarship Research Guide," http://guides.lib.uw .edu/research/dstools.

8. For more information about copyright and DS, see chapter 3.

9. These issues are also discussed in other chapters of this book, including chapters 6 and 8.

10. "UW Libraries ResearchWorks Archive," http://digital.lib.washington.edu/ preferred-formats.html.

11. Wikipedia, s.v., "Proprietary Format," https://en.wikipedia.org/wiki/ Proprietary_format.

12. "Design Help," http://depts.washington.edu/deshelp.

13. UW Information Technology, "UX Design Guides," http://uxdesign.uw.edu.

14. "Software Carpentry," https://software-carpentry.org/.

15. "eScience Institute," https://escience.washington.edu/.

16. UW Information Technology, "Activating Shared Web Hosting," *IT Connect,* https://itconnect.uw.edu/connect/web-publishing/shared-hosting/activat ing-shared-web-hosting/.

17. Miriam Posner, "How Did They Make That," *Miriam Posner's Blog,* August 29, 2013, http://miriamposner.com/blog/how-did-they-make-that/.

18. Andrew Johnson, Alix Keener, Brianna Marshall, Chelcie Juliet Rowell, and Joel B. Thornton, "Activity 1: Worksheet 2 Deconstructing Digital Scholarship Consultations in the Library," https://acrldigschol.github.io/ deconstructing-consultations/activity-1/worksheet-2/.

19. Paige Morgan, "How to Get a Digital Humanities Project off the Ground," June 5, 2014, www.paigemorgan.net/how-to-get-a-digital -humanities-project-off-the-ground/#more-158.

20. University of Washington Libraries, "Going Public," www.lib.washington .edu/commons/events/going-public.

21. University of Washington Libraries, "Hacking the Academy Program Series," www.lib.washington.edu/digitalscholarship/ hacking-the-academy-programming-series.

JENNIFER MUILENBURG

8

Data Services

D ata services in libraries are not new, but they are related in many aspects to digital scholarship in libraries. Although the term "data services" tends to lean toward researchers working in data-intensive sciences, many of the practices that comprise data services mirror those necessary to digital scholarship research. To that end, the University of Washington's (UW) data services librarian and digital scholarship librarian have discussed the type of services they provide to campus users and have collaborated on campus programming and events. They also collaborate on planning future services. This chapter will outline the similarities and differences between data services and digital scholarship and will describe the data services assessment work, training program, and strategy for marketing services at the UW Libraries.

DEFINING DIGITAL SCHOLARSHIP AND DATA SERVICES

Before we can talk about digital scholarship and data services, we need to discuss some terminology and definitions. The concept of data services is confusing to many, even in the context of academic library services.[1] Similarly, as explained in the Association for Research Libraries' article "Digital Scholarship

Support in ARL Member Libraries: An Overview," "Digital scholarship [DS] is not new and its panoply has evolved over time. DS is a shifting range of scholarly endeavor that can incorporate a number of definitions, methods, tools, and research outputs."[2] Even within this book, slightly different definitions of digital scholarship are used by different authors—despite the fact that all of us work at the same institution, if not on some of the same projects.

The term data services is also a common source of confusion, in part because "data" is a term that can mean multiple things. At UW, the Libraries has adapted a definition from the UK Data Archive: Data is "that which is collected, observed, or created, for purposes of analyzing to produce original research results. . . . Research data may be created in tabular, statistical, numeric, geospatial, image, multimedia or other formats."[3] In the book *Databrarianship,* the editors provide several examples of what data might mean in different disciplines before announcing a wide-ranging, catch-all working definition for the purposes of their text: "The data we are concerned with here are the product of taking that raw informational input and assembling it into a structure form for analysis. Data are a product of research as well as an input for research."[4]

There is also a lack of common, established definitions of several data-related terms, including "digital archiving" and "digital preservation," to name a few. For this reason, staff working in libraries may have different understandings of what it means to curate, archive, or share a digital item, unless specific institutional definitions are provided. This lack of common understanding extends to other disciplines are well. For example, a review of data management plans (DMPs) at UW in 2015 showed that terminology was an obstacle in implementing DMPs, especially around the terms "archive" and "sharing." For example, the review showed that researchers would use the word "sharing" when they meant anything from putting data on a shared drive in a lab, providing data upon emailed request, a verbal presentation at a conference, or depositing data in a disciplinary web-based repository with accompanying metadata.[5]

All of this is used to illustrate that when proceeding with descriptions of data or digital scholarship services at a particular institution, it will be in everyone's best interests to provide explicit definitions of various terms, along with relevant citations or links to specific software programs, metadata standards, or similar information so that all players have the same base information. In a nutshell: "the term digital scholarship itself is quite fluid and seems to offer many interpretations depending on a particular university's culture, institutional organization, and environment."[6] This means that the types of support services and education libraries can provide will also be in constant evolution. The case is similar with data services in libraries: although there are, generally speaking, a set of agreed-upon services that define "data services," the specifics of those services will vary not only over time, but at each institution. Tenopir et al. listed the most common data services offered by libraries (items marked with an asterisk are services offered at UW), which include:[7]

- Consulting on data management plans*
- Consulting on data and metadata standards*
- Outreach with other data service providers on campus*
- Providing reference support in finding and citing data sets*
- Creating guides for finding data*
- Directly participating in research projects
- Discussing data services with others on campus*
- Training librarians and others on campus*
- Providing repository services, which includes:
  - Deaccessioning of data from a repository
  - Preparing data sets for deposit into a repository*
  - Creating or transforming metadata*
  - Identifying datasets that could be candidates for repositories

Working from the 2012 Associations of College and Research Libraries (ACRL) list of research data management activities in libraries, one can draw parallels to equivalent services for digital scholarship. In table 8.1, each of Tenopir's major data services activities are listed in the first column, with the second and third columns providing examples of what such services might look like for either research data services or digital scholarship services.

TABLE 8.1

Tenopir's Research Data Management activities and digital scholarship equivalents

Service	Research Data Management	Digital Scholarship
Consulting on data management plans	Library staff help researchers complete DMPs from various funding sources, including creating metadata and other documentation, finding appropriate repositories, and data curation. Example from NSF: https://www.nsf.gov/eng/general/dmp.jsp	Library staff help researchers complete DMPs from various funding sources, including creating metadata and other documentation, finding appropriate repositories, and digital object curation. Example from NEH: https://www.neh.gov/sites/default/files/2018-06/data_management_plans_2018.pdf
Consulting on data and metadata standards	Library staff help identify disciplinary metadata standards, if available, or general standards in their absence. www.dcc.ac.uk/resources/curation-reference-manual/chapters-production/scientific-metadata, www.dcc.ac.uk/resources/metadata-standards	Library staff help identify disciplinary metadata standards, if available, or general standards in their absence. http://dh101.humanities.ucla.edu/?page_id=35, www.dcc.ac.uk/resources/subject-areas/social-science-humanities

(cont.)

TABLE 8.1 (cont.)

Tenopir's Research Data Management activities and digital scholarship equivalents

Outreach with other data service providers on campus	Library staff works for information technology departments, scholarly communications and publishing experts, as well as experts in various departments and/or labs on campus. This keeps both sides aware of current research, any opportunities for new or improved services and tools, and helps create partnerships and collaborations for the entire campus.	Library staff works for information technology departments, scholarly communications and publishing experts, as well as experts in various departments and/or labs on campus. This keeps both sides aware of current research, any opportunities for new or improved services and tools, and helps create partnerships and collaborations for the entire campus.
Providing reference support in finding and citing data sets	This falls under the work of what is considered more traditional librarianship.	For digital scholarship, this is extension thereof—in both cases, oftentimes a researcher has created/gathered her own dataset or other digital research objects, but may need assistance supplementing their data, or may need help starting a project. Library staff can help locate data sources and/or help negotiate licensing terms.
Creating guides for finding data	Traditional librarianship	Traditional librarianship
Directly participating in research projects	Library staff can work alongside researchers as information specialists, research assistants, etc. Services can include metadata creation, data curation, research methods, acquiring research papers or datasets, etc.	Similar to data services—library staff can participate in many types of research projects, offering varying levels of expertise, from metadata creation at the beginning of a project, to curation at the end.
Discussing data services with others on campus	This is essential to creating and maintaining a robust research data community on campus. Networking, collaborations, wayfinding (pointing people to the right experts on campus)—all of these create opportunity for collaboration, consultation, and connection for campus researchers.	The same applies for digital scholarship, sometimes even more so since it is such an interdisciplinary methodology.
Training librarians and others on campus	Providing training to librarians on tools such as DMPTool, persistent identifiers, metadata creation, online research tools such as Open Science Framework, and possibly data analysis tools or methods.	Providing training on various software tools and how they might be appropriate for various projects.
Providing repository services	Library staff can either assist with deposit into local repositories, or help locate external repositories and provide assistance with remote deposit.	Although there are fewer repositories for digital humanities/scholarship work, the same consultation services would apply here to digital scholarship.

Adapted from Academic Libraries and Research Data Services: Current Practices and Plans for the Future. Prepared by Carol Tenopir, Ben Birch, and Suzie Allard. Chicago: Association of College and Research Libraries, 2012.

THE HISTORY OF DATA SERVICES AT UW

Staff have been working on data services issues in the UW Libraries since 2010, when the first UW data services librarian position was created to support campus use of research data. The position was created in response to growth in data-intensive research on campus. As with most campuses, at UW there are multiple centers or departments on campus that support researchers with data, including the Center for Social Science Computation and Research, the Center for Studies in Demography and Ecology, and the eScience Institute. Several departments have also historically been data-intensive, including the health sciences and social sciences, departments using geographic information systems (GIS) analysis and software, and physics/astronomy. As computer power and data availability have grown (along with the concept and analysis of "big data"), the Libraries have added a librarian dedicated to support and facilitate research data issues.

In addition to meeting with researchers from across campus and establishing the libraries as a "data concierge" for all campus users, one of the first big projects undertaken by the new data librarian was a campus-wide survey to assess the data needs of UW researchers. The survey and accompanying interviews were instrumental in developing UW's first set of data services, which included data management plan consultations, data acquisition, data-related referrals around campus, classroom teaching and workshops for library staff and campus researchers, and work with campus partners to create a community of practice around research data issues.

To further bolster the development of the data services program, a data services team was created, which included the geographic information systems (GIS) librarian, metadata librarian, staff from the Libraries' information technology and technical services, health sciences librarians, and the government documents librarian. The team participated in the activities listed above and helped disseminate information to their particular areas and from those areas to the data services team for discussion. Eventually, a second, part-time librarian was hired to support marketing and outreach for library data services across campus.

Over time, data-related work within the UW Libraries has evolved to include efforts and services that overlap strongly with digital scholarship. These include assessment work, staff training, and outreach and marketing services.

NEEDS ASSESSMENTS

Before deciding what services should be provided, libraries should perform an assessment to determine what digital scholarship work is currently underway, what needs the community has, and where any gaps might be. This type of work should also include a frank assessment of library staffing and technological support, as well as identifying potential campus partners who can contribute to the effort.

The following are two examples of key assessments that have taken place within the data services team, or in collaboration with other UW Libraries units.

EXAMPLE 1

2012 Data Needs Assessment Survey[8]

In 2012, after several months of talking with library staff and campus departments, a more formal campus-wide survey was performed by the data services librarian to clarify the research data management needs of UW researchers. The key research questions for this assessment helped us to understand the level of awareness of data management plan requirements; determine the size and typical storage locations of researchers' datasets; and identify the attitudes of researchers toward data sharing, thus helping to shape our service priorities for UW researchers. Questions were reviewed by discipline to determine disciplinary need.

The survey targeted UW primary and co-primary investigators (PI and co-PI) who submitted grant proposals from 2010–2012 (see table 8.2). According to our records, the survey pool included over 3,100 individuals, of which 323 responded to the survey. When analyzing the data, we noted uneven response rates across academic disciplines, with a large number of respondents from the Health Sciences. This made it challenging to generalize results across disciplines.

To minimize the likelihood of confusion, at the start of the survey the data services team provided definitions for several data-related terms that were identified as ambiguous in pilot testing. These included:

TABLE 8.2

Respondents from 2012 UW Libraries' data needs assessment survey

	# Respondents	% of Respondents	% of Total Survey Population
Health	183	60.8	59.7
Sciences	82	27.2	28.5
Social Sciences	19	6.3	8.3
Humanities	5	1.7	.7
*Other**	12	4.0	2.8

*The category of "Other" included members affiliated w/ departments outside the four broader disciplinary areas (e.g. UW-IT, School of Business, Law School, Interdisciplinary Arts & Sciences, etc.).

Data: By data, we do not mean a synonym for information. We mean research data; that which is collected, observed, or created, for purposes of analyzing to produce original research results. Research data may be created in tabular, textual, statistical, numeric, geospatial, image, multimedia, or other formats.[9]

Data management: Data management pertains to the collection, cleaning, analysis, storage, sharing, disposal, and/or archiving of research data.[10]

Metadata: Metadata refers to the description of the content and context of data files. Examples include how, when, and by whom data was collected and how it is formatted.

Data cleaning: Data cleaning is a process used to detect and correct errors in a dataset. This can include the coding of missing data, correcting typing errors made in data entry, adjusting for column shift, and so forth.

In the main body survey, participants were asked to sort a number of services into low, low-medium, medium, medium-high, and high priorities. These levels were assigned values of 1 to 5, with a low value of 1 and a high of 5, and a mean priority level for each service was taken. According to results, the highest rated priorities were:

ensuring that data is secure—3.95

backing data up—3.95

short-term storage (5 years or less)—3.73

long-term storage—3.66

controlling/providing access to data—3.59

Other sections of the survey covered data storage needs and concepts around data sharing. For example, one section of the survey surfaced important trends in the duration of data storage needed by respondents. Only 9 percent indicated a need for storage for one to five years, while 27 percent were interested in "indefinite" storage. Additionally, 43 percent of the respondents were interested in storing their data for six to ten years, and 20 percent were seeking storage for longer than ten years but less than indefinitely. Separately, at least 68 percent of those responding wanted to be able to share their data over time (another 18 percent were unsure if they wanted shareable storage).

Respondents were also asked if they were willing to share data beyond the project team. A little more than half of respondents (55 percent) said that they were willing to do so. If health fields are excluded, this average rises to two-thirds (67 percent). Respondents in the health fields appeared less likely to share data with people outside of their research team; responses to the follow-up question asking for clarification indicated this was primarily due to concerns about the protection of anonymity and personal information of human subjects. Respondents in the sciences appeared to be most likely to share their data; again, according to responses from the follow-up question, this may have been due in part to sharing requirements of various funding bodies. Researchers were most willing to share their final reports and least willing to share raw data.

Humanities respondents comprised only 1.7 percent of the total respondents to the survey. Nevertheless, by combining the information provided by both our report and a separate needs assessment by UW's digital scholarship librarian (see chapter 4), we were able to make connections between our units' target populations.

The data services team considered the survey and interview results in terms of what services the library was offering, what researchers said they'd like to have offered, and where there were gaps. In response, the team adjusted some of our outreach and created many more training opportunities for researchers of all levels (as well as librarians) on both tools and data management concepts. LibGuides were modified to reflect the types of information researchers were seeking, and we created a stronger relationship with our Office of Research as well as data-intensive departments on campus to make sure lines of communications were open in both directions. In response to the survey's findings that many researchers would share data more easily if there were a simple mechanism to do so, the library began investigating the possibility of building a UW data repository to accompany our institutional repository. Information on that project is detailed in chapter 6.

EXAMPLE 2

UW Libraries' Triennial Survey

The data services team also relies on the UW Libraries' Triennial Survey, a survey sent every three years to faculty and graduate students at all three campuses (Seattle, Bothell, and Tacoma), to all undergraduates at Bothell and Tacoma, and a sample of undergraduates at the Seattle campus. Results of the surveys are used for facilities or service improvements, library budget narratives, UW student technology fee proposals, and to demonstrate the library's impact on research, teaching, and learning.[11]

The most recent survey was completed in 2016. Respondents to the 2016 survey included 1,527 faculty (35 percent response rate) and 2,780 Seattle campus graduate and professional students (22 percent response rate).[12] The survey included several data-related questions.

> *Does your research and teaching involve any of the following digital activities/tools? Please check all that apply.*
> - ☐ My work does not involve any of these
> - ☐ Text/data mining
> - ☐ Data visualization (using tools such as Tableau)
> - ☐ Web authoring or publishing (using tools such as Scalar or Omeka)

- ☐ Digital mapping/digital map making (using tools such as ArcGIS, Neatline, Google My Maps)
- ☐ Digital annotation (using tools such as hypothes.is and Lacuna)
- ☐ Other (please specify)

Responses indicated that 40 percent of both faculty and graduate student respondents said that their work uses one or more of the above activities and tools. Highest-ranked individual activities were data visualization and data/ text mining, followed by digital mapping.

Another digital scholarship and data services question of interest that was included on the survey looked at services to support researchers' work:

Which of the following library services would be helpful to your academic work, research, and scholarship?

- ☐ Citation management software
- ☐ Consultation with a subject liaison librarian
- ☐ Help managing, archiving, and preserving research data
- ☐ Questions related to publishing issues
- ☐ Submitting theses and dissertations electronically

Surprisingly, 51 percent of graduate student respondents said that help on managing, archiving, and preserving research data would be helpful to them and 57 percent of faculty respondents said the same.

On the faculty side, survey respondents were asked:

Which of the following library services would be useful to your research and scholarly activities:

- ☐ Managing, archiving, and preserving research data
- ☐ Assessing the impact of your work or research
- ☐ Questions related to publishing issues
- ☐ Depositing your scholarship into ResearchWorks, UW's institutional repository
- ☐ Development of data management plans

44 percent of faculty said they would be interested in depositing their research into ResearchWorks, and 37 percent said that help developing data management plans would be useful (figure 8.1).

Results of the Triennial Survey are used to help library staff reassess current offerings, compare to what survey responses indicate is desirable, and to identify opportunities where there are service gaps. Data services staff used the 2016 survey results to develop an online research data management workshop offered via Canvas (described below), and to improve our educational materials, LibGuides, and workshops offered on tools such as DMPTool and Open Science Framework (OSF).

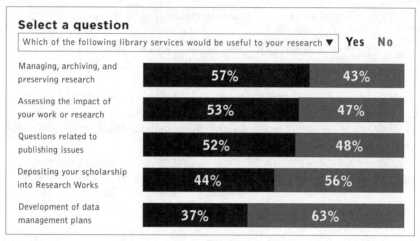

Select a question

Which of the following library services would be useful to your research ▼ | **Yes** | **No**

	Yes	No
Managing, archiving, and preserving research	57%	43%
Assessing the impact of your work or research	53%	47%
Questions related to publishing issues	52%	48%
Depositing your scholarship into Research Works	44%	56%
Development of data management plans	37%	63%

FIGURE 8.1

Faculty responses to "Which of the following library services would be helpful to your academic work, research and scholarship?"

KEEPING UP WITH NEEDS ASSESSMENTS

As with all technology, changes are rapid and constant. The solutions a library picks today to fit digital scholarship needs will change, whether that be in two years or ten. The tools researchers use now will likely change at the same pace; indeed, there are no doubt technological tools on the horizon that will allow types of research we have yet to imagine. To keep pace with these changes, libraries and librarians will need to make sure they stay on top of changes in the field. This can be done through partnerships with digital scholarship researchers and centers on campus, attending workshops, continuing education via software training and research methodologies, and by attending conferences. Professional organizations such as Research Data Access and Preservation and the International Association for Social Sciences Services and Technology are excellent places to find colleagues, continuing education, discussion groups, and conferences.[13] Keeping in touch with what other universities and data archives are doing in terms of facilities, programming, technology, and services will help library staff stay informed about changes in the field. Locally, designating a librarian or library staff member as a liaison to the various departments working on digital scholarship projects will help establish these relationships, as well as encourage their continuation.

Needs "re-assessments" will be essential to understanding an individual library's researchers and technological status. Although an extensive primary needs assessment is typical for a library new to digital scholarship, subsequent reassessments can be done on a smaller scale. For example, the library can

- interview a particular population of the researchers each year on a rotating schedule;
- create a community of practice (COP) that meets on a regular basis that includes library participation, which can be an important source of information; and
- make sure the COP knows the library is a resource and includes library staff in conversations on needs, projects, research, presentations, curriculum support, and so on to enhance and support this relationship.

This type of constant reassessment is essential when dealing with fast-paced changes in technology and methodology.

Once relationships are established that allow the library to understand the data and digital scholarship environment in which the University is working, the next step is keeping library staff and campus researchers aware and trained on services and tools available at the library.

COMMUNICATIONS, MARKETING, AND OUTREACH

Once you have decided on the kind of services that will be offered by your library, the next step is making sure the campus population is aware of those services. To get information and messages out, a communications and marketing plan can be an excellent tool to keep communications consistent, constant, and available via multiple channels.

The UW data services staff created the inaugural version of its own communications plan in 2014 (see appendix G). This plan included an outline for what types of communications would come from the unit, on what time line, on what channel (for example, Twitter, Facebook, Instagram, blog, etc.), and listed responsibilities by staff position. The intended audience for data-related communications was, ambitiously, anyone on campus—the idea being that parts of our services are relevant to undergraduates, research staff, faculty, graduate students, research assistants, and so on. It also included a calendar of when items are to be published, a crucial piece of any communications plan.

Locally, the data services staff also participates in groups for social media managers, both within the UW Libraries and the University as a whole, to hear about the trends, tools, and time lines they use. We follow other library social media accounts, as well as the accounts of data-intensive researchers or departments on campus, to learn about their events and to stay aware of various approaches to using social media when advertising services. Another, broader resource of interest to library staff is the annual Library Marketing and Communications Conference, which offers sessions and presentations on a variety of issues of interest to marketing and communications in a library setting.[14]

Many libraries already have certain communication channels in place: outreach to other library staff, particularly liaisons or subject librarians who work closely with departments; calendars of events; email newsletters; building signage; Twitter and other social media channels. However, sometimes these efforts are distributed among staff, and efforts may be duplicated, or individual items or channels may fall through the cracks. An organized communications plan is a good tool to prevent duplication and provide maximum impact for the library's message.

If your library has existing staff or guidelines for developing a plan, you'll want to start there. But even if there is an overall plan for your library, having an individual plan for your department will enhance your message and your presence on campus. Getting your own message out independently, or in addition to the library's overall message, will enhance patron's awareness of your services.

While creating the plan, make sure to consult with your library's social media and marketing staff (if any) to determine what channels are most effective. Twitter, for example, might be heavily used but perhaps only by a subset of your population. It may be that Instagram and SnapChat will have more uptake with your users. Connecting with your campus social media department or staff will help you find out what has the most impact and will help you keep up with trends, both by students as well as administrators.

You should determine the frequency that items will be posted to various forums (Twitter, Facebook, Instagram, blogs, etc.) and then create a calendar that anyone associated with marketing will adhere to. Put a point person in charge to remind writers when they're due to create content and to remind them when it's time to share information online.

As with all social media, be careful about operating in a vacuum: if you're not careful with your follows and followers, your consistent and useful messaging may only be reaching other library staff or campus users that are already aware of your services. Care must be taken to cultivate awareness of other groups, departments, and leaders on campus who are well-positioned to spread the library's message to their own constituencies. Having the library's message rebroadcast via retweets, email, newsletters, and so on by a respected professor, dean, or department head can have more impact than repeated messages from little-known accounts. Cultivating personal relationships will help improve the chances of this type of message rebroadcasting.

The communications plan is an excellent first step in creating a flow of information; however, personal relationships are what will give any marketing messages the weight and validity they need to impact user populations. One way to ensure that the library's message is distributed is to create and foster partnerships with various campus groups and departments. Subject and liaison librarians are a logical beginning, but outreach to other groups will work in the library's favor as well.

At UW, the Libraries has a strong connection with both the eScience Institute, UW's home for data-intensive science (not coincidentally located in a former Libraries-owned space), and the Walter Chapin Simpson Center for the Humanities. These types of close partnerships, if bolstered by regular meetings and conversations, will enable a two-way chain of communication that will keep both parties aware of the other's activities. Librarians at UW work with individuals from both the institute and the center to collaborate on programming, consult on areas of expertise, and solicit feedback on activities and events in the library and the individual departments.

Essentially, the message is this: communications outreach must come from multiple outputs, multiple times, and you will still have to rally constantly to make sure your message is heard. Marketing and communications channels are being used not only to create awareness around issues relevant to data-intensive research but also to broadcast information about training and education offered by the library.

TRAINING

Libraries and their staffs are in excellent positions on campus from which to offer various types of trainings on the tools and services that support contemporary research. This is because libraries tend to be centrally located on campus, are discipline-agnostic, and their offerings are typically available to researchers of all levels. Libraries' trainings are also usually offered in various convenient formats: drop-in sessions within the building, collaborations with other campus departments, educational series, presentations, and online classes or workshops are only some examples of the education and training a library can provide.

CASE STUDY

Staff Training

The UW Libraries' data services team has taken the approach of first offering in-person data-related trainings to library staff, then turning to the campus community. These staff sessions are usually an hour long and deal with a single tool at a time, unless there are several tools that relate to one topic (e.g., UW has several tools that offer various persistent identifier capabilities). Each session typically provides a short introduction to the tool and what it is used for, followed by either hands-on time or a question-and-answer period (or both) at the end of the session. Workshop offerings have included training on tools such as DMPTool, Open Science Framework (OSF), ORCID, and Data-Cite, for example.[15] The idea behind these sessions is to provide introductory-level information to staff, who will then have enough information about a tool to refer patrons to it when appropriate. Data services staff still handle reference-level questions about the tools, but the greater awareness about their capability allows more users to be directed to tools by word of mouth, instead of relying on Google searches or library reference guides.

The UW Libraries has also offered information sessions about products that are not supported by UW, but that could be acquired by individual interested parties. For example, data services staff helped electronic lab notebook company LabArchives offer a drop-in educational session to UW researchers, even though UW does not currently have a sitewide license for the software.[16] Having LabArchives demonstrate their software and be available for questions gave researchers an opportunity to determine whether or not this software would meet their needs. Although the UW Libraries isn't in a position to acquire the software on behalf of the campus, knowing about the software's abilities helps Libraries staff inform interested parties about free trials, grant-based allocations of the software, and helps the Libraries' staff advocate when necessary for other parties to acquire their own versions of the software.

Trainings can also be a worthwhile strategy for libraries looking to increase awareness of data-related issues beyond the uses of individual tools. Over the last few years, the UW Libraries has turned more of its attention toward developing this type of training, especially in combination with the Libraries' online learning efforts. One outcome has been the creation of a successful online multiday workshop on research data management skills, which we offer via the Canvas learning management system.

CASE STUDY

Research Data Management Skills Workshop

The Research Data Management Skills Canvas workshop was based on a 2013 UW workshop created from the New England Collaborative Data Management Curriculum (NECDMC).[17] The NECDMC was developed to teach research data management skills to researchers primarily in STEM disciplines. Each of the seven modules included a lecture, a slide presentation (sometimes with notes), activities to illustrate the learning concepts, extensive background information in the form of a Word document, and case studies.

In spring of 2013, librarians from UW's main campus and the health sciences library worked together to pilot all seven modules in a weekly, hour-long format. Staff worked to edit, enhance, and customize module content to reflect the culture, disciplinary realities, and technical tools available to UW's campus researchers. The resulting course was widely marketed, and had more than seventy-five enrollees, primarily from engineering, nursing, forestry, and biology. Unfortunately, the course suffered significant attrition over the seven weeks, with only seven of the seventy-eight enrolled researchers completing all modules. Although those who finished the class gave the content and instructors high ratings, the librarian instructors felt that the overall impact of the course was minimal. Discussions followed among the data services staff about how the content could be reoriented and better delivered to more researchers in a more efficient way.

Luckily, a collaborative solution to this issue arose in the form of the UW Libraries' instructional design librarian, Robin Chin Roemer, who had already been piloting a new series of online Canvas courses to graduate students on how to acquire key research skills. Chin Roemer had attended several of the in-person NECDMC workshop sessions and suggested the content might do better if delivered in a multiday online format, similar to the asynchronous Canvas classes her team had been designing. The data services librarians agreed, and development of a new online workshop began.

Content for the new workshop was plentiful, as much of it could be drawn from previously customized NECDMC modules. That said, the most difficult task for the data services team was limiting the content to the most salient and helpful data management best practices, tips, and links to resources, both at UW and externally, that would provide the highest impact to attendees. Collaborating with the specialists within the UW Libraries' Instructional Design (LibID) unit was imperative to achieving this goal. Because they were not data experts, LibID staff were more easily able to focus on streamlining the content suggested by the data services team and formatting it for use in the online Canvas environment. The LibID team provided design assistance, utilized best practices in delivery and language, and helped the data services team members understand how best to "chunk up" the curriculum for maximum impact (see figures 8.2 through 8.4). Having this instructional design expertise at

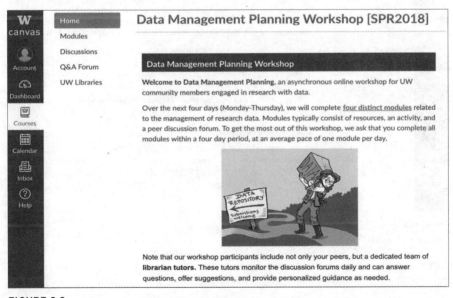

FIGURE 8.2
Homepage for Data Management Planning Workshop

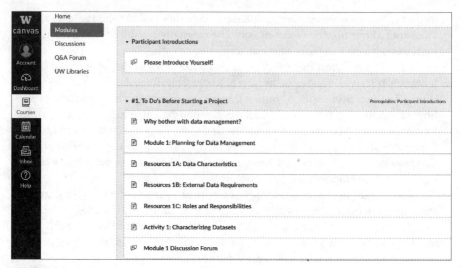

FIGURE 8.3

Example of Module 1's Content

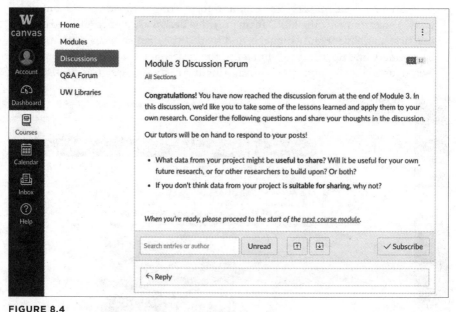

FIGURE 8.4

Module 3 Discussion Forum

hand made our revision work possible; without it, our course would have been ill-designed and overburdened with content.

The revamped Research Data Management workshop launched in August 2016. In consultation with LibID, we decided the class would be four days in duration, focus on asynchronous interactive learning between students and librarian "tutors," and would be limited in enrollment to forty students. Within days of its announcement, enrollment for this new non-credit class ran to sixty students, which forced us to create a significant waitlist. A 5:1 ratio of students to librarian tutors meant that every post was answered by a librarian in a timely fashion; in fact, because one of our tutors was working remotely from Germany, we had the benefit of the time difference to help make sure no query went too long without being answered. As with most online classes and massive open online courses (MOOCs), a minority of students did the majority of the participation, but that appears to be an issue with online, no-credit courses of all types.[18] Participants who completed the course rated the workshop highly and requested long-term access to the workshop materials in order to share information with peers.

The data services team followed up this class with a second offering in spring 2017, and then again in summer 2017. After looking at attendance numbers and seeing that a growing number of registrants were coming from health sciences, the data services librarian approached the librarians in the UW Health Sciences Library to ask if they'd be interested in creating their own workshop specific to their student populations. This quickly resulted in a new health sciences-focused version of the Research Data Management workshop, which was first offered concurrently with the sciences-focused workshop in spring 2018. For each instance of the workshop, maximum enrollment has been reached within a few hours or days of the initial marketing postings and waitlists are created each time. As of July 2018, a second iteration of the health sciences workshop was offered again during the summer term, concurrent with the sciences workshop. This concurrent two-workshop approach allows us to double the number of students and associated impact. It also allows librarian tutors for the two workshops to share information among themselves to better serve the students' needs.

The success of the health sciences-focused workshop has led to discussions among some UW librarians about offering other customized versions of the course to specific populations. These could easily include researchers who identify themselves with digital scholarship and digital humanities. Since a good portion of the workshop includes links to UW staff, IT support, and associated tools and resources—the portions of the workshop that don't require interpersonal connections to deliver the information—digital scholarship researchers would be well-served by a similar online workshop. Since many digital scholars are either unaware of or new to various relevant data management tools, a DS/DH class could provide up to 80+ researchers a year with information relevant to their fields of study and to the UW in particular. A workshop like this could also be developed to help walk researchers through the creation of a data management plan, whether that plan be for the National Science Foundation or the National Endowment for the Humanities.

WHAT'S NEXT FOR DATA SERVICES AND DIGITAL SCHOLARSHIP

Many of the tools and services provided by a library's data services staff are things that help ensure the long-term preservation and access to research outputs. However, the infrastructure required for both digital scholarship curation and archiving, as well as data science curation and archiving, is not currently something the UW Libraries is able to provide. Although there are people on the UW campus with the technical expertise required to provide these types of services, in an academic environment with constantly shrinking budgets and the ever-present competition for funds, finding the funding to provide such a service on a continuing basis is an issue. Librarians are available to provide curation services, but that lands us right back in an issue of definition: what, exactly, are curation services? Will they include metadata services, data validation, future format migration, hosting, and backup, or some combination thereof? What budget will be used to pay for these services to ensure their longevity? Long-term storage costs money and requires staffing to maintain. Right now, these questions and their solutions remain up in the air.

There are two issues of paramount importance to data-intensive science as well as digital scholarship for which there are no clear-cut answers. As discussed in chapter 4, "the number one question received during Office Hours centers around where to host and store projects for free or at low cost." The sciences have an increasing need to both archive and provide access to interactive content and very large datasets and the associated software. Even if libraries are not able to provide these services for either data-intensive science or digital scholarship, they have expertise in long-term storage and access of many types of materials—for all disciplines. Being able to participate in discussions and develop services or referrals for these kinds of services will help ensure that best practices for archiving are being considered and will ensure the best long-term outcomes for preservation.

CONCLUSION

This chapter outlined the similarities and differences between data services and digital scholarship by describing the data services assessment work and identifying opportunities for collaboration through training and marketing services at the UW Libraries. As noted above, there are many areas of library data services and digital scholarship that are similar, if not identical to, each other. Assessing its own library environment will help library staff develop high-demand services and will keep those services current. A staff knowledgeable about both data services and digital scholarship basics, trends, and technology will improve communication and community among library users. Using marketing strategies to get a library's message out will help ensure that library users know what the library can provide to assist them in their research. All of these efforts will foster a robust culture of digital scholarship and enhances researchers' experience—and success—creating and sharing their work.

Takeaways

■ Data services and digital scholarship are both technology-driven fields with meanings that vary greatly from context to context. Establishing definitions and context local to a specific library or institution is essential to ensure that library staff and patrons understand what is being discussed.

■ Assessment is important when introducing a service, but constant reassessment is necessary to deal with fast-paced changes in technology and methodology.

■ Partnerships and personal relationships are essential, both within and external to the Libraries.

■ Outreach must come from multiple outlets, be repeated multiple times, but you'll still have to work hard to ensure that the message is heard.

NOTES

1. Amanda J. Swygart-Hobaugh, "Data Services in Academic Libraries—What Strange Beast Is This?" *SLIS Student Research Journal* 6, no. 2 (2009): 1.
2. Association of Research Libraries, "Digital Scholarship Support in ARL Member Libraries: An Overview, https://perma.cc/ZVD2-LGM3.
3. Robin Rice, DISC-UK DataShare Project: Final Report, (JISC, 2009): 16, http://repository.jisc.ac.uk/336/.
4. Lynda Kellam and Kristi Thompson, *Databrarianship: The Academic Data Librarian in Theory and Practice* (Chicago: ALA Editions, 2009), 4-5.
5. Report internal to UW.
6. Heather McCullough, "Developing Digital Scholarship Services on a Shoestring: Facilities, Events, Tools, and Projects," *College and Research Libraries News* 75, no. 4 (2014): 187.
7. Carol Tenopir et al., *Academic Libraries and Research Data Services: Current Practices and Plans for the Future,* (Chicago: Association of College & Research Libraries, 2012).

8. Stephanie Wright et. al., *Fall 2012 Research Data Management Needs Assessment Results* (Seattle: University of Washington Libraries, 2013).

9. Adapted from Rice, DISC-UK DataShare Project, p. 16.

10. Adapted from University of North Carolina, Research Data Stewardship Report, https://sils.unc.edu/sites/default/files/general/research/UNC _Research_Data_Stewardship_Report.pdf, 2012, p. 11.

11. Funds from UW's student technology fee are used to pay for various technology resources for student use.

12. University of Washington Libraries Assessment Program, "Triennial Survey," www.lib.washington.edu/assessment/surveys/triennial.

13. More information on the International Association for Social Sciences Services and Technology may be found at www.iassistdata.org/. More information on Research Data Access and Preservation may be found at https://www.asist.org/rdap/.

14. More information on the Library Marketing and Communications Conference may be found at www.librarymarketingconference.org/.

15. DMPTool (https://dmptool.org/) is a tool that simplifies the creation of data management plans for many funding agencies. Open Science Framework (https://osf.io/) is a cloud-based collaborative research platform. ORCID (https://orcid.org/) is a provider of persistent identifiers for researchers. DataCite (https://www.datacite.org/) is a provider of digital object identifiers for research data.

16. LabArchives, (https://www.labarchives.com/), is an electronic lab notebook tool.

17. "New England Collaborative Data Management Curriculum," accessed October 3, 2018, https://library.umassmed.edu/resources/necdmc/index.

18. Amy Ahern, "The Flip Side of Abysmal MOOC Completion Rates? Discovering the Most Tenacious Learners," EdSurge, February 22, 2017, https://www.edsurge.com/news/2017-02-22-the-flip-side-of-abysmal-mooc -completion-rates-discovering-the-most-tenacious-learners.

JOHN VALLIER and
ANDREW WEAVER

9

Media Services

The rise of digital scholarship (DS) brings with it a parallel need for technologically intensive services, tools, and spaces. Whether it's text mining, GIS mapping, web scraping, or 3-D modeling, library patrons are increasingly seeking out support for such computationally intensive work. In this chapter, we describe how University of Washington (UW) Libraries has somewhat haphazardly met patron demand for intensive digital technologies such as sound recording, video, and moving image-based media.[1] We describe how UW's forty-year-old Media Center morphed from a traditional, circulation-oriented service point into two distinct units: a community-focused digital media lab and staff-side AV preservation lab. We will describe the two spaces and their concomitant missions to support the creation, preservation, and dissemination of media. From supporting media-oriented faculty research and teaching to preserving and disseminating unique media-based cultural heritage materials, we will review opportunities and barriers readers may face when developing similar spaces and services in their own institutions.

UW LIBRARIES MEDIA ARCADE

Inception and Growth

The Media Arcade was born out of a legacy library unit, the UW Libraries Media Center. Established in 1974, the Media Center, located within UW's Odegaard Undergraduate Library, was charged with collecting and providing noncirculating access to the University's undergraduate curricular media materials. Students who wanted to access audio or video media in the collection had to make requests at a service desk, where they were then directed to a designated cubicle. Once seated, students could dial into the content, which was then played back to the cubicle in real time from behind the service desk.

The Media Center operated in this fashion until about 2006, when John Vallier, a coauthor of this chapter—then a librarian and now the head of Distributed Media—arrived at UW from the University of California Los Angeles (UCLA). With the support of then undergraduate director Jill McKinstry, Vallier oversaw the installation of stand alone DVD players and VCRs in the carrels, equipment that students and other community members could operate without the intervention of Media staff. It was at this time that Vallier also opened up the media collection for circulation. As patrons increasingly learned of the new policy, the Center's collection of DVDs, CDs, and other media soon became the highest circulating collection of items in the UW Libraries system.

In 2012, the Odegaard Undergraduate Library began to undergo a major physical renovation. To facilitate the project, it was decided that the Media Center would permanently move to a new location on the third floor of the Suzzallo and Allen Libraries, another main branch of the UW Libraries system.[2] Unlike its home of nearly forty years, this new location did not have adequate space at its service desk for patrons to access media playback equipment. The new service area for patrons was also unusually cramped; in essence, it was a hallway cordoned off by rows of book stacks on one side. In response to this problem, Vallier requested some of books be moved elsewhere to widen the service area, but this solution could not be realized. The resulting lack of space left Media Center patrons without a place to adequately access media equipment in the library. Although Media Center staff managed to awkwardly squeeze a few playback stations at the edge of a stacks, demand—especially for course reserves—overwhelmed the Center's ability to support patrons' media viewing and listening needs.

This setup forced the Media Center to face some difficult questions. How were patrons now expected to access the Media Center's physical media collections? Under the reconfigured model, they would need to use one of the few playback stations or find off-campus solutions for screening the content, both of which were inconvenient for patrons. Additionally, the lack of an adequate viewing and listening facilities meant that the Libraries was not complying with ACRL's Guidelines for Media Resources in Academic Libraries.[3] The issue required resolution.

In an effort to recreate a space for listening and viewing, as well as to provide students, faculty, and staff with an expanded capacity to digitize, create, edit, and share audio and video content—Vallier began to scout for an alternative solution within the building. By way of lobbying internal stakeholders (e.g., the head of Facilities, as well as the director of the Reference and Research Services) and identifying a couple of underutilized rooms in the library, Vallier was able to garner support for a potential new service point that supported media access and creation.

Two fundamental obstacles stood in the way:

- Funding to purchase new equipment and software was needed.
- The two potential spaces, although underutilized, were in use: one housed PhD study cubicles, the other a librarian's office.

The funding obstacle was tackled first. At UW, all students pay a self-imposed Student Technology Fee (STF) that is used to fund technology resources for student use. Funding generated from this fee is pooled each quarter and distributed by a committee of students, who vote on proposals received from members of the campus community, including faculty and staff.[4] The Committee reviews each proposal's merits, favoring those that have the most direct and positive impact on students.

In 2014, Vallier wrote such a proposal, in which six iMacs with a unique suite of software would be installed in a new media-oriented library space. In it, Vallier stressed the following unmet media-based needs of undergraduate and graduate UW students:

- Equipment to access our audio, video, and film collections, which come on a variety of contemporary and legacy formats
- Hardware and software to create and remix content for new works
- Equipment and expertise to help with the digital conversion and preservation of analog media
- A discipline-agnostic space where students, staff, and faculty can meet to work on media-related projects

Since the STF committee is made up of students and, as noted above, favors proposals that benefit the greatest number of students, Vallier asked several students who were familiar with the Media Center or interested in audio/video production to write recommendations to include in the proposal.

In June 2014, Vallier, the primary proposal author, was called before the STF committee in order to answer questions about the mission and feasibility of the space. Following this conversation, the committee voted unanimously in favor of the proposal, releasing some $70,000 in STF funding. With external funding now approved, Vallier was able to convince Libraries Administration to release one of the identified spaces, the former librarian's office, as a home for this new service point. Once approved, staff spent the six months frantically clearing the former office, ordering equipment, purchasing hardware and software, imaging computers, creating policies and signage, and assembling many an Ikea table. Officially opened in January 2015, this new digital media lab came to be known as the Media Arcade.[5]

Inside the Media Arcade

An undergraduate student studies a waveform and hunches over a turntable, lining up another LP for a remix. As part of a fieldwork in Tibet project, a professor digitizes Hi8 video shot on another computer. Four more workstations in the room are occupied by students, staff, and faculty working on a variety projects: video editing, typographic design, cassette digitization, and DVD ripping. A student employee bounces back and forth between projects, helping patrons find solutions to their media challenges. The big screen TVs are also in use. A group of Swedish-language students gather around one, watching Girl with the Dragon Tattoo *(in Swedish, of course). A couple of students sit in front of second screen, using it to display slides and rehearse an upcoming presentation. Our last TV is mobbed by student gamers (most of them bio-engineering majors) bonding over numerous rounds of Smash Bros. It's an ideal day in the Media Arcade, a diverse array of needs is being met in an atmosphere that mixes seriousness and good-natured comradery.*

The Media Arcade sits in an open and rectangular room on the third floor of the Suzzallo and Allen Libraries on the Seattle campus.[6] At twenty-four feet wide and thirty-eight feet long, its proportions are close to that of a golden rectangle. Windows on three exterior walls filter in sunlight. Although this effect can be pleasant in sun-starved Seattle, it is simultaneously frustrating when attempting to work with video. All in all, the room has a relaxed atmosphere in which the UW community's projects are encouraged and supported.

A variety of hardware and equipment fills the room: iMacs, TVs, video game consoles, and vintage playback equipment. Due to the configuration of electrical outlets, this gear lines all four walls. The Media Arcade also offers a collection of portable equipment and peripherals available for checkout by UW students, staff, and faculty (check-out times vary from one to seven days). These includes digital cameras, digital audio recorders, USB drives, data projectors, and VCRs (yes, still in demand!). Peripherals cover a wide and ever-evolving array of chargers, cables, adapters, and dongles (see appendix H for a more detailed breakdown of the Arcade's circulating and noncirculating equipment).[7] Figure 9.1 shows the floor plan with workstations.

A service desk at the entrance is staffed by an Arcade tech, either a student employee or one of the Media Center's three full-time employees. These techs are on hand to assist visitors with media creation and viewing, as well as to check the Arcade's circulating equipment and peripherals in and out. They also are the initial point of contact for the Arcade's small but eclectic series of collections, including:

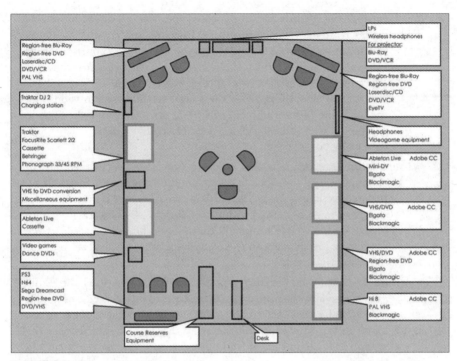

FIGURE 9.1
Floor plan of the Media Arcade

Course Reserves. The Media Arcade serves as the sole access point for Seattle campus students who need to access video that has been put on reserve by instructors. This is a rotating collection of between forty to one-hundred DVDs and other physical media titles that changes each term based on the needs of instructors. The collection is located in the Arcade because the space has the equipment necessary for viewing it. Course reserves can be checked out for several hours but cannot leave the Arcade (unless requested by the instructor of record).

Video Games. A modest collection of about 200 video games is also housed in the Media Arcade. Developed in collaboration with UW iSchool faculty and graduate students, the collection offers video games researchers and practitioners a broad range of noteworthy titles. The collection is browsable and available for one-week check-out. A variety of consoles—from Ataris to Playstations—are available for in-room use with one of the TVs.

Vinyl LPs. A small portion of the Libraries' LP collection is available in the Media Arcade. To increase browsability and to draw attention to the existence of records within the collection, the LPs are in browsable record store-like storage furniture. They are curated with an eye to keeping an eclectic mix of music (local sounds from the Sonics, Shabazz Palaces, etc., as well as historically significant releases across different eras and genres), spoken word (prose, poetry, and historic speeches), and sounds (sound effects, whale songs, satellite transmissions and the like). The LPs are adjacent to several turntables and a cell phone charging station, thereby giving patrons an analog activity to engage with while powering up.

Dance DVDs. The Arcade is also home to two large DVD collections of contemporary dance. Due to rights and licensing related restrictions, these collections—*Eye on Dance* UW's own Chamber Dance Company Archive—must be viewed within the Libraries. By housing them, the Media Arcade is able to uphold these legal obligations while at the same time providing both the equipment and technical support for screening these videos.

Archival Jukebox. Similar to the physical dance DVD collections, the Media Arcade provides the primary form of access to digital media materials that must be restricted to access within the physical confines of the Libraries (e.g., archival audio materials that were digitized under the section 108 exemption of US Copyright law). This access is created through a computer station known as the Archival Jukebox, which uses commonly available tools such as iTunes, with certain settings and modifications in place to restrict any attempts at copying materials off of the Jukebox. Unlike the Arcade, the Jukebox is available to those who come into the library, whether or not they are affiliated with the UW. Collections hosted on the Jukebox include thousands of hours of local music, speeches by esteemed UW faculty and visiting scholars, radio broadcasts from World War II, remixes created by UW students, and more.

Since the goal for the Media Arcade is to encourage a wide range of simultaneous uses while also upholding the educational mission of the Libraries, a minimum but practical number of policies were implemented to govern the use of the space. It is the arcade tech's job to implement and, if needed, explain these policies, which include the following points.

Access to the space. The space is open to patrons who have current university affiliation (students, staff, and faculty) with priority given to student use. Current affiliation is verified at the entrance to the Media Arcade with the presenting of valid University ID. These limits to usage are tied to the STF funding model initially used for creation of the Arcade. Although exceptions are made from time to time, they must first be cleared by the head librarian for the Arcade.

Priority for use. Although all kinds of activities are encouraged in the arcade, from relaxation and personal artistic creation, in times of high usage academic projects take precedence. Additionally, priority is given to audio-, video-, and design-related projects because other activities, such as word processing, can be conducted using other Libraries' resources (however, during times of low usage patrons are free to use the Arcade computers and stations in any appropriate manner within the bounds of the Libraries' Code of Conduct).[8]

Food and Drink. No food is allowed in the Media Arcade, and drinks must be in spill-proof containers. This policy is essential as the Arcade holds not only computers, but a wide range of unique and sensitive audiovisual equipment as well. And although the Media Arcade is staffed during all hours of operation, patrons are encouraged to be responsible for their property in the same manner as in any other part of the library. This helps to avoid placing an undue burden upon the student staff of the Arcade. Finally, although the Arcade is not a quiet study area, and indeed is often home to discussion and conversation, cell phone use is discouraged in the interest of maintaining the desired atmosphere and functionality of the space.

What DS is Practiced and Produced?

Digital scholarship is part and parcel of the Media Arcade's existence. In the Arcade, we have helped patrons digitize unique Noam Chomsky videos, home movies showing long-lost loved ones, audio postcards from Vietnam, and one-off instantaneous recordings from our Special Collections. We've also helped students compose new music, access their video course materials, and simply commune with one another after finals by playing video games. It is a discipline-agnostic space that students, staff, and faculty from all departments and backgrounds are welcome to use. That said, the Arcade tends to work most closely with—and within—such subject areas as gaming studies; information and archival studies; music, cinema, and media studies; ethnic studies; gender studies; and other social sciences fields. However, whatever the discipline or topic, the Arcade supports media access, reformatting, creation, and criticism. Some examples of real-life digital scholarship scenarios include:

- Students, staff, and faculty reformatting archival collections— sound recordings, video, films, slides, photographs, documents— for use in their research and study
- Students composing and creating music and editing multimedia on computers.
- Students, staff, and faculty digitizing personal media
- Students using software to create multi-model course assignments, such as podcasts or remixes

- Faculty and students accessing vintage media that can't be viewed at home (e.g., VHS, 16-mm film,)
- Faculty bringing their students to the arcade for instruction on such topics as copyright, preservation, and media production
- Students attending a media-centric library event (such as screenings of vintage films)
- Library employees and student workers using lab resources for reformatting projects (e.g., special collections)
- Instructors booking instruction sessions in the arcade for their classes about copyright and fair use or media production
- Faculty reserving computers in the arcade for office hours with students in media-intensive classes
- Community members from Native American and other off-campus communities accessing archival collections of media originally recorded within their communities
- Students defending dissertations on music, copyright, and preservation
- Students and staff creating cassette mix tapes from a thumb drive of mp3 files (yes, digital to analog conversion!)

MEDIA ARCHIVING AND DIGITIZATION LAB (MAD LAB)

Inception and Growth of the MAD Lab

The UW MAD Lab and its previous iterations predate the Arcade by several years. Its origins go back to 2006, when John Vallier came to UW. Vallier's experience as UCLA's ethnomusicology archivist drove him to establish a single AV reformatting station within what was, at the time, the Media Center. By slowly building out the Center's capacity to reformat analog media, the Media Center was able to better meet such patron needs as streaming media course reserves and reformatting the Libraries' collections for both preservation and access.[9] As the popularity of physical media formats began to wane in favor of commercial streaming services—and the Media Center's DVD and VHS circulation statistics began to decline—what was once an ancillary function of the Media Center took on an increasingly prominent role. In other words, due to its possession of vast audiovisual collections, along with the relevant equipment and expertise to digitize these collections, a natural and unplanned evolution of the Media Center's functions occurred.

In addition to the organic evolution of functions for the Media Center, an external factor motivated the growth of the MAD Lab: the magnetic media crisis. For the latter half of the twentieth century, magnetic tape was a crucial element in the creation and dissemination of audiovisual materials.

This practice resulted in an extensive amount of AV materials that are held on unstable and rapidly decaying carriers dependent on specialized playback machines for all forms of access. Not only are playback machines and parts across all formats increasingly scarce, but the knowledge and expertise required to repair and maintain these machines are also being lost as previous generations of technicians retire. The simultaneous deterioration of both materials and means of access means that the window for preserving magnetic media is rapidly shrinking and that active preservation must be undertaken for as many materials as possible. The ongoing expansion of the MAD Lab has been a direct response to the need for increased intervention with the audiovisual collections housed in the UW Libraries.

There has been, and continues to be, a more subjective impulse motivating us to build and work in the MAD Lab: the content. Much of the material we work with in the Lab represents traditionally marginalized communities (e.g., recordings from the Ethnomusicology Archives) or content that documents tragic acts of institutionalized hatred (e.g., CBS Radio broadcasts about Japanese-American incarceration). When we in the MAD Lab digitize such material to preserve it for the long-term, we believe we are pushing back against grand narratives, colonial impulses, and the ever-increasing commercialization and standardization of media content. As author Arundhati Roy writes, "There's really no such thing as the 'voiceless.' There are only the deliberately silenced, or the preferably unheard."[10] Through the work of the MAD Lab to digitize these sensitive media, the UW Libraries works to make sure that doesn't happen.

Inside the MAD Lab

The sound of 1960s garage rock floats quietly out of a pair of speakers as a vintage studio reel-to-reel spins tape at fifteen inches per second. The graduate student who is conducting the ongoing archival transfer is simultaneously monitoring the tape output on one computer while using a neighboring station to run digital preservation processes on the output of prior transfers, electronically packaging them for long-term storage. Across the room a technician is finishing up migrating a VHS tape (an early 1990s interview with a NASA astronaut). The technician shuts down the monitors and tape machine before walking over to the Media Arcade for a scheduled consultation with a professor about digitizing research materials. Meanwhile, a curator from Special Collections stops by to use one of the Labs' iMac programs to retrieve data from an encrypted RAID array.[11] In an adjacent space, another student is inserting a cassette into a player, one of four running concurrently to complete the preservation of a University of Washington lecture series dating from the 1970s. On this day, the MAD Lab is humming at full capacity, helping to safeguard the audiovisual heritage of its community.

The MAD Lab is housed within the former Media Center's closed collection and staff-side space in Suzzallo Library. It is essentially a large cubicle of

120 square feet. Its repurposed push-pin office divider walls support a locking door. The Lab houses audiovisual reformatting stations along two walls, with one side focused on video and the other on audio. A fifth computer is dedicated to digital file management and audio restoration. The audio stations are primarily intended to play back quarter-inch reel-to-reel tape. Two Studer A-802s, one Ampex ATR-100, and a collection of other assorted reel-to-reel decks are available for use. Other audio formats are also supported on these stations as needed, including compact and micro cassette, DAT, analog disc, and MiniDisc. These stations have Apple computers with Apogee Symphony A/D converters running WaveLab software for audio capture.

The video stations in the MAD Lab enclosure have access to a full rack setup with video players ranging from VHS to U-matic and MiniDV to BetacamSP bolted into a vertical stack, along with associated hardware and monitors to aid in high-quality captures. A 16-mm Tobin Telecine is available for integration in the signal chain as necessary for film. Two Apple computers on this side of the Lab use Blackmagic hardware. The open source capture software vrecord handles the analog to digital conversion. FinalCut is used for editing and simple post-production rendering.[12]

The fifth Apple computer in the Lab sits along a back wall in the lab. In both a physical and virtual sense, this workstation bridges the Lab's audio/video divide. Its primary function is to describe, manage, and store all files created in the Lab, whatever their type. Tethered to the computer are three RAID arrays, totaling some 50 TB storage. One of the arrays (a Drobo) acts as a primary storage for projects and as a platform that can support post-production work such as metadata embedding, editing, and restoration. The remaining two Raids (Synology Nas) supply the station with secondary storage, a kind of intermediary step between post-production and lolo, our institution's cloud tape-based repository.[13] Lolo is effectively our preservation repository and tertiary storage solution (see figure 9.2). The few remaining work areas within the Lab's enclosure support hands-on efforts to maintain, repair, and organize equipment and collections.

Space Advantages and Challenges

Space is both a challenge and an advantage to the functioning of the MAD Lab. Although its relatively small area can create complications during equipment movement and setup, being located in an enclosed physical space makes it much easier to secure the valuable equipment contained within the lab. The enclosure, and resulting lack of distractions, promote focus. At the same time, the confined nature of the space encourages collaboration among those working in the Lab, creating a small purpose-driven world within the greater Libraries environment.

Due to limited space, the function of the MAD Lab must extend beyond its confines. Outside of the space and around the corner, four Apple computers

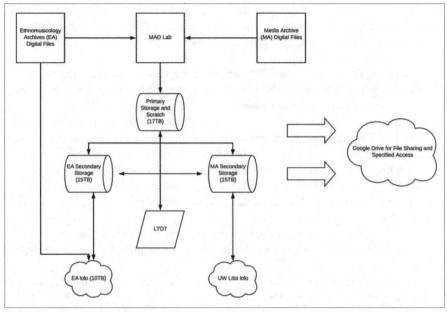

FIGURE 9.2

Schematic of the MAD Lab's Digital Storage and Preservation Infrastructure

sit in a row, repurposing what was once the staff side of the Media Center's service counter. Each of these four Macs is outfitted with Apogee A/D audio converter and compact cassette deck. This quad setup allows a single operator to run four transfers at a time, averaging between twenty and forty digitized cassettes per day. Four stories down, in the bowels of Suzzallo Library, a closed storage space waits for collections associated with the MAD Lab, the Arcade, and recently the Ethnomusicology Archives. This surge space also accommodates ingest processing of archival collections (see figure 9.2).

What Digital Scholarship Is Practiced and Produced?

Just as digital scholarship is a presumption of the purpose of the Media Arcade, the MAD Lab exists within the same value-space as the field of digital scholarship. The MAD Lab is primarily driven to preserve and provide enduring access to the media collections housed within the UW Libraries. Although it serves more of an auxiliary function as compared to the Media Arcade, there is a symbiotic relationship between the two, with the MAD Lab contributing to digital scholarship within the University in several key ways. First, through its ongoing shepherding of physical holdings into the digital realm, the Lab is a key component of the maintenance of these items' utility. Second, through its ongoing reformatting efforts and its capacity to digitize on demand, the

MAD Lab ensures that legacy and archival media collections are usable in a digital context. This role in turn is linked to the collections available within the Arcade, with a significant portion of the contents of the aforementioned Archival Jukebox being products of the MAD Lab.

Having this direct connection between a digitization lab and a digital creation lab not only increases the visibility of archival collections, but also helps overcome one of the primary barriers to the digital preservation of audiovisual materials, namely, the byzantine restrictions placed on them by copyright law. Due to copyright it can be problematic to add digitized audiovisual materials to online collection access systems; however, with the critical issue of the magnetic media crisis, it would be an ethical failing to let this obstacle stand in the way of preservation. Having a dedicated and clearly established station for creating legal access to archival materials helps overcome logistical difficulties and institutional objections to engaging in proactive digitization. Although this connection may seem a small component of the Media Arcade's overall functions, it is of far-reaching importance for the MAD Lab and digital media collections.

By building out a related set of equipment, tools, and workflows for preservation of UW Libraries-owned collections, the MAD Lab serves both as a cornerstone of Libraries infrastructure and a crucial ground for training and knowledge transfer, for Media Arcade support staff and aspiring archival professionals.[14] The MAD Lab has also been an active contributor in the Open Source preservation community, alternatively relying on and contributing to open projects and workflows.[15] This balance allows the Lab to take advantage of recent community developments while also expanding its impact outside of the University.[16]

CONSIDERATIONS

Although the physical space of the Media Arcade is critical in fostering its open and inviting atmosphere, it does provide some functional limitations that should be considered by any institutions planning a similar space. For instance, the large windows in the Arcade, although part of its appealing environment, also bring a degree of light that can be detrimental to the use of screens, which is problematic for an audiovisual oriented space. Additionally, there is no sound isolation either within the Arcade itself or between the Arcade and the Suzzallo and Allen Libraries at large. This means that patrons are dependent on headphones for all sound-producing activities in the Arcade. Because the Arcade is stocked with headphones, this does not create a barrier to access per se, but nonetheless can be an inconvenience for certain activities such as group media viewing.

The constraints of the space also arise from the Arcade's overall physical location on the third floor of a main campus library. The adjacent space to the Media Arcade houses a group of study carrels that, until recently, was designated as a quiet study area. Although this area is no longer designated for quiet study, there still have been periodic tensions with patrons in the surrounding library stacks. Because the Arcade's doors are kept open to enhance visibility and create an inviting atmosphere, a certain amount of noise spillage does occur during periods of active use.

The makeshift nature of the MAD Lab's space offers similar challenges. Since it is situated within a shared office environment (one in which cubicles of catalogers hammer out MARC records nearby), use of the MAD Lab must be headphone-based. When we have deviated from this policy in the past, sounds from the Lab have disrupted the work of our Libraries colleagues. The open-top nature of the Lab also raises potential concerns about the security of the equipment and collections, as well as our inability to keep its environs free from dust and other airborne particulates.

Equipment maintenance remains another consistent challenge in the Media Arcade and MAD Lab. Because it is used for a wide range of functions, it can be complicated to maintain the variety of software and hardware available in both spaces. Adding to this issue, both the Arcade and Lab use Apple computers, which are not supported by the Libraries' IT department. Therefore, all IT imaging, formatting, and computer support must be done internally. Even setting these IT considerations aside, expertise in both antiquated analog playback machines and digitization technology demands a specialized skill set not easily found in Libraries staff. In the case of the Media Arcade, this knowledge gap is effectively covered through its close relationship to the MAD Lab, where there is often an overlap in Library staff and student workers. Libraries looking to create similar spaces dedicated to patron media digitization activities would strongly benefit from forming a similar relationship with the relevant preservation staff.

Due to the wide variety of activities supported by the Arcade, it is necessary to have staff available on-call to assist patrons in using the space. The Arcade's desk is primarily staffed by student employees of the UW Libraries, who must be trained by the Media Center staff to be reliable jacks of all trades for low-level functions while directing more in-depth question to full-time staff.[17] Because this can be difficult, especially for newer student workers who lack the confidence to provide first-line technical support in technical matters, it results in high demand for help from on-call staff. Some of this difficulty can be ameliorated by encouraging patrons with specific projects or technical needs to make appointments with appropriate experts in advance, but to rely completely on appointment-based services would negatively impact the creative and impromptu spirit at the core of the Arcade's mission. Institutions planning similar ventures should expect to invest in dedicated staff time in order to realize the full potential of the space.

The Media Arcade and MAD Lab have also had to grow and operate within an organizational structure that has been ambiguous about its support for DS.

Up to this point, the UW Libraries' approach to supporting DS has been decidedly laissez faire, tolerating individual agency over centralized efforts and coordination. This hands-off approach, in which individual staff are given the freedom to pursue the development of DS-related services and spaces, elicits both opportunities and challenges for the development of digital scholarship across the UW community as a whole. On the one hand, having a decentralized approach to DS—especially as it relates to media—encourages staff to respond flexibly and creatively to unmet patron needs. This organizational receptivity to user-centered nimbleness was critical to the birth of the Media Arcade and MAD Lab.[18] By allowing those of us on the ground to listen, understand, and creatively respond to our users' needs, the Libraries encourages staff to meet evolving demands, such as those found in DS. When coupled with staff expertise and external funding sources (e.g., grants and endowments), this approach embraces a positive culture of risk-taking and, consequently, the possibility of developing new services that may succeed.

On the other hand, such an approach to digital scholarship also presents challenges. For example, although the UW Libraries values individual agency, the organizational reality of the Libraries is hierarchical, departmentalized, and siloed. The resulting clash of laissez faire values with legacy organizational structures could result in stasis, which the Libraries attempts to temper by highlighting collaboration as an aspirational value.

CONCLUSION

Challenges aside, the sister spaces of the Media Arcade and the MAD Lab have had a tangible impact on their surrounding community through facilitating the creation of new digital scholarship while also expanding the relevance of analog collections to the digital realm. Our example is offered as a case study of a successful grassroots implementation, as well to encourage those of you who are looking to usher traditional media services into a new role that creates and supports a culture of multimodal digital scholarship.

FURTHER READING

Kroski, Ellyssa. *The Makerspace Librarian's Sourcebook*. Chicago: ALA Editions, 2017.

Walton, Graham, and Graham Matthews. *University Libraries and Space in the Digital World*. London: Routledge, 2016.

Webb, Katy. *Development of Creative Spaces in Academic Libraries: A Decision Maker's Guide*. Cambridge, MA: Chandos Publishing, 2018.

Willingham, Theresa, and Jeroen DeBoer. *Makerspaces in Libraries*. Lanham: Rowman and Littlefield, 2015.

Takeaways

- The question of the shifting roles and evolution of media centers and media collections in academic libraries is not unique to the University of Washington. When faced with changing technologies and user needs, many institutions are now unsure of how to best use these materials in teaching, research, and study. The Media Arcade and MAD Lab combination shows that media resources need not be viewed solely as a dichotomy of digital versus analog. With a DIY spirit, commitment to infrastructure, and collaborative sensibility, existing collections can be effectively blended into ongoing digital initiatives.

- Institutions considering the creation of digital media labs and digitization facilities should consider the staff resources that can be devoted to the space. Making equipment available without adequate support will create barriers to use for a wide range of patrons. Establishing a system of triage with a combination of front-line generalists and on-call area experts can be beneficial.

- If traditional funding sources and other internal sources of support are scarce, consider going directly to your patrons and making your case.

NOTES

1. For the purposes of brevity, the authors refer to sound recordings, videos, and moving images simply as "media." Although the term "media" is imperfect, libraries have adopted it to describe such collections, services, and tools. See Lori Widzinski, "The Evolution of Media Librarianship: A Tangled History of Change and Constancy," *Simile* 1, no. 3 (2001).
2. The Media Center's former collections, staff, and patrons spaces would soon be reconfigured into staff offices and meeting rooms.
3. "The necessary equipment to access media resources should be available and maintained to provide ready access to collections" (www.ala.org/acrl/standards/mediaresources).
4. Tech Fee Committee, https://depts.washington.edu/thehub/home/in-the-hub/tech-fee-committee/.
5. Most libraries—be they public or academic—with similar kinds of spaces tend to call them "digital media labs" or "digital media commons." Our somewhat unorthodox choice of the word *arcade* grew out of discussions with and suggestions from staff and student employees. *Arcade* is a word perhaps most popularly associated with a video game arcade. In this sense, it is apt, because the space provides access to a video game collection and complementary assortment of consoles. Along these lines, we also thought it would draw students into the space. Further solidifying our use of *arcade* was Walter Benjamin's critical treatment of the term in his *Arcades*

Project (Cambridge, MA: Harvard University Press, 2002). This work, at once commentary on bourgeois consumerism and a creative example of collage technique in literature, mirrored on our values of supporting critical investigation of popular culture and encouraging the remix and creation of new works.

6. University of Washington Libraries, "Media Arcade," www.lib.washington .edu/media.

7. In this way the Arcade is well situated with the existing framework of a Digital Media Lab. "A digital media lab (DML) is a library creative space devoted to the creation of multimedia, including digital video, video games, audio, and images. The focus of one of these labs in an academic library environment is normally on helping students realize their projects, although faculty and course assignments may also be supported." Amanda Goodman, "Digital Media Labs in Libraries," *Library Technology Reports* 50, no. 6 (Chicago: ALA TechSource, 2014).

8. The full code of conduct available online at https://www.lib.washington .edu/about/policy/conduct.

9. Because of the age of the Media Center and rapid evolutions of media formats over the years, with each new format resulting in the attrition of certain available titles, a not insignificant portion of the Media Center's circulating collection became unique enough to require the planning of proactive preservation. Concurrently, due to active outreach efforts over the years, the Media Center's noncirculating archival materials had become considerable.

10. Arundhati Roy, "2004 Sydney Peace Prize Lecture," http://sydney.edu.au/ news/84.html?newsstoryid=279.

11. RAID (Redundant Array of Independent Disks) is used at the MAD Lab to create duplicate copies of archival information as insurance against drive failure.

12. As of the time of writing, the vrecord project is available for participation and download at https://github.com/amiaopensource/vrecord.

13. "Shared File System for Research Archives (lolo),"IT Connect, https:// itconnect.uw.edu/service/shared-central-file-system-for-research-archives -lolo-archive/.

14. The iSchool at the University of Washington does not have an archives-specific path of study and does not offer classes relating to media preservation. The MAD Lab has been an invaluable resource for providing instruction and hands-on work experience to students interested in careers in this area.

15. This ethos is effectively described in the call to action "Digitization Software Obsolescence, Too?" by Dave Rice, originally published in *IASA Journal* 45 (October 2015) and available in an open-access form via the author's website at http://dericed.com/papers/digitization -software -obsolescence-too/.

16. Much of this output is available through the "pugetsoundandvision" Github repository, actively maintained by Weaver at https://github.com/pugetsoundandvision.

17. The Arcade employs roughly eight students per year. They work solo shifts on a rotating basis. The Arcade is open nearly 100 hours per week during the academic term.

18. These values are highlighted in the Libraries' Strategic Plan. For example, on flexibility and responsiveness: "We align our services and programs with the needs of our communities and strive to create shared ownership of the Libraries. We do this by . . . being flexible in response to evolving user needs and leveraging the expertise of our staff to guide decision-making in partnership with user communities (www.lib.washington.edu/about/strategicplan). Creativity is one of the Libraries' core values: "We embrace a culture of exploration, experimentation, and reflection to improve services, anticipate needs and manage change. We do this by: Creating a culture of openness to alternative solutions and empowering staff to propose new ideas that address shared challenges; Developing robust and respectful feedback loops to ensure ongoing organizational and individual learning; Providing spaces, services, resources and tools that facilitate interactivity and creativity for our organization and our user communities." (www.lib.washington.edu/about/strategicplan).

JUSTIN WADLAND and
MARISA PETRICH

10

The Urban Serving University

Gauging an Emerging Digital Scholarship Program

Universities located in urban settings have complex, rich interrelationships with their host cities and locally influence social issues, economic vitality, and quality of life. Libraries too contribute significantly to this dynamic, to the extent that they support and engage with the mission of these same universities. In this chapter, we address a gap in the literature about academic libraries with urban serving missions by offering a case study of the digital scholarship program at the University of Washington Tacoma (UWT), one of three campuses of the University of Washington, and a campus that has relied on its urban serving university (USU) designation to shape its identity.[1] To contextualize our study, we also conducted an environmental scan of digital scholarship programs at other urban serving universities and reviewed the literature around scaling and institutionalizing digital scholarship programs. Through this process, we seek not only to understand how the urban serving university values articulated at our institution have influenced and oriented our approach to digital scholarship, but to discern the past, present, and future direction of our work at UWT so that we might more consciously and strategically align staffing, resources, and projects to these values. As an initial foray into the intersection of digital scholarship at USUs, we believe our inquiry will be useful for making visible the thought processes necessary for aligning activities of urban serving or community-oriented digital scholarship programs.

BACKGROUND: UNDERSTANDING THE UW TACOMA CAMPUS

UWT first opened its doors to 187 students in the fall of 1990. The campus was established as a direct result of synergy between local community activism to establish a public university in Tacoma and statewide efforts to expand access to higher education. Initially, the University offered only upper division classes in an interdisciplinary Liberal Studies program and primarily served "placebound students" seeking to complete bachelor's degrees. Over the years, the University has expanded significantly, becoming a four-year campus in 2005 and adding twelve graduate degrees.[2] As of 2017, UWT has 5,185 students enrolled in eight schools or programs.[3] The student body is exceptionally diverse, with the majority of students identifying as minorities, and continues to draw primarily from the greater Tacoma area.[4] UWT began to formally identify itself as an urban serving university in 2011, based on the terminology and values established by the Coalition of Urban Serving Universities, an organization of thirty-seven public urban universities that was formed in 2005 and now focuses on enhancing student and community success through local partnerships.[5]

BEFORE AND AFTER UWT

Located on a 46-acre parcel in Tacoma's historic warehouse district, UWT has played a pivotal role in revitalizing and transforming the city's urban core. Figures 10.1 and 10.2 show views before development, and figures 10.3 and 10.4, after. The university moved to its permanent site in 1997, relocating to previously derelict industrial buildings that it renovated. At that time, an estimated 33 million dollars in public financing were invested in downtown Tacoma; since then, the University has continued to rehab old buildings to accommodate growth. From the very beginning, the University has rented out commercial spaces to local businesses and organizations. The campus has a porous boundary that makes it difficult to determine where the University and the city begin and end.[6]

The UWT Library (hereafter "Library") has expanded and evolved along with campus. The UW Libraries "operate[s] as one library serving three campuses," and as a result, the resources and expertise available from the wider system have consistently served as invaluable assets for extending our work

FIGURE 10.1

BEFORE: Intersection of Commerce St. and S. 17th Ave. in 1994, Snoqualmie Falls Transformer Station (Powerhouse) is located on the right.

FIGURE 10.2

AFTER: Intersection of Commerce St. and S. 17th Ave. in 2010

FIGURE 10.3
Last Burlington Northern freight train passing through campus in 2003

FIGURE 10.4
Opening of the Prairie Line Trail in 2014

locally.[7] From a modest collection on a single floor of a downtown build-ing, the Library now occupies most of two central buildings on campus. The Library's largest quiet study area and reading room is located in the iconic Powerhouse, a historic building that once held transformers that provided electricity for Tacoma's street cars. The staffing has increased from two librar-ians in the early years to seven full-time equivalent (FTE) librarians, eight FTE staff, and approximately seventeen student workers. It is important to note that although the campus has more than doubled in size over the past decade, the number of library staff overall has remained about the same. As a result, the Library has had to consider how to strategically respond to increas-ing demands.

Over the past few years, the Library has started consistently to use the term "digital scholarship" to describe the work that supports our digital repository services and support for digital collections. We use the term out of pragmatism and convenience more than any other reason—it unites our work to a larger community of practitioners in the UW Libraries and the wider professional community. Many faculty members are still learning what digital scholarship means at UWT, but they understand and appreciate it when con-textualized by the past, present, and future work we and others on campus are doing.

UWT Library Staff currently supporting the Digital Scholarship Program

- The *Associate Director/Head, Digital Scholarship Program* provides leadership for the digital scholarship program in the library and supervises librarians and graduate students carrying out work and guiding overall direction; oversees and administers the campus digital repository; and participates and contributes to the tri-campus Digital Scholarship Group. This role requires expertise in digital oral history. The associate director/head seeks to create more opportunities for faculty development and make contacts with partners in the community and has served as point of contact for setting up digital collections in bepress and CONTENTdm.

- The *Instructional Design Librarian* assists faculty with using digital tools and resources in classroom instruction and working with digital pedagogy; contrib-utes to the program's communication strategies, program design, and scaling efforts; and participates in the UW Libraries Scholarly Communication Outreach and Education Team; and provides information regarding Open Access and Open Educational Resources; and coordinates campus events and workshops focused on digital tools and resources.

(cont.)

- The *Data and Digital Scholarship Librarian* is currently an open, unfilled position that will provide much-needed expertise in data services and management. The full scope of activities will be determined by the hire, but the Library foresees the data and digital services librarian participating and enhancing every aspect of the research lifecycle. Other duties will include acting as a liaison to the Urban Studies Program and the Milgard School of Business and enabling deep relationships with faculty doing community-engaged research and/or using data in innovative ways.

- *The Digital Projects Specialist keeps* faculty profiles and publication data up-to-date, cleans up metadata for digital collections, writes blog posts for the Tacoma Community History Project blog, performs digitization as needed, and performs many of other tasks. This position has been consistently filled by an MLIS candidate at UW iSchool who seeks a career in digital scholarship or archives/special collections.

FOUR ELEMENTS OF AN URBAN-SERVING UNIVERSITY: THE INFLUENCE OF URBAN SERVING VALUES ON THE UWT DIGITAL SCHOLARSHIP PROGRAM

Although the landscape and architecture of the campus are perhaps the clearest signs that "the mission of an anchor or an urban serving university is indeed within the DNA of UWT," there are others as well.[8] For instance, in 2016 the campus also explicitly defined the urban serving mission of the University and articulated the following four elements of the USU mission at UWT:

1. Expand access to higher education in an environment where every student has the opportunity to succeed.
2. Foster scholarship, research, and creativity to address the challenging problems of our time and place.
3. Partner and collaborate for common good.
4. Catalyze the economic and social vitality of the region.[9]

To underscore how this mission has shaped the development of the Library's digital scholarship program, we will review the program according to these four elements.

1. Expand Access to Higher Education in an Environment Where Every Student Has the Opportunity to Succeed

When it was founded, the intent of the University was to serve adult transfer students whose commitments to jobs and families made it impractical for them to travel to existing public universities in the state to complete their degrees.[10] Although the campus has grown significantly since then, and now includes first-year students, dorms, and services for residential students, "access to education and opportunity" is still identified as UWT's central value, along with ongoing commitments to diversity, community, innovation, and excellence.[11]

The campus also sees equity as an impact goal for its new strategic plan; reducing disparities in achievement across diverse groups and increasing both the number and satisfaction of traditionally underrepresented faculty and students are indicators of success.[12] More than half the student population at UWT is made up of first-generation students.[13] Ensuring that such students have equitable access to the support systems and practices designed to facilitate their success is part of this work. For example, to improve student success and retention, the UWT campus has initiated a number of efforts to adopt High-Impact Educational Practices (HIPs), that is, a set of ten practices introduced in 2008 by George Kuh, the founding director of the National Institute for Learning Outcomes Assessment. HIPs were developed using data collected from the widely used National Survey of Student Engagement (NSSE) and reflect approaches to active learning that "have been shown to be beneficial to students from many backgrounds."[14] These include support for undergraduate research, including culminating projects or experiences in degree program requirements.

When first developing its digital scholarship program, the Library specifically sought to incorporate values of access and equity, most notably through partnerships with specific programs to make visible student work online. We also engage directly with HIPs by gathering and providing access to culminating and exceptional student works through the UWT Digital Commons institutional repository, thus expanding access to research produced at UWT for all.

In 2012, the UWT Global Honors Program became the first to openly share capstone projects and theses via Digital Commons. This collection now has over sixty-one papers, many of which are listed in the repository's top ten downloads. Since then, we have set up an additional ten repository collections, with several others in development. Some collections—such as the Gender and Sexuality Studies Collection—gather exceptional student work at the discretion of a department or faculty member, whereas others—such as the *ACCESS*: Interdisciplinary Journal of Student Research*—are journals with a formal review process.[15] In all cases, these works were collected and stored offline prior to a partnership with the Library. By providing a platform in which student work can be shared online with anyone, not just other members of the University, the Library encourages engagement between students and the surrounding urban environment. This is especially important for programs like the Geographic Information Systems certificate, in which UWT students often create detailed digital maps based on local issues, sourced through direct engagement with community members.

Although the Library's Digital Commons offers many benefits in relation to access and equity, the logistics of using it to showcase student work can sometimes be tricky. Right now, we have a highly flexible and distributed approach to integrating student work into our digital repository. In many cases, students upload their work directly to the repository, and then a faculty or staff member reviews and posts their work. This process shares the labor with digital scholarship stakeholders outside the Library, although at times our digitization specialist does the batch uploading on a student's behalf. With this hands-off model, we have been able to develop a large number of student-focused collections, but as a result, we've lost some quality and consistency in the repository's metadata.

Even with the significant progress we've made incorporating student work in our digital repository, the UWT campus has not yet fully embraced or prioritized open access when it comes to the culminating works of graduate students, let alone undergraduates. Individual departments currently decide whether or not culminating student work is openly shared, and we have encountered reluctance to sharing it. Some departments do not want to release proprietary information, although others question what the quality standard should be for sharing student work. Still others are hesitant because their students' projects fall outside of traditional thesis or paper formats. Ironically, one key sticking point comes directly out of the urban-serving values of the University: quite a few culminating student projects originate in collaboration with local partner organizations, and some departments fear that these partners might not want sensitive information about them shared online.

These concerns raise larger questions about the accessibility of student work that the campus as a whole has not yet considered. How does online open access to student work alter the nature of that work, and how does the student's relationship to the work change if it becomes available online? To what extent do these practices affect student privacy and agency over their work? And what new and novel relationships to audiences does open access sharing of student work enable? Further conversation about these issues is needed, especially because each UWT program will likely have its own answers and approaches. Although the Library's digital scholarship program is developing the capacity to lead such discussions, it is challenging to find an appropriate venue to propose a systemic approach that recognizes the mutually beneficial relationship between the campus' urban serving values and the larger principles of open access.

One of the opportunities that the Library has identified in furthering the scope of student digital scholarship is to offer more faculty development related to open access. Faculty members who advise students need to know the benefits of open access on the potential reach of student work. They must understand the pedagogical implications of employing digital technologies to create and share student work and become versed themselves in the affordances and risks platforms offer. The Library has valuable insight to offer here, particularly by collaborating with faculty to create learning experiences that integrate digital scholarship tools and openly shared student work through-out the process rather than including them as an afterthought.

Policy represents another area in which UWT has an opportunity to pro-mote the benefits of digital open access to student work. In conducting an environmental scan of other USUs, we found a number of examples of insti-tutions that have prioritized access to student work this way. Georgia State University, for example, has passed an open access policy for all theses and doctoral dissertations. The policy seeks to "unlock the underutilized result of graduate education for the scholarly community" with the goal of "hav-ing graduate students learn about electronic publishing and digital libraries, applying that knowledge as they engage in their research and build and submit their own ETDs."[16] The wording in this policy, though not aimed specifically at the urban environment, expresses values that align closely with HIPs and the value of student success.

2. Foster Scholarship, Research, and Creativity to Address the Challenging Problems of Our Time and Place

School violence and mass shootings, landslides caused by climate change, food insecurity in Tacoma, Lushootseed language revitalization—follow the news stories of faculty research on the UWT homepage, and the many different ways that faculty engage in research that responds to the unique challenges of our time in place become clear. The UWT Strategic Plan further under-scores the importance of this type of "current" research in its promotion of community-engaged scholarship. According to Virginia Commonwealth Uni-versity—another officially designated USU—community-engaged scholar-ship "addresses community needs through research, teaching and service in a mutually beneficial partnership."[17] To support faculty who do this type of work, the UWT campus offers a Collaborative Publicly Engaged Scholarship (CPES) Fund, which has funded six faculty teams for research projects in a variety of areas.[18]

Within the Library, we have always evolved our services to partner with faculty in their research and creative work, including community-engaged scholarship. In the context of the digital scholarship program, this includes our efforts to digitize and amplify the products of faculty activity, such that others locally and globally will be able to better discover and benefit from their work. For instance, in 2011, a faculty member in the Urban Studies program approached the Library to start an occasional paper series to be made dig-itally accessible with the aim of bringing together work from a wide range of contributors that would explore the "inherent dynamism and vitalities of cities and urban processes throughout the world," and much of the work that would appear in it would engage with issues and developments merging from

Tacoma and other cities.[19] The need for a digital platform to host this content prompted an investigation into digital repository solutions.

We explored a number of options before ultimately settling on bepress and its Digital Commons product as the most viable. Many factors influenced the decision, such as the SelectedWorks author profiles, which enable faculty to feature their publications, and the bepress service model, but the Library leadership group at the time was particularly attracted to how it would support UWT's distinct identity and scholarly mission. UW Tacoma Digital Commons launched in 2012, populated with publications and profiles for twenty-four faculty members included in the IR Kickstart package offered by bepress. Since then, with the help of interns and graduate student workers, we have significantly grown the number of faculty members with profiles. As of October 2017, 193 faculty (57 percent) had profiles, while 148 did not have profiles.[20]

In developing profiles and related collections of published scholarship, we generally take the initiative to reach out to faculty and make it as easy as possible for them to keep their information up-to-date. Also, rather than emphasizing open access, we recognize that faculty members want to offer access to their entire publication record, not just those works that can be shared openly. As a result, we create comprehensive profiles, linking to licensed electronic versions whenever possible. Although not every faculty member is doing publicly engaged research with community partners, we recognize that enabling open access to content unlocks the research and can enable the bidirectional scholarship described in a case study of UWT published by the Coalition of USU.[21]

Just as the repository has connected us with published scholarship, it has also enabled emerging forms of scholarship that are directly community-engaged. For instance, the repository hosts the teaching materials of the Lushootseed Language Institute and the Puget Sound Environmental Justice Interviews, both of which have strong connections to the local community.[22] More recently, we have recognized the need to move beyond capturing the artifacts of scholarship to participating in the whole lifecycle of scholarship and creative work and are initiating efforts to encourage a culture of digital public scholarship at UWT. Library staff have begun offering faculty development opportunities, such as hosting a quarterly book discussion group on digital scholarship, organizing trainings on topics such as digital storytelling, and engaging the public with social media, among other topics of interest. These projects provide opportunities to contribute to the evolving discussions of community-engaged scholarship on campus and advocate for the central role open access can have in making the products of academic research available to the general public.

Recognizing our common interest to promote and share the whole lifecycle of faculty scholarship, in the last year, the Library has begun partnering with UWT's Office of Research. The Office of Research wanted to better capture and share the scholarly output of campus, and because we already had a workflow in place for systematically gathering citations, it seemed a natural collaboration. Now, the Office of Research sends out quarterly calls for new publications, referring faculty to our online form, and we provide a formatted list of citations that can be shared with the campus and make sure that publications are also gathered in our digital repository. One faculty member recently pointed out that this was a significant coup for UWT Digital Commons and represents its further institutionalization as a platform for faculty scholarship. It also makes it much easier for us to keep faculty profiles up-to-date.

Although we can point to impressive strides made in support of digital scholarship, a closer look at the faculty publications, collections, and specific projects also illustrate some of the limitations of our current approach. As of 2017, for instance, only 12 percent of the faculty publications in the UWT Digital Commons were shared open access (203 out of 1,683 total). Also, nearly all of the faculty profiles in the repository were created and are maintained by Library staff. We have at least three schools or programs that only have only partial coverage in the faculty profiles because of the complexity of the outreach that must be done to accomplish this work.

Recently, the UW Faculty Senate that governs all three UW campuses passed an Open Access Policy that will apply to all scholarly articles published by faculty. As a result, there are many questions within the UWT Library about the infrastructure and services that will support faculty as they make their future work digitally available: how will the development of Libraries-wide systems and procedures change our local branch's digital scholarship activities? What is the future of the local UWT digital repository for supporting faculty publications? What kinds of outreach needs to occur to educate local faculty about the Open Access Policy? Many of these questions were also brought to the fore by Elsevier's acquisition of the bepress platform in August 2017 and will become more central to our work over the next few years.

The Library seeks to position itself as an advocate for the ways that digital scholarship practices and open access framework can significantly enhance community-engaged scholarship and is therefore approaching this as a rare faculty development opportunity. Faculty are conducting outstanding and interesting work, often relying on a wide array of digital technologies and tools, but most of the campus discussion tends to focus primarily on the core elements of this work—locality in the Tacoma/Pierce County area, involvement of local partners, and the scholarly impact—without clearly delineating the ways that open access and digital technologies might enhance and extend this work. Yet even as we encourage communities of practice among the faculty, the Library is only beginning to formalize its own local infrastructure, staffing, and service models to effectively interface with faculty research teams.

UWT can look to USUs throughout the country that are engaging with faculty scholarship in innovative ways that support the full scope of scholarly inquiry, from applying digital tools to support traditional scholarship to actively participating in emerging forms of scholarship. The University of New Mexico has a series of services that help in this area, including consultations with its Digital Scholarship Services office and introductions to current issues from its Office of Innovative Scholarly Initiatives.[23]

The University of North Carolina at Charlotte facilitates collaboration with its Faculty Connections tool, which helps individuals with shared interests find each other.[24] This type of tool is particularly intriguing because of UWT's origins as a highly interdisciplinary institution. A version of this tool could be just as valuable for helping faculty members from different departments create collaborations as it could be to connect them with important community stakeholders. Having it housed or supported by the library increases the interdisciplinary feel of the resource and ensures that librarians and non-faculty experts may also be "connected" to interest groups and projects.

3. Partner and Collaborate for the Common Good

As a USU, UWT is characterized by many strong institutional partnerships at multiple levels of the University. The Center for Urban Waters, a partnership of the campus, the City of Tacoma, and the Puget Sound Partnership, is one of its signature examples. Specific UWT faculty members also engage in numerous, complex partner activities. One Psychology professor, Chris Beasley, is creating a "pipeline" for formerly incarcerated students to go from prison to higher education, including institutions like UWT;[25] Anne Wessels, an Urban Studies faculty member, is codirecting the Livable City Year in Tacoma, a broad-based initiative to make more sustainable communities.[26] To champion, and to some extent, coordinate these kinds of efforts, the campus also has established the Community Engagement Council, and is now applying for a Carnegie Community Engagement Classification. The campus has entered into this process so that it will be "more intentional and systematic as an institution about how we develop community engagement infrastructure in alignment with national best practices."[27]

UWT's partnership culture has provided key opportunities for the Library to become an active part of research groups with digital scholarship components. For example, one of the Library's initial forays into digital scholarship, the Tacoma Community History Project, was born out of a mutually beneficial partnership of the Library, faculty and students, and members of the local community.[28] Professor Michael Honey has taught the Doing Community History Class since the early 1990s. In this class, students learn oral history methodology and conduct an oral history project on an organization, institution, neighborhood, event, or prominent individual. The collection now includes over eighty interviews with individuals who represent the diverse and underrepresented voices of Tacoma: civic leaders, ethnic and indigenous groups, the LGBTQ+ community, labor unions, military personnel, and veterans, among others. It contains a trove of primary sources on the lived experiences of peoples in Tacoma and the wider region.

In 2010, Professor Honey received a grant from the Puyallup Tribe to digitize existing oral histories, and these funds—combined with additional support from the Friends of the UW Libraries—went toward hiring student workers to digitize the projects and make them available online in a public collection. Up to this point, the projects were created in the class and then deposited in the Library at the end of the quarter. Students received little to no oversight or guidance about the specific recording technologies, and as a result a wide array of media formats and recording qualities were in the collection.

The challenges of digitizing this material and making it available online underscored the importance of consistency and guidelines for the students conducting oral histories in the future. We developed a LibGuide for the class that not only provides links to resources but offers templates for the documents and guidance for creating digital files.[29] More recently, we have introduced a blogging component to the course; after the students have conducted their oral history, they also select clips from the interview and write a brief blog post about it.[30] The Library features these posts in its social media, and we were surprised that some of these posts became the most popular items in our feed.

The Library's digital scholarship program has built on its experiences with the Tacoma Community History Project and is now engaged in several other collaborative partnerships with faculty that use oral history to document the history of Tacoma and the south Puget Sound. While we look forward to our involvement in these additional oral history projects, the digital scholarship staff recognize that we will likely have to alter the ways that we support them, perhaps shifting to an approach that assists the overall design and implementation of projects.

As our perspective broadens to include the multiplicity of research projects and partnerships occurring at UWT, determining the role of the digital scholarship program can be both inspiring and daunting. On one level, we observe a high degree of community-engaged scholarship already occurring on campus, but on another, it raises questions about how far the Library can extend and enhance this work through digital scholarship approaches without more extensive infrastructure and staffing. How do we prioritize projects that engage with the community? With limited staffing, how do we do outreach to demonstrate the value that intentional digital scholarship approaches can have in the lifecycle of projects? To what extent do we participate in the planning and implementation of projects?

At the same time that we are tracking community engagement initiatives and conversations on campus, we also are beginning to expand the culture of digital scholarship by establishing some of our own partnerships with local museums, public libraries, and heritage organizations that may lead to new and novel digital scholarship activities. Some of these partnerships are relatively small one-time events, such as the Tacoma History Keepers event for a local ethnic heritage organization, although others are much larger projects, such as grant applications with local institutions to respond to community needs. Yet threaded through all of these projects are a host of complex questions: How are formal partnerships established at UWT? Is the partnership with UWT or the UW Libraries or both? The UWT Library tends to focus on supporting the academic side of the University, yet it does not regularly offer or teach any classes, so to what extent can faculty and students become involved in these partnerships?

Many of the digital scholarship programs we examined in our environmental scan of USUs have established mutually beneficial partnerships that have significant impact on the region. Cleveland State University, for instance, hosts the Center for Public History and Digital Humanities, which has incubated a number of local history projects, notably Cleveland Historical, an interactive website that features narratives of the city's built environment.[31] It is important to note, however, that this project comes out of the history department rather than the Library and reflects the importance of tying work to faculty research and teaching.

We also found a number of larger institutions that have clearly delineated digital scholarship services that enable partnerships to benefit the common good of their surrounding regions. Some, such as Indiana University-Purdue University Indianapolis, Temple University, and the University of Memphis, have well-developed services that emphasize the metropolitan or regional emphasis. The Center for Digital Scholarship at IUPUI identifies extensive list of partners that range from local historical societies, public libraries, museums, and government agencies, and these partners have contributed to a wide variety of collections.[32]

4. Catalyze the Economic and Social Vitality of the Region

The Coalition of USUs was created in part to "to leverage the intellectual capital and economic power of urban universities" and its commitment to this idea is still apparent in initiatives focused on workforce development and partnerships with prospective employers.[33] In the case of UWT, the assessment of the University's economic impact reveals that the campus tends to focus on the built environment, grant funding, and the educational opportunities the University has generated. Tacoma and the larger Pierce County region in which it sits are now seeing dramatic population and economic growth, and many news articles credit the University for its impact.[34]

In March 2018, the Tacoma Economic Development Board gave the campus a Golden Shovel Award for its role as an economic engine in the region.[35]

The award recognized the campus role "in downtown Tacoma's physical transformation to a thriving urban hub" and specifically identified the influence of the Milgard School of Business, the Institute of Technology, and the Urban Studies program. This announcement reinforces similar themes in the Anchoring for Change case study of UWT.[36] The roles of student learning and faculty research and scholarship may be acknowledged, but its actual economic contribution remains unclear and unquantified, perhaps because of the difficulty of defining the scope of this impact. Of the four elements of an urban serving university, this is perhaps the least developed for the UWT digital scholarship program. Yet we do have several projects underway that reflect our growing awareness of this element. We also acknowledge the conflict that prioritizing economic development can bring to models of higher education and hope that our efforts retain a strong sense of social consciousness and emphasis on scholarly inquiry, community, and student well-being.

To the extent that the digital scholarship program supports the full spectrum of scholarship and learning across campus in meaningful ways, it also functions as an "economic and social vitality." Libraries are usually seen as social or cultural assets, but their economic functions can also be significant. Most studies of economic and social impact have been conducted in public libraries, but a body of literature recognizes the key roles academic libraries play in student success and retention and faculty research, among others.[37] Because the digital scholarship program connects and collaborates with faculty and students in novel ways, it has the potential to extend the innovation, creativity, and inquiry that contributes to the region.

One example is the UWT Oral History: Founding Stories project, which uses digital scholarship practices to document and share the economic and social impact of the University. The oral history project, which is being co-led by Professor Charles Williams and Justin Wadland, head of the Digital Scholarship Program, is collecting interviews with founding faculty members and staff, community leaders, and (eventually) students of the University. Many people can easily observe the dramatic transformation that UWT has brought to the urban core. Less visible are the political, social, and educational exchanges that occurred within these buildings and are now being carried out into the city and beyond. The oral history project takes advantage of digital tools and technologies so that the materials can be openly shared.

As the program continues to evolve, we can foresee developing initiatives that more explicitly recognize the economic, social, and cultural impact of digital scholarship activities, especially in terms of those that better prepare students for employment in the region. Yet it is important to note that the intersection of economic development and the educational and research mission of UWT quickly draws us into larger debates about both the future of universities and the role of digital scholarship in the academy. As state funding has decreased and tuition dollars have increasingly funded the University, how does the campus serve students seeking skills and competencies that will make them employable? How do faculty balance the economic realities of higher education against their academic freedom to determine the curriculum and research agendas? Since most of the digital scholarship projects are carving out new virtual and physical spaces at UWT, as well as new staff positions, how might digital scholarship activities ensure academic rigor and social value against the entrepreneurial drive that inspires projects? How does the digital scholarship program reflect the positive values of the institution without replicating its disparities?

The faculty, staff, and administrators we work with at UWT hold a spectrum of opinions on these perspectives, but there seems to be unity—and pride—in the access mission of the University. It was centrally placed in the values compass, also created in the strategic plan.[38] As this review has revealed, there are multiple ways the digital scholarship program has supported this value, but in planning, access should be a guiding principle.

In our environmental scan, we didn't find any examples of digital scholarship programs that articulated their specific economic or social impact, but we did find attractive approaches that could enhance both economic and cultural development. The first is providing students (and faculty, for that matter) clear venues to develop the skills of digital scholars. For instance, Temple University offers a Digital Scholars Program for graduate students.[39] It provides funding and training for students to design and implement projects. The second approach involves partnering with local institutions to digitize and share regional history. The University of Central Florida launched a Center for Humanities and Digital Research that has incubated and supported cross-institutional collaborations that have focused on its region. In addition, Virginia Commonwealth University has a particularly well-developed program focused on the history of its host city and offers a Community Digitization Program.[40]

PRIORITIES FOR THE FUTURE

As evidenced above, these four elements of a USU, as defined by UWT, have laid the foundation for the UWT Library's digital scholarship work and brought it in sync with the mission and values of the institution as a whole. However, a number of challenges remain for our emerging program, especially with regard to how to work within the institutional constraints to communicate, institutionalize, and scale these efforts that are central to much of our current work.

To address these challenges and help strategize next steps, we have looked to the existing literature on how to grow and sustain library digital scholarship work. All of the literature and professional conversations about establishing and sustaining a digital scholarship program emphasize that there is no template to follow. Yet there are some discussions and bodies of literature that can serve as sign posts.

Two works in particular have been useful for establishing a framework as we move ahead. The first, Kathryn K. Matthew's blog post, "Biscuits vs. Granola: Innovative Ways for Libraries, Archives, and Museums to Scale Up," suggests a process in which program development is divided into four main phases—testing, piloting, scaling, and mainstreaming.[41] Although more established elements of UWT's digital scholarship program, like our institutional repository, have reached the point of scaling or mainstreaming, other elements are still very much in the testing or piloting process, including upcoming trainings for DS tools and resources. The other work that we have found helpful is Dan Cohen's closing plenary speech on institutionalizing digital scholarship at the 2017 CNI-ARL Digital Scholarship Planning Workshop (as summarized by Craft). In it, Cohen presents a related perspective to Matthew's, which includes the suggestion that libraries find ways to routinize, normalize, and depersonalize their services in order to institutionalize and sustain our work.[42] Keeping this framework in mind, we have identified and summarized three key areas for future development.

1. Drafting an Effective Communication Strategy and Mission Statement for an Urban Serving Digital Scholarship Program

Communication is one of the main areas of focus as we grow our digital scholarship program. The literature suggests several priorities for effectively communicating the scope of a digital scholarship program: defining digital scholarship terms and practices to establish a shared vocabulary, clearly describing the library staff roles and responsibilities, providing a meaningful framework for collaboration and partnerships, and creating means of formally sharing faculty development and training opportunities.[43] Communication strategies are also an important part of scaling a program. Libraries need to make clear decisions about their capacity (in terms of space, equipment, storage, hardware, software, and staff) to support digital scholarship work and convey that to stakeholders.[44]

Equally important to the future of UWT's digital scholarship program is a public-facing mission and vision statement that will clearly tie our program activities to the priorities of UWT and its urban serving focus. The Digital Scholarship Center at IUPUI Library offers a particularly useful example of this, not only because it is located at a USU but because it provides bullet-pointed lists of the center's objectives, activities that will help the center achieve those objectives, and selection criteria the center will use to assess digital projects.[45] The literature generally recognizes that a clearly articulated mission can enable a program to convey how it engages in the entire cycle of research activities, keep it from getting bogged down with highly local or short-term goals, and help with the overall sustainability of the program by establishing its relationship to long-term, strategic goals.[46] This has obvious importance to UWT and its urban-serving focus.

2. Strengthening and Formalizing the Relationships of an Urban Serving Program

Although relationships are arguably already a strength of the UWT Library's approach to digital scholarship, we must remain conscious of their importance as we continue to scale and grow our digital scholarship program. The literature consistently highlights the tension between traditional client or service models with emerging partnership models, which position libraries as experts on and contributors to the projects they support. Some authors argue that the partnership models have more "positive, sustainable" results than traditional models. These models require digital scholarship programs to delineate roles and manage the expectations of partners.[47] That said, it will come as no surprise that strong interpersonal relationships (both inside and outside the library) are frequently cited as critical aspects of fostering this work.[48] In this respect, UWT faces challenges for depersonalizing certain aspects of its partnerships so they do not rely too heavily on the presence of a particular individual to survive;[49] communicating and fostering new partnership models with campus constituents; and creating strong internal support networks so that new staff and library liaisons feel empowered to pursue digital scholarship work.

3. Fostering the Flexibility of an Urban Serving University Digital Scholarship Program

Digital scholarship work can be fast-moving, challenging, and difficult to predict. In general, keys to a successful program include teamwork, responsiveness to changing needs or constituent requests, and attentiveness to emerging tools and technologies.[50] Flexibility is helpful when dealing with these and other common challenges to digital scholarship work. We must plan for resources years in advance even as digital tools and trends rapidly evolve and we must find inspiring, innovative ways to collaborate while also continually shifting our own mental models of scholarly practices along with faculty, staff, and administrator allies.[51]

The UWT Library hasn't had the personnel to accommodate as many program needs as we might hope. Craft's recommendation for working with these challenges is to hire for aptitudes and attitudes rather than a particular skill set. Libraries should work to establish a range of different skills and expertise on a team rather than in an individual.[52]

CONCLUSION

Through this chapter, we have gauged the past, present, and possible futures of the digital scholarship activities at UWT, and we have evaluated them against the core values and characteristics of the urban serving university as articulated by UWT. Together, all of this creates a contextualized, nuanced portrait of our program, circa September 2018. However, talk to us six months or a year from now, and things will inevitably look different. As we consider these different priorities, we see them less as a sequence and more as series to be braided over the near and long-term. Their ultimate shape will be governed by intention, emergent opportunities, unexpected outcomes, accidents, and failures.

We open up our thought process in this public way so that it might serve as a model for others. The approaches of USUs, we believe, can serve as a helpful framework for institutions of higher education with strong community orientations, even if they are not formally a member of the USU coalition. USUs provide novel ways for understanding the roles of a student learning, faculty teaching and research, community partnerships, libraries, and digital scholarship within an urban context. The university and the city become interrelated and even in some ways interdependent, and a strong library-based digital scholarship program can better position both the institution and the community to achieve their shared goals.

Takeaways

■ The Urban Serving University model provides a valuable framework for any digital scholarship program located at an urban university.

■ Open access and digital scholarship can contribute to campus-wide efforts to enhance community-engaged scholarship and student success.

NOTES

1. The only article we could find on the intersection between USUs and libraries was Tom Bielavitz, "A Content Analysis of the Strategic Plans of the Coalition of Urban Serving Universities' Academic Libraries," *Urban Library Journal* 17, no. 1 (Spring 2011): 1–19.
2. Justin Wadland and Charles Williams, "University of Washington Tacoma," HistoryLink.org, November 11, 2017, http://historylink.org/File/20469.
3. University of Washington Tacoma, "UW Tacoma 2017–18 Facts," https://www.tacoma.uw.edu/about-uw-tacoma/uw-tacoma-2017–18-facts.
4. Ibid.

5. Coalition of Urban Serving Universities, "Coalition Overview," http://usucoalition.org/about/overview/.

6. Justin Wadland, "UW Tacoma Opens Permanent Location in Downtown Warehouse District on September 27, 1997," HistoryLink.org, November 11, 2017, www.historylink.org/File/20471.

7. University of Washington Libraries, "One Library: Three Campuses," www.lib.washington.edu/dean/tri-campus.

8. Andrea Craft et al., *Anchoring for Change: The Deepening Role of Urban Universities* (Coalition of Urban Serving Universities and Association of Public and Land-Grant Universities, 2016), 12.

9. These values have been shortened and have also been incorporated into the mission statement of the University. For the sake of consistency, we refer to the shortened versions throughout this chapter. See UW Tacoma, "What Is an Urban-Serving University?," https://www.tacoma.uw.edu/strategic-planning/what-urban-serving-university and UW Tacoma, "Vision, Mission and Values," https://www.tacoma.uw.edu/about-uw-tacoma/vision-mission-values.

10. Wadland and Williams, "University of Washington Tacoma."

11. "Charting Our Course: UW Tacoma's Strategic Plan 2016–2021," https://www.tacoma.uw.edu/sites/default/files/sections/Chancellor/ChartingOurCourse-2018.pdf.

12. Ibid.

13. University of Washington Tacoma, "Quick Facts," www.tacoma.washington.edu/node/43452.

14. "High Impact Educational Practices: A Brief Overview," Association of American Colleges and Universities, https://www.aacu.org/leap/hips.

15. The Gender and Sexuality Studies Collection is available at https://digitalcommons.tacoma.uw.edu/gender_studies/; the *ACCESS*: Interdisciplinary Journal of Student Research* may be viewed at https://digitalcommons.tacoma.uw.edu/access/.

16. Georgia State University, "Mandate for Deposit of ETDs: University Policy 2.10.16 Electronic Master's Theses and Doctoral Dissertations," https://scholarworks.gsu.edu/univ_lib_dadocs/6/.

17. University of Washington Tacoma, "Community Engagement Terms and Definitions, www.tacoma.uw.edu/community-engagement/community-engagement-terms-definitions.

18. "UW Tacoma Collaboratively Engaged Public Scholarship Fund," https://www.tacoma.uw.edu/office-research/uw-tacoma-collaborative-publicly-engaged-scholarship-cpes-fund.

19. The occasional papers series was name *Conflux* and launched in 2014; see https://digitalcommons.tacoma.uw.edu/conflux/.

20. For more about the extent of faculty sharing of open access materials, see Justin Wadland, "UW Tacoma Faculty Profiles and Open Access," *UW*

Tacoma Profiles in Research (blog), October 26, 2017, https://blogs.uw.edu/taclibdc/2017/10/26/uw-tacoma-faculty-profiles-open-access/.

21. "Imagined in this manner, the educational, research, and development goals of the campus move from a unidirectional model (of experts to non-experts) to a bidirectional model in which the University and its activities are shaped by regional stakeholders as much as the University affects its external constituents." In Craft et al., *Anchoring the Community*.

22. The Lushootseed Language Institute collection is available at https://digitalcommons.tacoma.uw.edu/lushootseed_institute/; The Puget Sound Environmental Justice Interviews are available at https://digitalcommons.tacoma.uw.edu/ej_interviews/.

23. University of New Mexico Libraries, "Digital Scholarship Services," https://library.unm.edu/services/escholarship.php; "An Introduction to Scholarly Communications," University of New Mexico Libraries, https://scholarly.unm.edu/scholarly-communications/index.html.

24. University of North Carolina Charlotte, "Faculty Connections," https://pages.uncc.edu/connections/.

25. Eric Wilson-Edge, "Chris Beasley Builds a Pipeline," *University of Washington Tacoma News and Information,* September 30, 2017, https://www.tacoma.uw.edu/news/article/chris-beasley-builds-pipeline.

26. University of Washington Tacoma Urban Studies, "Anne Wessels Faculty Co-Director for 2017–18 Livable City Year," https://www.tacoma.uw.edu/urban-studies/article/anne-wessells-livable-city-year.

27. University of Washington Tacoma, "Carnegie Community Engagement Classification 2020 Overview," https:/www.tacoma.uw .edu/community-engagement/carnegie-community-engagement-classification-2020-overview.

28. University of Washington Libraries Digital Collections, "Tacoma Community History Project," https://content.lib.washington.edu/tacomacommweb/index.html.

29. University of Washington Tacoma, "TIAS 515 and THIST 437 Doing Community History-Honey," http://guides.lib.uw.edu/c.php?g=344264&p=2318468.

30. *Tacoma Community History Project* (blog), http://blogs.uw.edu/tchp/.

31. Center for Public History and Digital Humanities, https://csudigitalhumanities.org; Cleveland Historical, https://clevelandhistorical.org.

32. A listing of IUPUI's partners can be found at www.ulib.iupui.edu/digitalscholarship/partners; IUPUI's collections is available at www.ulib.iupui.edu/collections.

33. "Coalition of Urban Serving Universities," http://usucoalition.org/.

34. Jack Stubbs, "'Placemaking in Tacoma': Economic Drivers Shaping the City," *The Registry,* July 18, 2018, "https://news.theregistryps.com/placemaking-in-tacoma-economic-drivers-shaping-the-city/.

35. John Burkhardt, "Take That Golden Shovel And . . . Do Even More," *University of Washington Tacoma News and Information,* March 16, 2018, www.tacoma.uw.edu/news/article/take-golden-shovel-do-even-more.

36. Craft et al., *Anchoring for Change.*

37. Megan Oakleaf, *The Value of Academic Libraries: A Comprehensive Research Review and Report* (Chicago: Association of College and Research Libraries, 2010), www.ala.org/acrl/sites/ala.org.acrl/files/content/issues/value/val_report.pdf.

38. *Charting Our Course: UW Tacoma's Strategic Plan 2016–2021* (Tacoma: University of Washington Tacoma, 2016), 9, http://digitalcommons.tacoma.uw.edu/strategic_plan_16–21.

39. Temple University Libraries Digital Scholarship Center, "Digital Scholars Program," https://sites.temple.edu/tudsc/research/digital-scholars-program.

40. Virginia Commonwealth University Libraries, "Digital Collections and Online Exhibits," https://www.library.vcu.edu/research/digital-collections/.

41. Kathryn K. Matthew, "Biscuits vs. Granola: Innovative Ways for Libraries, Archives, and Museums to Scale Up," *Institute of Museum and Library Services News and Events*, June 8, 2018, https://www.imls.gov/blog/2018/06/biscuits-vs-granola-innovative-ways-libraries-archives-and-museums-scale.

42. Anna R. Craft, "Digital Scholarship Planning: A Perspective on the CNI-ARL Workshop," *Serials Review* 44, no. 1 (2018).

43. John Cox, "Communicating New Library Roles to Enable Digital Scholarship: A Review Article," *New Review of Academic Librarianship* 22, no. 2–3 (2016): 132–47; A. Miller, "DS/DH Start-Ups: A Library Model for Advancing Scholarship through Collaboration," *Journal of Web Librarianship,*10, no. 2 (2016): 1–18.

44. Cox, "Communicating New Library Roles."

45. IUPUI Libraries Digital Scholarship Center, "Mission," www.ulib.iupui.edu/digitalscholarship/mission.

46. Cox, "Communicating New Library Roles"; Joan Lippincott and Dian Goldenberg-Hart, *Digital Scholarship Centers: Trends and Good Practice* (Washington, DC: Coalition for Networked Information, 2014), https://www.cni.org/publications/joans-pubs/dsc-2014-workshop-report.

47. See Cox, 2016, p. 138: "Managing the library's involvement in digital scholarship is challenging and there needs to be clarity around what can and cannot be done within finite resources in a climate of high expectation and demand . . . Without clear communication strategies, resources will be spread too thinly, or invested inappropriately, and the library's reputation as a key player in digital scholarship will be compromised."

48. Cox, "Communicating New Library Roles"; Joan Lippincott and Dian Goldenberg-Hart, *Digital Scholarship Centers: Trends and Good Practice,* (Washington, DC: Coalition for Networked Information, 2014), https://

www.cni.org/publications/joans-pubs/dsc-2014-workshop-report; A. Miller, "DS/DH Start-Ups: A Library Model for Advancing Scholarship through Collaboration," *Journal of Web Librarianship* 10, no. 2 (2016), 1–18; Craft, "Digital Scholarship Planning."

49. Craft, "Digital Scholarship Planning."
50. Lippincott and Goldenberg-Hart, *Digital Scholarship Centers.*
51. Ibid.
52. Craft, "Digital Scholarship Planning."

VERLETTA KERN

Conclusion

The Culture of Digital Scholarship Continued

We hope you have enjoyed coming along with us on a journey of our strengths, struggles, and aspirations in growing a culture of digital scholarship at the University of Washington (UW). Perhaps our stories are similar? Perhaps our struggles are your struggles and our successes are your successes? Regardless, we hope we were able to provide some inspiration and guidance along the way.

Although the culture of digital scholarship is disparate at UW and perhaps within the Libraries itself, we are unified in a core set of characteristics and inquiry that lead us as an academic library to become a focal point for the culture of digital scholarship at UW. We see the importance in our role as translators—from translating infrastructure needs to an internal understanding of how we should, may, and can develop infrastructure and related services for users (chapter 6) to fluidly bringing together the data services and digital scholarship services to better support cross-disciplinary research needs (chapters 4 and 8) to translating a researcher's digital scholarship dreams into reality (chapter 7). We see the role of communicator and connector play out through digital scholarship-supported community-engaged research to assessing the impact of digital public scholarship to building and continuing relationships beyond library assessments (chapters 1, 4, 7, 8, and 10). We see the importance of being a champion for digital scholarship in designing spaces and services to meet their needs (chapter 9). We see how a culture of digital scholarship is supported through entrepreneurial approaches to space and service design along with new approaches to teaching (chapters 2, 5, and 9).

We see the importance of flexibility and responsiveness to changing needs (chapters 4, 6, and 8). We see strong connections between the culture of digital scholarship and equity through innovative program design and teaching (chapters 1, 2, 3, and 10). And arguably most importantly, throughout our discussions in this book, we see how an academic library's work in growing a culture of digital scholarship supports expanding opportunities for research to reach the public and make a considerable contribution to the public good. Each of these soft skills and entrepreneurial initiatives has resulted in the cascading effect of influencing a culture of digital scholarship at UW.

So, what's next for the UW Libraries as we press forward with our admirable goal of growing a culture of digital scholarship at UW? As so eloquently put by our dean of libraries and UW vice provost for digital initiatives, Betsy Wilson:

> The UW Libraries will continue to use its significant user assessment capabilities and liaison librarian program to anticipate the digital needs of scholars and to demonstrate the value that librarians bring to the enterprise. In its 2018–2021 strategic plan, the Libraries commits itself to growing as a learning organization by investing in developing staff who can advance digital scholarship and new areas of research support.[1]

Indeed, the mix of traditional user assessment paired with a new focus on creative problem-solving—a foundational element of a learning organization—will put us in an excellent position to be adaptive to changing needs as our culture of digital scholarship continues to evolve.[2] After all, as Miriam Posner, digital humanist and assistant professor at UCLA's Information School, rightly points out, "To succeed at digital humanities, a library must do a great deal more than add 'digital scholarship' to an individual librarian's long string of subject specialties. It must provide room, support, and funding for library professionals to experiment (and maybe fail)."[3] Although the authors of these chapters have already been doing great experimental work to build a culture of digital scholarship, shifting to a learning organization focus provides expanded room for experimentation. Rather than grassroots efforts across the Libraries to grow a culture of digital scholarship, this is our opportunity to bring aboard more collaborators to systematically plan, experiment, and iterate, in the hope of growing a robust culture of digital scholarship. Although it is all well and good for us to have a plan and a renewed enthusiasm for supporting digital scholarship, what does this mean for you, the reader? What's next in growing a culture of digital scholarship beyond institutional silos?

Let's take a quick step back and review a few findings from the book. For one thing, we've found that digital scholarship is a tricky term. It is hard to define and even more challenging for researchers to see themselves as part of a digital scholarship movement (chapters 4, 5, 7, and 8). What we do see is more and more researchers interested in including voices from underrepresented populations (chapters 2, 5, and 10) and extending their research beyond the walls of the academy for the public good (chapters 1, 3, 6, and 9).[4] In this way, digital scholarship is a means to a greater goal of open scholarship.

How does a culture of digital scholarship support open scholarship, and what is an academic library's role in supporting open scholarship? As questions of higher education's value loom large in today's societal dialog and as funding agencies for large-scale research projects are routinely placed on the chopping block in order balance government budgets, we in the academy come to the hard and fast realization that although we've done a great job sharing the value of our research with each other, we have done so at the expense of cutting the general public out of the conversation.[5] Just as Gutenberg's printing press opened up knowledge to lead Europe from the Middle Ages into the Renaissance and Enlightenment, we are seeing a similar impact as digital publishing and social media cast open a wider information net. As so aptly put it in chapter 2's discussion of digital scholarship and global citizenship:

> Today's researchers and students have ready access to an abundance of information and perspectives, from peer-reviewed secondary literature to Tweets directly from the president of the United States. Digital self-publishing and social media have especially altered the landscape of whose voices get to be heard, breaking down traditional print-based publishing barriers. Virtually anybody with a device and the ability can now publish for free via a wide selection of online blogging platforms and services, which provide authors with the opportunity to give life to perspectives, partnerships, and voices that are not fully represented or promoted in academia.[6]

In a world where virtually anyone can publish information digitally, academics must work even harder to connect with communities and get research into the hands of the public. Because we no longer live in a space where people will come to us to find quality information, we must increase our efforts to not only get information to them but also to involve them in the information creation process. This is where digital scholarship, open access, and open scholarship join forces. We see this work trickling down through libraries such as MIT, which has adopted its library vision as, "We envision a world where enduring, abundant, equitable, and meaningful access to information serves to empower and inspire humanity."[7] MIT provides an aspirational example of how libraries can combine open scholarship through a social justice lens to provide access to information for all, not just those who walk onto our campuses or are part of an elite group of people who can access licensed content through the library.

So how can a culture of digital scholarship move us closer toward a goal of open, equitable access to information and how do libraries get there?

1. *We need to change the way we think about our users.*

Traditionally, academic libraries have considered our user population to be those enrolled at our institutions. Although we will always see this group as our primary set of users, we need to think more broadly. If you work at a large state institution, such as UW, how are you supporting those within your community? Are there opportunities such as those presented in chapter 10 to partner with and serve the immediate community? Beyond the immediate community, what more can be done to get research into the hands of constituents across the state who could benefit from the work being done at your institution? How can the library partner with and support researchers who engage in community-engaged scholarship, participatory scholarship, citizen science, public scholarship, and so forth? How can a culture of digital scholarship help elevate their work and celebrate the work of community contributors in the research process?

2. *We need to help researchers share their work widely.*

From creating spaces where digital scholarship can be produced such as the one described in chapter 9, to understanding what it takes to invest in digital infrastructures as discussed in chapter 6, to helping researchers locate places to share their research findings ethically as examined in chapters 3, 7, and 8, we need to be active promoters in developing opportunities to share research widely. It doesn't just stop with infrastructure development though.

3. *We need to invest in training.*

This training may fall outside of what has traditionally been thought of as a library's purview. We need to help researchers develop their online identities, whether it be through training opportunities for creating an ORCID iD, writing a researcher biography, creating a researcher's web presence, or helping to demystify the process of creating a social media presence. By assisting researchers in this area, we are helping them share their expertise with wider publics who will then find it easier to locate the researcher and connect with areas of shared interest. We can also help by training researchers how to communicate their research to wider publics. In their book, *Being a Scholar in the Digital Era: Transforming Scholarly Practice for the Public Good,* CUNY scholar Jessie Daniels and CUNY's chief librarian Polly Thistlethwaite point out, "for scholars who want to reach a wide public audience through digital media technologies and don't know how to use these tools, there are few options available in the way of training that is tailored specifically to academics."[8] Although seemingly unconventional to some, libraries provide the perfect discipline-agnostic, low-stakes space to train researchers how to communicate the story of their research. As discussed in chapter 5, digital storytelling can be an excellent way to share the story of your research. We can coordinate efforts to train researchers on how to interact with the media, how to write op-eds, how to pitch a story to the media and more. After all, our mission is to connect people with knowledge.[9] Although infrastructures can provide access, promotion of research is an obvious next step in getting research out of the academy and into the hands of the people.

4. *Think of students as creators of new information and incorporate information creation skills into information literacy work.*

This concept has been around for quite a while, but how does it relate to a growing culture of digital scholarship? We have excellent examples of incorporating conversations around digital citizenship into the classroom in chapter 2, the importance of scale and project management in chapter 7, and incorporating discussions of copyright, author rights, and Creative Commons licensing into classes in chapter 3. More can be done here. We can use our expertise with metadata to include critical thinking exercises with students on the verge of developing guided metadata strategies for their own work. We can mainstream teaching our students to become critical consumers, and thus producers, of data and data visualizations.[10] We can fold conversations of "algorithmic literacy" into our teaching to raise awareness of how students interact with information online, help students to think critically about how information they encounter is being presented, and aspire to make change in how future information systems are constructed.[11]

5. *Break down disciplinary silos.*

Again, this one requires us to think outside of our traditionally constructed liaison roles to look at new models of organization. As we think about supporting a culture of digital scholarship, we must also acknowledge that it crosses disciplinary boundaries. As researchers increasingly produce digital and public research reaching across disciplinary lines, so too must we adapt to support this work. At UW, for example, in the last few years an amazing community-engaged research program called Urban@UW has emerged that brings together researchers from across disciplinary silos and even across our tri-campus boundaries to solve a pressing community need.[12] Although a recent shift in organizing UW liaison librarians into disciplinary teams offers broader opportunities for collaboration, the interdisciplinarity of programs such as Urban@UW spans across our team structure and even our defined lines of how campus librarians support faculty within their own unique campuses. Although we can support these programs through the potential training opportunities and infrastructure outlined previously, the need remains to create interdisciplinary liaison contacts who can serve as embedded concierges to support programs such as these. As academics work with the community to solve research problems and as libraries move toward creating and sharing research for the public good, having a librarian member of these interdisciplinary research teams will become increasingly important.

6. *Help researchers assess their digital safety.*

As our culture of digital public scholarship moves toward the admirable goal of opening up research beyond the academy, it may draw unexpected attention to researchers that lead to unanticipated consequences such as online bullying or doxing. As libraries push researchers to open up access to their research to wider publics, we must educate researchers on how to assess their digital footprints in efforts to mitigate risk. These are also important conversations to incorporate into library information literacy sessions to ensure students understand their own digital footprints. Topics to cover might include considerations of merging personal and professional social media accounts, online data brokers, developing secure passwords and password managers, or better understanding public records requests. Clearer knowledge of digital safety and digital risk can go a long way toward a researcher's willingness and comfort level when working openly.[13]

7. *Help researchers assess the impact of their work.*

Last, but certainly not least, our culture of digital scholarship will never become robust unless we help researchers understand and evaluate their digital public scholarship. Chapter 1 reviews several ways in which libraries already have and can continue to help determine scholarly impact. For better or for worse, demonstrating the value of scholarly work remains a cornerstone of life in the academy. We can increase the reputability of digital scholarship and open scholarship by demonstrating the reach and impact of the work.

Throughout this book, we've looked at how a culture of digital scholarship has taken shape through the lens of our own institution, the University of Washington Libraries. We've looked at where we've come from, where we've struggled, and where we would like to go in the future. We've shown you the soft skills and characteristics that have helped lead us to our culture of digital scholarship. As with digital scholarship itself, we've shown you how our process of experimenting and iterating has led us to where we are today. Perhaps the same is true for you, too? Perhaps this book serves as a guide on how to (or how not to) move forward in developing your own culture of digital scholarship?

We thank you for reading this book and leave you with an inspirational quote, again from our dean of libraries and UW vice provost for digital initiatives, Betsy Wilson, about why academic libraries are the perfect place to grow a culture of digital scholarship:

> Academic libraries are uniquely positioned to help create and lead robust digital scholarship cultures and infrastructures at our universities. Librarians are proven collaborators who thrive in an interdisciplinary world. They bring a holistic perspective on the entire research lifecycle, scholarly publishing, and digital technologies to the scholarship table. They not only connect people with knowledge but with each other, which is foundational for a productive digital scholarship culture and institutional framework.[14]

With this in mind, we encourage you to charge ahead on the journey of building your own culture of digital scholarship! The path is not straight, and the road can be twisted and bumpy, but the journey is inspiring, filled with beautiful stops along the way.

NOTES

1. Betsy Wilson, interview by Verletta Kern, September 14, 2018.
2. The term "learning organization" was coined by Peter M. Senge in his book *The Fifth Discipline: The Art and Practice of the Learning Organization* (New York: Currency Doubleday, 1990). Members of a learning organization work together to continuously learn and adapt in order to achieve collective goals and understandings. For more information on how libraries can transition into a learning organization, see Joan Giesecke and Beth McNeil, "Transitioning to the Learning Organization," *Library Trends* 53, no. 1 (2004): 54-67.
3. Miriam Posner, "No Half Measures: Overcoming Common Challenges to Doing Digital Humanities in the Library," *Journal of Library Administration* 53, no. 1 (2013): 51.
4. While we recognize that not all digital scholarship is produced with a goal in mind of being made open immediately or even to all communities, we also recognize the fact that the mere act of digital scholarship provides opportunity for this work to reach a wider audience at a time deemed appropriate.
5. Scott Janschik, "NEH on the Chopping Block," *Inside Higher Ed,* January 20, 2017, www.insidehighered.com/news/2017/01/20/humanities-advocates -alarmed-reports-trumps-first-budget-will-seek-kill-neh-and-nea; Andrew Kreighbaum, "Senate Appropriations Bill Cuts NSF Funding," *Inside Higher Ed,* July 26, 2017, www.insidehighered.com/quicktakes/2017/07/26/ senate-appropriations-bill-cuts-nsf-funding.
6. Reed Garber-Pearson, "Digital Citizenship: Teaching Research Identity and Accountability to Undergraduates," in *The Culture of Digital Scholarship in*

Academic Libraries, ed. Robin Chin Roemer and Verletta Kern (Chicago: ALA Editions, 2019), 24.

7. MIT Libraries, "About Our Organization," accessed September 26, 2018, https://libraries.mit.edu/about/organization/. For more inspiration, please see MIT's Future of Libraries Report at https://future-of-libraries.mit.edu/.

8. Jesse Daniels and Polly Thistlethwaite, *Being a Scholar in the Digital Era: Transforming Scholarly Practice for the Public Good* (Bristol, UK: Policy Press, 2016).

9. University of Washington Libraries, "2018-2021 Strategic Plan," www.lib .washington.edu/about/strategicplan.

10. See the much beloved UW course, Calling Bullshit: Data Reasoning in a Digital World, created by Carl Bergstrom and Jevin West for tips and materials to incorporate into your own work, https://callingbullshit.org/.

11. The term "algorithmic literacy" comes from Safiya Umoja Noble's book *Algorithms of Oppression: How Search Engines Reinforce Racism* (New York: New York University Press, 2018).

12. Urban@UW, "Initiatives," accessed September 28, 2018, https://depts .washington.edu/urbanuw/initiatives/.

13. The Library Freedom Project, https://libraryfreedomproject.org/, and the Electronic Frontier Foundation, https://www.eff.org/, are excellent sources of information on this topic.

14. Wilson, interview.

Teaching Community Accountability Worksheet

Research Skills Worksheet

1. What is your topic?

2. What is your central claim or research question?

3. What types of experiences or perspectives might answer these questions?

4. Where might you find these perspectives (e.g., government report, blog, journal article, a family member, etc.)?

5. What people or communities might be most impacted by your research questions? If you had the time, what is one way you could envision collaborating with this community?

Jigsaw Activity

This activity can be used in a "flipped" classroom so that students may explore evaluation techniques before the session, using in-class time for group work. This activity can also be used in an online classroom, assigning distinct discussion groups and forums. In an asynchronous classroom, this activity may take anywhere from 50–120 minutes, depending on the amount of work assigned prior to the class.

Part I

Students break into small groups and are given a common article to look at. You may print out the first page of an article with a TinyURL so that they can access it online easily or do this as part of an exercise in using library search tools. Assign each group a different source type, without disclosing what it is. Some possible source types are:

- scholarly article
- scholarly book
- newspaper and magazine articles
- blog
- Tweet
- encyclopedia article

Students are given some prompts in how to evaluate that source. You can use CRAPP, 5 Ws, or another preferred method. You can also give them some questions to prompt them in considering not just *what* type of source the article is, but also *how* it might be used.

Part II

Students separate into different groups, generally with one person represented from the first group. The idea is that students now come together to share what they've learned about their source types, then to discuss how those sources could work together, how they could be used differently, etc.

At this point it can be helpful to talk about a bibliography as a topic panel. I've found it helpful to use an example of a topic panel on immigration. What voices would you want represented on that panel? Students often come up with answers like an immigrant (someone with that lived experience), somebody from government (creator of laws), and researchers. Then you can talk about where you might find those voices. Students can use this example to debate which of those sources you gave them in this exercise they might use on their topic panel.

Part III

Class discussion is where the juicy work started happening in my sessions. Students began debating about what kinds of voices should be represented and how they were detecting bias, and whether or not it was okay to use a source that was biased.

I try to stress that there are no right or wrong answers—it's all dependent on the context of each project, and that's why it's important to constantly consider the types of voices being represented and how "reliable" they might be.

At this stage we might talk about each of these sources one by one. I'll prompt students to let me know what the source is (encyclopedia articles tend to be the more difficult ones to identify). Then we talk about who wrote them and what that might mean, their currency, and so on. After that, we might discuss the topic and what kinds of sources and voices could best represent that topic. There are often many different and interesting thoughts that students have to share about this.

APPENDIX **C**

Activity in Pairs: Using Yourself as an Information Source*

Ask the following questions of your neighbor and jot down the answers.

1. What are you considered an expert at?

2. What did you have to do to acquire that knowledge or skill?

3. If you meet others with the same claims to knowledge as you, how do you know and evaluate that they are actually knowledgeable?

4. What is the difference between what you do to evaluate something in your area of expertise and what you do when you're not an expert?

*Hazel McClure, Patricia Bravender, and Gayle Schaub, *Teaching Information Literacy Threshold Concepts: Lesson Plans for Librarians* (Chicago: Association for Scholarly and Research Libraries, 2015).

Extra Credit Assignment: Meet with a Librarian

Overview

For this assignment, you will seek guidance on developing your social science writing or annotated bibliography from a UW librarian or writing tutor. A librarian can help you to find sources, think about the scale and scope of your research, and help you to formulate a plan for writing and finding sources. A writing tutor can help you to structure your paper and identify common issues in your writing. The goal of this assignment is to work collaboratively with a librarian or tutor to think about your topic and develop strategies for effective research and writing.

If you are looking for writing help, see a writing tutor at the Odegaard Writing and Research Center. Tutors have limited online appointments, so plan ahead! The same process for this assignment can be followed during your consultation with a writing tutor.

Directions

1. *Choose one subject librarian to contact for a consultation.*

   Your consultation can be via telephone, video conference, or in person. A synchronous interaction (via phone, chat, or video) can often be helpful in working through ideas together—and a lot can be accomplished in a short amount of time. Consult the list of UW Subject Librarians.

You can choose a librarian in a specific field or you can choose to contact the ISS Librarian.

2. *Prior to contacting the librarian, make sure you have a few questions written down.*

   The questions can be broad or specific. Sample questions include:

   a. Where is the best place to start researching my topic?
   b. What are some strategies for writing annotations?

   Even if you don't have specific questions, a librarian can still help you, so start with these basic questions and see where the conversation takes you.

3. *During your consultation, be sure to take notes.*

   For this assignment you will submit a one to two paragraph summary of what you learned from your consultation.

   In your summary, be sure to identify:

   a. The librarian you consulted and a link to that librarian's subject guide (if more than one subject guide, choose the one that best matched your topic).
   b. The question you asked the librarian.
   c. The results of your consultation. What specific suggestions did the librarian have and what specific steps or course of action will you now follow?

Focus Group, Interview, or Survey Questions

Focus Group, Interview, or Survey Questions were modified slightly for the Humanities and for the Sciences/Social Sciences. The Humanities interviews took place first and questions were tested and modified to work with The Sciences/Social Sciences faculty and graduate students.

Humanities Questions[1]

Thank you for coming to this focus group. We appreciate you taking time out of your busy schedules to help our project. The goal of the following session is to inform the libraries about what kinds of programs will best support your exploration of and work in digital scholarship. We want to know what you know about this field, where your training gaps are, and what support you most need.

1. What got you interested in digital scholarship? Project? Colleague? Workshop? Article?
2. How many of you are currently working on digital projects related to your academic, research interests?
3. What do you think of the term digital scholarship? Is digital scholarship (or digital humanities) a relevant term in 2016?
4. How do you describe your digital project(s) to your colleagues? How do your colleagues react to digital scholarship?

5. How can we build a community of digital scholars at UW?
6. Does your department leadership support your interest in digital scholarship?
7. Does your department offer financial support of digital scholarship?
8. What are your biggest obstacles to digital projects?
9. What skills would most help you to better do your digital work?
10. Where do you currently go for support for digital scholarship?
11. Have you attended workshops, lectures, or other events at UW specifically about digital scholarship, such as DMDH (Demystifying Digital Humanities)?
12. Have you attended workshops, lectures, or other events at UW not specific to digital scholarship but nevertheless helpful to your work in that area?
13. What makes you more or less likely to attend an event or a workshop?
14. How do you think the library can better support digital scholarship?
15. What tools or technologies (specific to digital scholarship) would you like to see the library acquire?

Science/Social Sciences Focus Group/ Interview Questions[2]

Thank you for coming to this focus group. We appreciate you taking time out of your busy schedules to help our project. The goal of the following session is to inform the libraries regarding what kinds of programs and services will best support your exploration of and work in digital scholarship.

Background Questions

1. The libraries are charged with supporting the needs of researchers across disciplines, both in the sciences and the humanities. We've struggled to come up with a unifying term that points to the needs of researchers working with digital materials. Although "digital humanities" designates a new and evolving realm of scholarship, "digital sciences" is redundant almost to the point of meaninglessness. With respect to your field of research, how do you feel about the term "digital scholarship"? Do you see a distinction between research and digital scholarship? Would you recognize yourself as a constituent for library services supporting "digital scholarship"?
2. Are you currently working on digital projects related to your academic, research interests? What form do these projects take? What type of data is included?
3. We would like to know a bit more about your data needs. Are you required to archive your data as part of a grant project? If so, where are

you archiving data? Are you using a subject-specific repository? Do you have data storage needs mid-project?

4. Are digital tools or software (R, Python, Tableau, etc.) incorporated into teaching and/or theses and dissertation work in your department?
5. What tools does a new graduate student in your lab need to master, or have mastered, in order to take part in your research?

Support for Digital Scholarship Work

1. What are your biggest obstacles to digital projects?
2. What skills would most help you to complete your digital work?
3. Where do you currently go for support for digital scholarship?
4. Have you attended workshops, lectures, or other events at UW related to digital scholarship, such as the Tableau Basics workshops, Software Carpentry workshops, or eScience Community Seminar?
5. What makes you more or less likely to attend an event or a workshop?

The Big Picture

1. How do you think the library can better support digital scholarship?
2. Do you think a community of digital scholars across disciplines at UW is an important goal?

NOTES

1. Humanities questions and interviews were designed and led by 2016 iSchool students Abigail Darling and Becky Ramsey Leporati as part of their Capstone project.
2. Verletta Kern, Khue Duong, Elizabeth Bedford, and Jenny Muilenburg co-designed and led the Science/Social Sciences focus groups.

Template: Message for Subject Librarians on Digital Pedagogy Study

The author wishes to acknowledge library volunteer Michelle Urberg's work co-designing and analyzing the data produced in this study.

Hello [Subject Librarian],

I wanted to check in with you on a digital pedagogy project we're working on in the hopes that you'll be able to help. We're trying to figure out which courses across campus are using digital tools and methods in the classroom. The tools and methods we're interested in include the following:

- 3-D modeling
- augmented reality
- community engaged research
- exhibits
- data presentation
- data visualization
- digital archiving
- digital objects
- digital storytelling
- GIS
- making or maker
- media creation
- multimodal
- Omeka
- oral history
- public scholarship
- Scalar
- text analysis
- virtual reality
- WordPress

We've been reviewing the time schedule and found a few [subject] courses that may include these methods. Courses we're interested in include:

[Insert List of Courses Here]

I'm wondering if you might know of any other courses that might include tools and methods from our list above? Sometimes it is hard to tell if digital tools and methods are part of a course because of the short course descriptions listed in the time schedule. We've also been trying to gather syllabi from courses across campus to text mine for our study. I'm wondering if you would be okay with us contacting [your department] to see if we can get these syllabi or if you would prefer to contact them on our behalf (we have a script that can be modified). Let me know what you think! I'm hoping we can use the data we collect in this study to try to advocate for more institutional support for this type of work. Wish us luck! Let me know if you have any questions about our work.

Best,

Verletta

Message Sent to Departments Requesting Syllabi

Dear [Departmental Administrative Assistant],

The UW Libraries is trying to gain a better understanding of how we might support instructors who incorporate or are already incorporating digital scholarship tools and methods into their classrooms. We are currently collecting syllabi to do a campus-wide survey of digital tools and methods used in teaching. We hope to use the survey findings to help plan for future student research support. In reviewing course descriptions for [department], we were interested to learn more about [course numbers]. Would you be willing and able to share those syllabi with us for this project? Thank you for your time and consideration. Do let us know if you have any questions about our project.

Best,

Verletta Kern and Michelle Urberg

UW Libraries Research Data Services Unit Communications Plan, 2014

Communication Initiatives for the Research Data Services Unit

The *purpose* of the University of Washington Research Data Services Communications Plan is to:

- *Inform Libraries staff* about services and projects we provide;
- *Inform the UW community* about data services the Libraries provides and data-related events at UW and in the region;
- *Exchange information and engage in discussion* with the larger community of international data librarians;
- *Announce* new datasets and relevant publications held by the libraries, such as those in GovPubs, Maps/GIS, Engineering/Business, etc.

To accomplish these goals, the Data Services Curriculum and Communications Librarian will:

- Publish a *quarterly newsletter* (January, April, July, October) that includes information about our services, current projects, featured current blog posts, and staff and student profiles. This newsletter is to be disseminated via:

- The Weekly Online News [internal Libraries communication tool], and then:
- Posted to ResearchWorks page
    - Posted to Staffweb [Libraries Intranet] with a link to ResearchWorks page
        - Emailed/shared to UW departments such as:
            - EScience Institute
            - Geography, Urban Planning, Oceanography, Business, Engineering, etc.
                - Announcement and bit.ly link posted to Facebook and Twitter
- Twitter @UWLibsData
    - Post and repost items of interest to both UW community as well as those pertaining to academic librarianship, open data/publications, etc.
    - Monitor feed for RT/MT opportunities
    - Post items of interest to UW and data communities
- Facebook
    - Post and repost items of interest to both UW community as well as those pertaining to academic librarianship, open data/publications, etc.
    - Monitor feed for reposting opportunities
    - Post items of interest to UW and data communities.
    - *Generally speaking,* the Twitter and Facebook feeds should mirror each other, but because Twitter is used with greater volume and frequency, and if Twitter posts are frequent (more than one/day), only the most important or relevant item should be posted to Facebook.
- Blog Data @ Libs
    - Maintained by Data Communications Librarian; both Data Librarians have author permissions. At least one post per month. Guest posts are allowed according to the following Guest Blogger Policy:
        - Guest bloggers will request permission to post and be approved by the Data Services Communications Librarian.
        - Guest bloggers will submit their posts to Data Services Communications Librarian prior to publication for editing and review.

- After review and editing, Data Services Communications Librarian will post items to the blog for the guest blogger, making sure to add a byline and a link to a professional blog or web page the guest blogger desires (as approved of by Data Services Communications Librarian).

- *Local contacts.* There should be a list of local contacts (that are used to market the newsletter), such as eScience Institute, Geography, Urban Planning, Oceanography, Business, Engineering. Certain items should be marketed directly to this list, which is only used for EVENTS and NEWSLETTERS and other CAMPUS DEVELOPMENT AND ANNOUNCEMENTS. Many of these announcements should also be shared with Facebook and Twitter.

About the Editors and Contributors

ROBIN CHIN ROEMER is the head of Instructional Design and Outreach Services for University of Washington Libraries, where she has worked since 2013. She previously worked as a communication librarian at American University in Washington, DC. She holds a BA and MA in English, and an MLIS from the University of Washington. Robin is the author of the 2015 handbook *Meaningful Metrics: A 21st Century Librarian's Guide to Bibliometrics, Altmetrics, and Research Impact,* as well as numerous professional articles on altmetrics and digital pedagogy.

VERLETTA KERN has served as digital scholarship librarian at the University of Washington Libraries since 2016. She has presented on digital scholarship topics at venues such as the Digital Library Federation and the Humanities, Arts, Science, and Technology Alliance and Collaboratory (HASTAC). She received her MS in Library and Information Science from the University of Illinois.

■ ■ ■

ELIZABETH BEDFORD is a scholarly publishing outreach librarian at University of Washington Libraries. She supports the scholarly conversation by helping researchers share their data, publications, and educational resources with the world. Before joining UW, she was a digital preservation and data curation consultant, working with such clients as the Digital Curation Centre and the University of Edinburgh Archives. She earned her MS in Information from the University of Michigan iSchool.

MARYAM FAKOURI is a scholarly publishing outreach librarian at the University of Washington. She monitors developments in information law and policy that affect higher education and offers guidance about copyright issues. She has designed educational programs about copyright, fair use, open access, and related topics. Prior to specializing in scholarly communication, Maryam was a reference and teaching librarian. Maryam has a Master of Library Science from Indiana University and a Juris Doctor from DePaul University College of Law.

REED GARBER-PEARSON is the integrated social sciences and online learning librarian at the University of Washington whose work includes embedded online teaching, curriculum development, and creating learning programs for professional students. Reed's interests focus on antiracist and feminist pedagogies and strategies for digital safety in teaching.

BETH LYTLE is an instructional technologist with UW Learning Technologies, where they support students, staff, and faculty in the use of UW teaching and learning tools. Beth received an MLIS from the University of Washington.

JENNIFER MUILENBURG is research data services librarian in the Scholarly Communication and Publishing department of the UW Libraries. She focuses on supporting the data needs of UW researchers; data curation, publishing and archiving; and data repositories. Previously Jenny was a geographic information systems librarian. She holds a BS in journalism from the University of Illinois, and an MS in Information from the University of Michigan.

MARISA PETRICH is the instructional design librarian at the University of Washington Tacoma where she supports digital scholarship work by consulting on digital tools and resources, contributing to programming efforts, developing resources, and assisting with program design and communication strategies. As a former community college librarian, she has strong commitments to student support, library-community partnerships, and providing equitable access to higher education.

ELLIOTT STEVENS is the English Studies and Research Commons librarian at the University of Washington Seattle. He has published about problems with Problem-Based Learning in library instruction as well as the value of written reflection done by student workers while on the job. He is intrigued by digital storytelling, podcasting, multi-modal education, and online text-based games.

JOHN VALLIER is ethnomusicology curator and head of media for UW Libraries. In these roles he collects, preserves, and provides access to an array of media collections, including the UW Ethnomusicology Archives. He also oversees the Libraries' Media Arcade makerspace and media preservation lab. Before coming to UW, John was archivist at the UCLA Ethnomusicology Archive, a writer for *All Music Guide,* and a drummer for such bands as Swell, Santa Cruise Control, and Climax Golden Twins.

JUSTIN WADLAND is the associate director and head of the Digital Scholarship Program at the UW Tacoma Library, where he has worked as a librarian in various position since 2003. In his current role, he administers the campus digital repository, collaborates on digital projects, and employs direct and indirect approaches to cultivating reflective, open cultures of digital scholarship. As a creative writer, he has published reviews and essays in a variety of prominent literary venues. His first book, *Trying Home: The Rise and Fall of An Anarchist Utopia,* won the Washington State Book Award in 2015.

ANDREW WEAVER is the digital infrastructure and preservation librarian at Washington State University. He has previously worked in the University of Washington Libraries Media Center. John earned his MLIS from UW in 2015. His research is centered around audiovisual preservation, particularly with regard to developing and leveraging open source tools to benefit the preservation community. He has presented on digital and media preservation at both national and international venues, including annual conferences for ALA, the Association of Moving Image Archivists (AMIA), and the International Association of Sound and Audiovisual Archives (IASA).

PERRY YEE has served as online learning support manager for the University of Washington Libraries since 2014. He designs and develops online learning and instructional design resources, technologies, learning environments, and pedagogies. He earned an MA in Educational Technology in 2013 from San Diego State University.

Index